FOUNDERS AND FRONTIERSMEN

Artist's rendition of the signing of the Constitution, in Philadelphia. This painting by Howard Chandler Christy, which hangs in the U.S. Capitol, captures the spirit of the historic event. At Independence National Historical Park, the National Park Service has accurately restored the room.

FOUNDERS AND FRONTIERSMEN

Historic Places Commemorating Early Nationhood and

the Westward Movement, 1783-1828

ROBERT G. FERRIS

Series Editor

UNITED STATES DEPARTMENT OF THE INTERIOR

NATIONAL PARK SERVICE   WASHINGTON, D.C. 1967

This volume was prepared by the Division of History Studies, National Park Service, under the general supervision of the Chief, Robert M. Utley. One of a series designed to make available to the public the studies of the National Survey of Historic Sites and Buildings, directed by John O. Littleton, it incorporates survey and evaluation reports prepared by the following National Park Service historians: S. Sydney Bradford, Robert F. Fenton, Ray H. Mattison, Frank B. Sarles, Jr., Charles E. Shedd, Jr., Horace J. Sheely, and Robert M. Utley. These reports were reviewed by the Advisory Board on National Parks, Historic Sites, Buildings, and Monuments and the Consulting Committee for the National Survey of Historic Sites and Buildings. Members of these groups are listed in the Acknowledgments. The assistant editor for this volume was Richard E. Morris.

The background narrative for this volume was prepared by Charles H. McCormick.

LIBRARY OF CONGRESS CATALOG CARD NUMBER: 67—60015

For sale by the Superintendent of Documents, U.S. Government Printing Office, Washington, D.C. 20402 - Price $3.00

Contents

[v

B. National Historic Sites in Non-Federal Ownership · 167

C. Sites Eligible for the Registry of National Historic Landmarks · 169

Photographs are by the National Park Service except where specified

MAPS

Foreword

Between 1783 and 1828, the formative years when the foundations of our Nation were laid, Americans dreamed bright dreams and
faced harsh realities. Statesmen such as Washington, Hamilton, and Jefferson began to fashion the national political structure that the Constitution of 1787 created. Millions of pioneers struggled over the Appalachian
barrier and moved the frontier to the Mississippi and beyond. As the Nation surmounted obstacle after obstacle—internal political strife, international crises, and war—it gained in strength and confidence. The newly
emerging national spirit among the people began to give substance to the
Founding Fathers' hopeful motto, *E Pluribus Unum*.

The founders and the frontiersmen were pivotal figures in United States
history. They proclaimed the basic ideals of our heritage and initiated
courses of national action so consequential to the Republic. We can
profit immensely from knowing more about them and by sharing their
experiences.

Books and pictures help us accumulate facts and ideas about the past,
but visits to historic sites and buildings—the scenes of past events—provide us with a living sense of history. Books about George Washington
or Thomas Jefferson, for example, seldom impart so vivid a picture of the
men as visits to Mount Vernon or Monticello.

This volume describes many of the historic sites and buildings that are
associated with and commemorate or illustrate our early nationhood. It
is one of a series designed to make available the findings of the National
Survey of Historic Sites and Buildings, a nationwide program conducted

by the National Park Service of the U.S. Department of the Interior under authority of the Historic Sites Act of 1935. The Survey's purpose is to identify historic and prehistoric places of significance to the Nation. Such places are studied and evaluated by Service field historians and archeologists, screened by a Consulting Committee of outside scholars, and final selections recommended to the Secretary of the Interior by the Advisory Board on National Parks, Historic Sites, Buildings, and Monuments. When approved by the Secretary, sites and buildings judged of national historical significance are eligible for designation as Registered National Historic Landmarks. Upon application, their owners are provided with a certificate and bronze plaque attesting to the distinction.

Credit for the preparation of this volume is shared widely by persons both in and out of the National Park Service. In particular, the work of the Service in the general field of historic preservation has benefited inestimably from the assistance provided by the National Trust for Historic Preservation in the United States, a cosponsor of the Survey.

It is my earnest hope that citizens will use the volumes in this series to seek out and visit sites of interest to them, and that they will also encourage individuals, private groups, and State and local governments to unite with the Federal Government in an unremitting campaign to preserve our historic treasures, an indispensable part of our national heritage.

GEORGE B. HARTZOG, Jr.
Director
National Park Service

FOUNDERS AND FRONTIERSMEN

PART I

Founders and Frontiersmen:

Historical Background

DURING THE PERIOD 1783–1828, from the end of the War for Independence to the election of President Andrew Jackson, the people of the United States transformed their wartime alliance of 13 virtually autonomous States into a strong Federal Union of 24 States. Building upon the colonial heritage of self-government and English common law, they formulated and defined the institutions and ideals that enabled the Nation to survive and mature. During these years, growth was dynamic. The national bounds doubled and the population nearly quadrupled. All these achievements were possible only because of the efforts of many men—famous and forgotten, founders and frontiersmen.

From 1783 to 1789 the 13 United States continued their wartime political system, defined by the Articles of Confederation. The State governments and the Second Continental Congress made some progress toward the solution of postwar problems. But many Americans called for a stronger, more effective, and truly national union. So in 1787, at Philadelphia, the Constitution came into being. The distillation of months of proposal, debate, and compromise, it created the machinery of the Federal Government, defined the limits of its powers, and specified its relation to the States. Above all it provided the framework for an enduring Union.

Opposition to the adoption of the Constitution was strong, the major criticism being the absence of a bill of rights that would guarantee hard-won individual liberties. The promise of the addition of such a bill weakened the opposition, and, by 1789, 11 States had ratified the Constitution—enough to win it a trial as the law of the land. Once in effect, it quickly gained the confidence of the people. In large measure this resulted from the integrity and achievements of the First Congress and President George Washington.

The political parties emerging in the 1790's made it possible for dedicated and honest men to express their differences and afforded effective vehicles by which the people could pass on their views to their representatives. The personal and philosophical differences between Hamilton and Jefferson and the partisanship arising out of the philosophical, diplomatic, and economic ramifications of the wars of the French Revolution divided the Nation into Federalists and Democratic-Republicans. In the 1790's party warfare was fierce. Washington's successor, John Adams, bore the brunt of it. A Federalist but not a Hamiltonian, he steered a course between the policies of Hamilton and Jefferson, one that avoided a declared war against France but defended U.S. sovereignty on the high seas.

In 1800 vigorous grassroots campaigning enabled Jefferson to win the Presidency and inaugurate 24 consecutive years of political ascendency of the Democratic-Republicans. The Federalists, repudiated after 12

George Town and the city of Washington in 1801. From an aquatint by T. Cartwright, after a painting by G. Beck. Courtesy, Library of Congress.

years of power, would never elect another President. Although they had not been optimistic about the potentialities of democracy, they had left a substantial political legacy. They had launched the Government and put it on a solid fiscal and legal base.

In 1801 Jefferson brought informality, simplicity, and economy to the Government. In contrast to Adams, Jefferson showed more concern for the future of agriculture and a deeper interest in the West. His foremost success, in 1803, was the acquisition of the vast Louisiana Territory. His greatest disappointment was the failure of the Embargo of 1807 as a substitute for military force in the effort to avoid war against Great Britain or France. In 1809 James Madison succeeded Jefferson. The major problem of Madison's first term was the need to obtain markets for U.S. goods in Europe—at the very time that Great Britain and France were struggling desperately to destroy each other's trade. Madison relied upon diplomacy in place of embargo, but it failed. In 1812 the United States and Great Britain went to war.

The war went badly. From the first, many New Englanders opposed it. The Army was a disappointment. It was for the most part poorly trained and led. The militia system proved ill-suited to offensive warfare. The victories at Put-in-Bay, the Thames, Plattsburgh, and New Orleans were mingled with such humiliations as the refusal of militiamen to cross into Canada and the burning of the Capitol and the White House. More than 2 years of war produced only a stalemate. Ship for ship, the U.S. Navy proved a match for the Royal Navy, but ships were too few; at the end of the war, the U.S. fleet rode restlessly at anchor, blockaded in its own ports. The Treaty of Ghent, in 1814, recorded no diplomatic victory for the United States; it only restored the status quo before the war. But in terms of morale and national purpose, the war proved a boon. The Nation had combated Great Britain, whose power had crushed the mighty Napoleon. And, twice tested, independence seemed more real.

A number of themes and trends characterized national development between the War of 1812 and the inauguration of Jackson. One was the acceptance of many Hamiltonian political programs by the heirs of Jefferson. Another was the upsurge of nationalism, which found expression in the nearly unanimous election of James Monroe and in the description of the first years of his Presidency as the "Era of Good Feelings." Still another was the Monroe Doctrine, which declared the Nation's intent to pursue its own destiny free from foreign interference.

There remained inequities in U.S. society, but the growth of humanitarianism and the reform spirit aimed to erase them. So did the movement toward white manhood suffrage and the growing faith in democracy symbolized by Andrew Jackson's election to the Presidency in 1828.

Another theme was America's romance with the West. Good land and adventure lay beyond the horizon. The Presidents from Washington to Jackson recognized that Western settlement was intimately related to the country's future wealth and power. And the people knew it, too. In 1783, 2 percent of them had lived west of the Alleghenies; by 1830 the figure was 28 percent. The Indians, the British, the Spanish—all retreated before the pioneer. Prosperous farms, plantations, and towns sprang up in the trans-Appalachian West, while soldiers, trappers, and traders explored and mapped the trans-Mississippi West. The settlement of the successive frontier zones from the Atlantic seaboard to the Pacific would become a major determinant in national growth.

By the time of Jackson's election, the Nation had come a long way since its founding, when its very survival had been at stake. It had not fully matured, but the patterns of thought and action that had begun to form during these critical years pointed to future trends and problems. Representative Government and democratic ideals would guide political development. The people would allow no hereditary or formal class distinctions. The United States would oppose European intervention in the affairs of the Western Hemisphere and avoid entanglement in European politics. Sectional rivalry would pose serious threats to national unity. The West would be a source of contention, as well as strength. Already it had become an article of the optimistic national faith that some would prosper and some would not. Likely as not, however, a man would be better off than his father, but not so well off as his son.

The Formative Years—Visions and Prospects of Nationhood

The War for Independence, which pitted the United States and its allies France and Spain against Great Britain, officially ended in 1783, when the negotiators signed the Treaty of Paris. At last, almost 2 years after Cornwallis' surrender to Washington, Great Britain recognized the independence of the United States. The dream of independence was a fact, but it brought serious problems. Challenge and promise were mingled with peril and uncertainty. Would the Nation survive? Would it endure?

INDEPENDENCE—PERILS AND PROMISE

In 1783 the United States encompassed more than 800,000 square miles, from present Maine to Georgia and from the Atlantic Ocean to the Mississippi River. The total population was more than 3 million people. Of these, 98 in every 100 lived in the 13 former British colonies, now independent States along the eastern seaboard. The other 2 percent had crossed the Appalachian Mountain barrier to seek the future in the forested, virgin territory between the mountains and the Mississippi. During the next century, millions more would follow and push beyond the Mississippi to the Pacific.

To provide the benefits of the land to the many under a representative form of government would be the challenge and the triumph of succeeding generations. In 1783 the land contained immense potential wealth. No one could even guess how much. But already Americans recognized the importance of land and knew that in their country it was in abundant supply. Nine-tenths of them made a living from it. From large tidewater plantations, elaborately organized for the production of a cash crop for sale in the world market, to frontiersmen's primitive subsistence farms, agriculture was the principal pursuit. Of course, most farmers were neither planters nor frontiersmen, but of the "middling sort," able to raise a modest surplus to exchange for goods in the nearest town—if they lived in the vicinity of a town or a navigable stream.

The problems of transportation required solution if the United States were to grow and remain united. The speed of communication was that of a man or animal—2 to 5 miles per hour for any long distance overland. Roads were rutted, winding, and often impassable. Water transportation was easiest and cheapest. As late as 1816 the cost of transporting a ton of goods 30 miles overland or 3,000 miles overseas was roughly the same. Under such circumstances cities were few and industrialization almost nonexistent.

Most towns were small; few had more than 2,500 inhabitants. But they had an influence beyond their size as centers of trade, culture, and the exchange of ideas. Several, owing to the energy of their merchants and providential locations where trade routes reached salt water, had prospered sufficiently to be called cities. Philadelphia, the Nation's metropolis, had in 1783 a population of perhaps 40,000. New York, Boston, and Charleston had more than 10,000 inhabitants and Baltimore would soon have that many. In the noisy and bustling cities, one could purchase a wide variety of plain and fancy manufactured goods. Gentlemen in powdered wigs and velvet and satin clothes passed among "mechanics" in felt hats, leather aprons, and buckskin breeches, and visiting farmers in homespun and moccasins. The towns and cities had no street lights, sewers, safe drinking water, or municipal police and fire departments as we know them, and epidemics often drove those who could afford to do so to flee to the country. Still the cities and towns offered entertainment and the chance to socialize. And from the town printing presses came the newspapers, pamphlets, and copies of the State and National laws that played such a vital part in fostering representative self-government.

The United States differed in many ways from the nations of Europe. It had no king, no hereditary aristocracy, and no national church. It did have an aristocracy of sorts, made up of ladies and gentlemen whose wealth, family, and elegance of manner, language, and dress marked them as special. But to a large extent talent was a prerequisite of social position. U.S. society, then as now, was open ended. The careers of the poor boy from Boston, Benjamin Franklin, and the immigrant from the West Indies, Alexander Hamilton, demonstrate that in only one generation an individual could rise from the bottom to the top. In the relatively simple society of the United States in 1783, few large fortunes had yet been accumulated and the confiscation of Loyalist estates at the time of the War for Independence eventually contributed to a wider distribution of property. The gulf between rich and poor was narrower than it would be a century later.

A widely held opinion in 1783 was the belief that men were entitled to equal treatment before the law. Related to this idea of equality, which Thomas Jefferson had stated in the Declaration of Independence, was a fundamental commitment to representative government. Just how representative government should be was a source of dispute, but most agreed that, for the good of society, in some way the will of the people must be expressed through representatives. In 1776 these two concepts had helped unite diverse groups in the Thirteen Colonies in defense of the rights of Englishmen. When political thinkers spoke of equality and representative government, they did not usually mean democracy as we think of it in the 20th century. Most 18th-century political theorists in the United States divided the state into three parts: The monarchy (executive), the aristocracy (legislature), and the democracy (the people). Each

More than any other man, George Washington symbolizes the ideals of the
Founding Fathers. From a mezzotint by H. S. Sadd, after a painting by
Gilbert Stuart. Courtesy, Library of Congress.

part had its function in government, and each was to act as a check upon the ambitions of the others. Should one of the three gain control of the state, evil was certain to result. Complete control by either the executive or the legislature was tyranny or oligarchy; complete control by the mass of people was "mob rule," or anarchy.

In practice, although variations existed from State to State, the country was more democratic than the theory suggests—even though only property owners were qualified to vote in national and local elections, only large property owners usually attained high office, slaves could not legally vote under any circumstances, and few women could vote. Property requirements for voting were modest. Most white adult males in the Thirteen States likely could vote and thus have a voice in government if they wished. Representative government and the belief in equality needed only time and logical development to become modern democracy. But first the perils that threatened the independence and unity of the Thirteen States had to be overcome.

In 1783 no one could be certain that the United States would endure—that it would be able to solve the many problems it faced in domestic affairs and foreign relations. True, the Atlantic Ocean posed difficult logistical problems to prospective invaders from Europe. Yet the British, though they had the most powerful navy in the world and bases in Canada and the West Indies, had been unable to subdue so large a country. But the Americans, who had a traditional distaste for large standing armies, relied primarily on the State militia system for defense, and the territory beyond the Appalachians had few inhabitants to fill militia ranks. The Spanish in the Southwest and the British in the Northwest were endeavoring to strengthen their domains in the trans-Appalachian country, and the United States lacked an effective Army.

Equally serious was the internal threat to the Union posed by extreme sectionalism and regionalism. Already the Northeast (New England), the Middle States (New York, New Jersey, and Pennsylvania), and the South (Maryland, Delaware, Virginia, the Carolinas, and Georgia) differed in economic interests and social structure. New England, the richest section, specialized in commerce and fishing. Its society was dominated by merchants, bankers, and shipowners. The Middle States had a more flexible society than either New England or the South, and the economy was more evenly divided between commerce and agriculture. Southern society was basically agrarian and rural. Planters and farmers grew tobacco and rice, and, after about 1800, cotton. Within

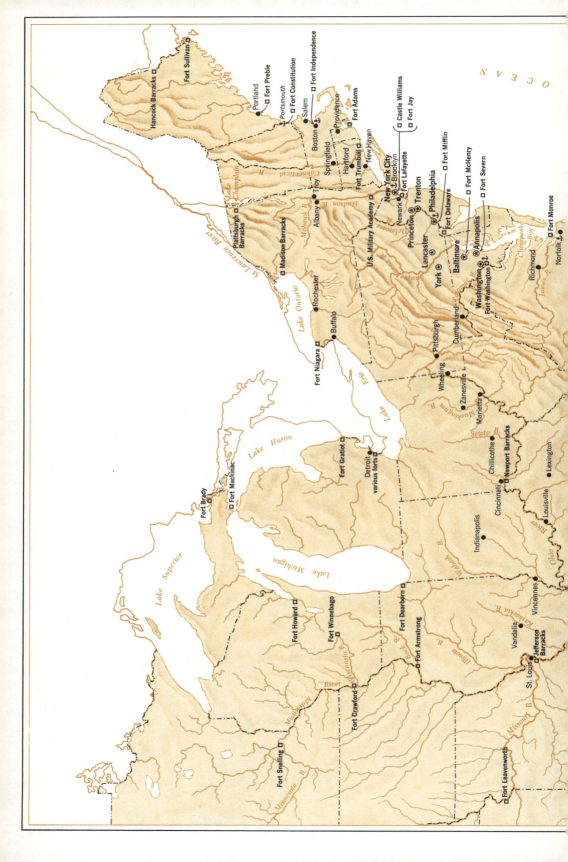

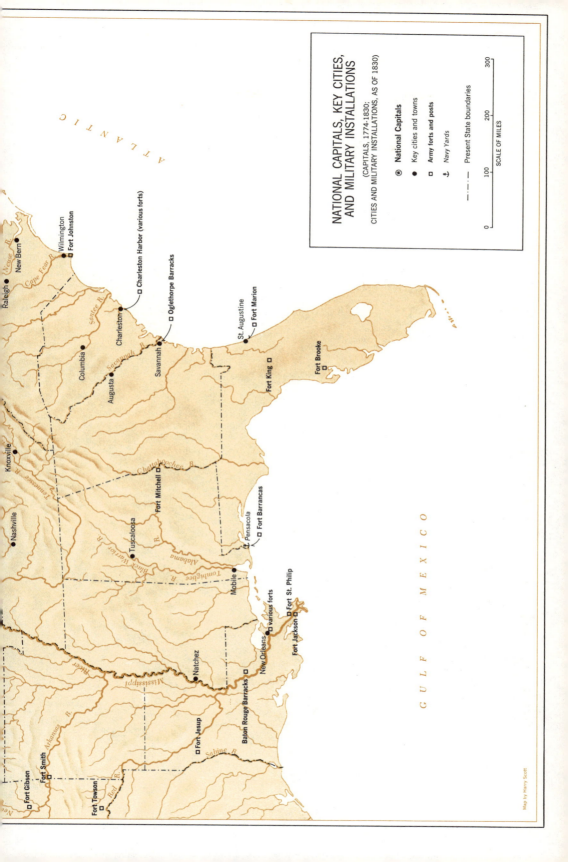

NATIONAL CAPITALS, KEY CITIES,
AND MILITARY INSTALLATIONS

(CAPITALS, 1774-1830;
CITIES AND MILITARY INSTALLATIONS, AS OF 1830)

⊛ National Capitals
● Key cities and towns
□ Army forts and posts
⚓ Navy Yards
— ·· — Present State boundaries

SCALE OF MILES

0   100   200   300

ATLANTIC

Raleigh
New Bern
Neuse R.
Cape Fear R.
Wilmington   Fort Johnston
Charleston Harbor (various forts)
Columbia   Oglethorpe Barracks
Santee R.
Augusta   Charleston
Savannah R.
Savannah   Fort Marion
St. Augustine
Fort King
Fort Brooke
Knoxville
Tennessee R.
Chattahoochee R.
Fort Mitchell
Fort Barrancas
Nashville   Pensacola   Fort Barrancas
Tuscaloosa
Black Warrior R.
Alabama R.
Tombigbee R.
Mobile
Fort St. Philip
various forts
New Orleans
Fort Jackson
Natchez
Mississippi
Baton Rouge Barracks
Arkansas R.
Fort Jesup
Sabine R.
Fort Gibson
Fort Smith
Red R.
Fort Towson

GULF OF MEXICO

Map by Harry Scott

each of the three regions were further divisions. For example, in the South, the culture of the Virginia tidewater planters was quite distinct from that of the planters of South Carolina. Both cultures contrasted sharply with that of North Carolina as well as with those in the western parts of their own States. The regional and sectional diversity placed a heavy burden on the Nation's founders. They would need to erect a national political framework large enough to accommodate individual and group differences, strong enough to contain them, and flexible enough to permit growth. Their first attempt at such a framework produced the Articles of Confederation.

THE CONFEDERATION: AN INTERIM GOVERNMENT

Between 1776 and 1789 the United States did not have a strong National Government. During this interim period the threat of British military power and the "firm league of friendship" created by the Articles of Confederation held the 13 independent States together. The Confederation won the war with Britain and laid some foundations for the future, but as time went on many Americans came to believe that it could not solve national problems. Many leaders clearly recognized that the United States must form a truly national government. As Alexander Hamilton phrased it, Americans needed to learn to think "continentally."

In the 1780's many Americans favored a national government of very limited powers. According to a widely held belief of the time, "republican," or representative, government would not succeed in large geographical areas. In 1776 colonists had rebelled against interference in their local affairs by a government that claimed superiority to their legislatures. Having repudiated the authority of the Crown, they were wary of erecting in its place a potentially tyrannical national government.

Many believed that the preservation of individual life, liberty, and the pursuit of happiness could more safely be entrusted to 13 independent republics than to a single central government. At the same time it was advantageous for the 13 republics to act in unison in military, diplomatic, and financial affairs. In 1781, when the last State ratified the Articles of Confederation, the States, at least on paper, surrendered certain powers to the Continental Congress. Each State, regardless of its population, had only one vote. Congress, acting upon instructions from the States, could make war, negotiate loans, regulate currency, manage Indian affairs, and operate an interstate postal service. It could not coin money or collect taxes. It could requisition money from the States, but had no power to enforce payment. The Articles did not establish a national executive or a system of Federal courts. The passage of national laws was difficult. The support of 7 States was enough to enact some laws, but 9

The Pennsylvania State House (Independence Hall), Philadelphia, in 1799. From a drawing and engraving by William Birch and Son. Courtesy, Library of Congress.

had to approve matters of war and all 13 consent to any changes in the Articles themselves. In a time of crisis, such a government could not act quickly or forcefully. The people placed their faith in the State governments, which could levy taxes and import duties, maintain militia, regulate commerce, and, when necessary, use force to maintain order.

The State governments accomplished much during the Confederation period. In most States, during the war, committees of leading citizens drew up new constitutions. Incorporated into these documents were principles that have been part of our system of government ever since. The British constitution was not and is not a written document. However, most of the American Colonies had begun with royal charters, and the colonial legislatures had evolved from governments under these charters. Americans, therefore, were firm believers in written constitutions. They viewed them as contracts or agreements between the people and the governments of the States that were drawn to promote understanding of the laws, define responsibility, and provide a measure for evaluating disputes between liberty and authority.

In the constitutions several of the States incorporated lists of the rights of individual citizens. Most notable of these was George Mason's Virginia Declaration of Rights of 1776, which later became the basis of the U.S. Bill of Rights. The constitutions generally encouraged government more responsive to the will of the people. Many reduced property qualifications for voting and outlawed titles of nobility. The Southern States abolished two feudal institutions, primogeniture and entail, that theoretically encouraged the preservation of large family estates from generation to generation. The idea of the separation of church and state found expression in State constitutional provisions that allowed citizens to specify which Protestant church their taxes would support. Virginia went further and passed a law, the Statute of Religious Freedom (1786), written by Jefferson, that declared in ringing words: "Almighty God hath created the mind free" and "no man shall be compelled to frequent or support any religious worship, place or ministry whatsoever."

The individual States faced the difficult problems of rebuilding after the war, paying off war debts, providing for defense, and improving transportation. Attempts to solve these problems met with limited success. By 1790 a few of the States had managed to pay most of their war debts, and some of them had undertaken road, canal, and bridge building. Yet progress was slow and cooperation between the States was less than perfect.

In one area the States and the Continental Congress, working together, achieved substantial success. They created a national domain west of the Appalachians and outlined a means of settling it. The first step in the process was to untangle the snarl of conflicting State claims to Western lands, which were based on the old colonial charters. Georgia claimed much of what is today Alabama and Mississippi—as did Spain—and North Carolina claimed Tennessee. Virginia, possessing the oldest charter, claimed almost all the rest of the Western United States. North of the Ohio River, her claims conflicted with those of Massachusetts, Connecticut, and New York.

The Western claims were a potential source of national disunion. Rhode Island, Delaware, New Jersey, Maryland, Pennsylvania, and New Hampshire had no such claims. These "landless" States feared that the "landed" States would sell their western lands to pay off debts or, worse, develop the lands and grow so large and powerful that they would threaten the independence of their neighbors. The landless States urged that, for the future of the Union, the landed States surrender their Western claims to Congress to administer for the benefit of all. South of the Ohio River, State land claims would not be completely settled until 1802. By 1786, however, New York, Virginia, Massachusetts, and Connecticut had surrendered sufficient lands north of the Ohio to give the Continental Congress clear title and allow it to begin the organization of Western settlement.

Settlers were eager to enter the old Northwest, and in a series of ordinances during the period 1784–87 Congress laid down rules for orderly settlement. These rules, somewhat modified, served as the Federal pattern for organizing westward expansion until the Civil War. The short-lived Ordinance of 1784 established the principle that temporary governments under Congress should govern Western Territories until they attained sufficient population for statehood. The Ordinance of 1785 spelled out the means of disposing of the lands to land companies and

Baltimore, Maryland, from Federal Hill, in the 1830's. From an aquatint by W. J. Bennett, after his painting. Courtesy, Library of Congress.

individual settlers. To avoid disputes over ownership, Government surveyors would divide the land into 6-mile-square townships made up of 36 sections. One section, consisting of 640 acres, in each township was to be set aside for the support of public education, and the remaining sections would be sold at $1 per acre.

The Northwest Ordinance of 1787 outlined the political path from wilderness to statehood. An appointed Governor and three judges would rule a Territory until the population reached 5,000. At that time, the citizens could elect a legislature, and, when the population numbered 60,000, the Territory could apply for admission to the Union as a State on a basis of full equality with the Original Thirteen. Other significant provisions of the ordinance guaranteed the protection of liberty, property, and religious freedom and also prohibited slavery.

Though the Continental Congress contributed to the organization of the West, in other fields it was less successful. After the war, the problems of political, social, and economic readjustment caught up with it. People blamed it for failure to solve problems that would have tried stronger governments. But the weaknesses of the Continental Congress were real—particularly in foreign affairs, national defense, mediation of interstate disputes, and fiscal matters.

Other nations showed contempt for the United States. In 1785 Great Britain received Minister John Adams, but not until 7 years later did she send a diplomatic representative in return. She refused to grant trade concessions needed by the United States if prewar outlets for American goods were to be restored, and she did not evacuate military posts in the Northwest Territory as called for in the peace treaty of 1783. As grounds for refusal to abandon the Western posts, the British contended that the United States had already violated the treaty by failing to pay Loyalist claims for confiscated property. Congress could not solve the problem, lacking as it did the military power to drive the British out of the Northwest and the authority to force States to pay the Loyalist claims.

France remained friendly and hoped to establish trade with the United States, but the trade amounted to little because the traditional and practical outlet for American raw materials was industrial Britain. Since the French Foreign Minister, the Comte de Vergennes, at the peace negotiations in 1783, had shown a willingness to sacrifice the American Western territory to the interests of French diplomacy, relations between the two countries had cooled.

Spanish-American relations had never been warm, even when Spain was an ally during the War for Independence. She did not recognize U.S. claims to portions of Georgia, Alabama, and Mississippi, and disputed the location of the boundary between Florida and the United States as defined by the Treaty of 1783. She also used her control of New Orleans and the mouth of the Mississippi to attempt to persuade Western settlers to forswear the United States and join her. Seeking accommodation, Congress authorized John Jay to negotiate with the Spanish. After 1 year of inconclusive talks, in 1785–86, he failed to obtain for U.S. shipping the right to pass freely through the mouth of the Mississippi.

In the meantime, Mediterranean pirates plundered and exacted tribute from U.S. ships on the high seas, and the Continental Congress did nothing about it.

The Congress also failed to provide an adequate national defense. In the Newburgh Addresses of March 1783, Army officers, with civilian support, brought pressure to bear on Congress to dispense backpay and pensions. Congress had no money to pay the men, but George Washington used his authority and prestige to calm them and avert a crisis. A few months later, when several hundred mutinous soldiers demonstrated outside Congress Hall demanding backpay and redress of grievances, Congress moved from Philadelphia to Princeton, N.J.

Under the Confederation, at the very time that westerners were clamoring for protection from the Indians and action against the British in the Northwest, the Army was in a weak and dissatisfied state. In 1783, in response to frontiersmen's pleas, the best Congress could do was call for an increase in the size of the Regular Army from 80 men to 700. Before the adoption of the Constitution, the goal was never reached, but enough State militiamen volunteered for Regular Army service to erect and garrison a few forts in the Ohio country and provide token evidence of U.S. authority. From 1784 until 1789 the Army consisted only of the Western garrisons, small detachments at West Point, N.Y., and the Springfield, Mass., and Pittsburgh supply depots. The "navy" of the War for Independence had almost disappeared. After the war, ships were sold and sailors discharged. Not until 1794 would there be a U.S. Navy and not until 1798 a separate Navy Department.

The failure of Congress to provide for national defense stemmed mainly from its reliance on State militia and from financial difficulties. To finance the War for Independence, it had issued more than $240 mil-

lion in paper currency. It had also borrowed heavily from foreign investors, chiefly in the Netherlands, and the States were reluctant to provide
enough money even to pay the interest on the foreign loan. Furthermore,
by 1784 inflation had made Continental currency almost worthless.
The Nation had no uniform currency, and Continental paper, State
paper, bills of exchange, and foreign coins circulated freely. Creditors
claimed that debtors were ruining them by paying old debts in worthless
money. But many debtors were too poor to pay in any kind of money.
Soldier-farmers had returned from the war to find their farms mortgaged.
Heavy State taxes resulting from the war caused many to lose their
farms. As a result, debtor political factions arose that advocated laws to
prevent foreclosures and print more paper, or "cheap," money. Congress
could do little to alleviate the situation.

In disputes among the States, Congress was no more successful. Lacking the power to enforce its decisions, it hesitated to make many. It could
not regulate interstate commerce or, for example, prevent New York from
passing restrictive measures against the importation of Connecticut firewood and New Jersey produce. When the "State of Franklin" (1784–88)
claimed independence from North Carolina and a faction within the
"state" sought annexation to Spain, Congress was powerless to resolve
the issue. And it could not settle the conflicting claims of New Hampshire and New York to the Vermont area, at a time when Ethan, Ira,
and Levi Allen were said to be discussing with the British Vermont's possible separation from the United States and annexation to Canada. By
the mid-1780's many of the men who had been leaders in the War for
Independence had reached the conclusion that the United States needed
a stronger National Government.

During the course of a conference and two conventions, in the years
1785–87, a movement developed for change in the National Government and resulted in the Constitution. The first, the Mount Vernon Conference, made no effort to amend the Articles, but it led to the Annapolis
Convention. This convention began as an interstate discussion of commercial matters, but ended in a call for another convention, in Philadelphia, to amend the Articles of Confederation. The Convention in
Philadelphia wrote the Constitution.

The Mount Vernon Conference of March 1785 resulted from efforts
to establish commercial ties between the East and the trans-Appalachian
West. George Washington and others recognized that the rivers that

The Maryland State House, Annapolis, in the 1780's. From an engraving in *Columbian Magazine*, 1789. Courtesy, Library of Congress.

flowed through the mountains could become commercial arteries. Washington considered the matter urgent, for, as he wrote, the West was "on a pivot" and a "touch of a feather" would, he feared, turn it toward Spain. He, therefore, took the lead in an attempt to cement the East and the West. He became the first president of the Patowmack Co., which attempted to make the Potomac River navigable above the fall line by dredging a channel in the river and building a series of short canals around the rapids. Because Washington's company had a Virginia charter and Maryland held title to the Potomac River, the two States needed to agree before the project could begin. The Mount Vernon Conference cleared the way for free navigation of the Potomac, and its success led to a call for another conference, to which all the States were invited.

The second conference convened at Annapolis, Md., in September 1786, for the purpose of seeking a national solution to commercial problems. Nine of the Thirteen States sent delegates. Travel being what it was, however, delegates from only five of the States arrived in time to take part. The participating States—New York, New Jersey, Virginia, Pennsylvania, and Delaware—made little progress toward a national solution of commercial problems. They did, however, through the efforts of Alexander Hamilton and other nationalists, agree to request the Continental Congress to invite all the States to another convention, to begin at Philadelphia in May 1787. Its purpose was to discuss all matters necessary to make the Articles of Confederation strong enough to meet the needs of the Nation. When the delegates rode away from the Annapolis Convention, they could not be sure that the meeting at Philadelphia would take place. The public seemed apathetic. But Shays' Rebellion convinced many people that a change was necessary.

Shays' Rebellion dramatized the weakness of the National Government. In the fall of 1787 farmers in western Massachusetts, many of them debtors, rose against the State government. They demanded abolition of the "aristocratic" upper house of the Massachusetts legislature and lower taxes, lawyers' fees, and court costs. The legislature reacted by calling up the militia. The rebels, choosing a veteran of the War for Independence, Daniel Shays, as their leader, took up arms. In February 1787, after some inconclusive military action, Gen. Benjamin Lincoln and the Massachusetts Militia defeated the Shaysites and crushed the revolt. Yet the episode gave many men pause. Debtors were dissatisfied in other States, and Congress had aided neither in putting down the rebellion nor in alleviating its causes. On February 21, 1787, Congress acted on the recommendation of the Annapolis Convention and resolved to call a convention at Philadelphia to discuss changes in the Articles of Confederation.

THE CONSTITUTION: A PERMANENT FRAMEWORK

For generations the people of the United States have revered the Constitution, and rightly so. It has provided an enduring and evolving framework for more than 175 years of national development. In some respects, it reflects the time of its creation, for it incorporates basic American tenets of the 18th century. These include the theory of the state as a compact between the people and the government and the idea that fundamental laws should be written. The Constitution reaffirms the commitment to traditional rights of Englishmen to the protection of life, liberty, and property that Americans defended in their rebellion against the British Crown.

Above all, the Constitution expresses, both in its provisions and in the process by which they were formulated, the Founding Fathers' abiding faith in man's willingness to reason—his ability to surmount political differences by means of rational discussion and compromise. Men sometimes disagree over the meaning of specific provisions of the Constitution, but within its broad framework and mechanism for compromise lie means to reconcile disagreement. The Constitution expresses the concerns of a past age, yet it is the embodiment of a spirit and a wisdom as modern as tomorrow.

The delegates from the various States brought a variety of political ideas and special interests to the Convention in Philadelphia in the summer of 1787. Only after about 4 months of secret debates, marked by compromise after compromise, did the ideas and interests merge into an improved framework for the National Government. Of the 39 delegates who signed the Constitution, few expressed complete satisfaction with it. The public was even less sanguine. The advocates of the Constitution labored for 1 year before enough States ratified it and made it the law of the land. Once in effect, it soon became the pride and bulwark of the Republic. It succeeded because the Convention had recognized and dealt realistically with the need to create a truly National Government.

A well-qualified body of 55 delegates from 12 States—only Rhode Island abstaining—drafted the Constitution. They represented a variety of professions and vocations, educational backgrounds, age groups, geographical areas, economic interests, and political factions. Some 34 were lawyers; 29 had graduated from colleges in England or the United States; and 8 had signed the Declaration of Independence. Of the total of 55 delegates, 18 derived their major income from farms or plantations, 15 from commerce, and the remainder from various professional or political pursuits. New Jersey's Jonathan Dayton, 27 years old, was the youngest delegate. World-famous Benjamin Franklin, 81 years old, was senior. Two delegates were reputedly the richest men in the country: George Washington and Robert Morris, "Financier of the Revolution." Others were poor. Roger Sherman of Connecticut, for example, was in dire financial straits. Some were well-to-do on paper but poor in fact. Madison, "Father of the Constitution," owned a respectably sized Virginia plantation, but could barely earn a living as a planter and also had to rely in part upon his small salary as a public official and upon gifts and loans from friends and relatives.

The delegates included many able and distinguished men: George Washington, James Madison, George Mason, George Wythe, and Edmund Randolph of Virginia; John Dickinson of Delaware; Benjamin Franklin, Robert Morris, and Gouverneur Morris of Pennsylvania; Alexander Hamilton of New York; Charles Coatsworth (C.C.) Pinckney, Charles Pinckney, and John Rutledge of South Carolina; William S.

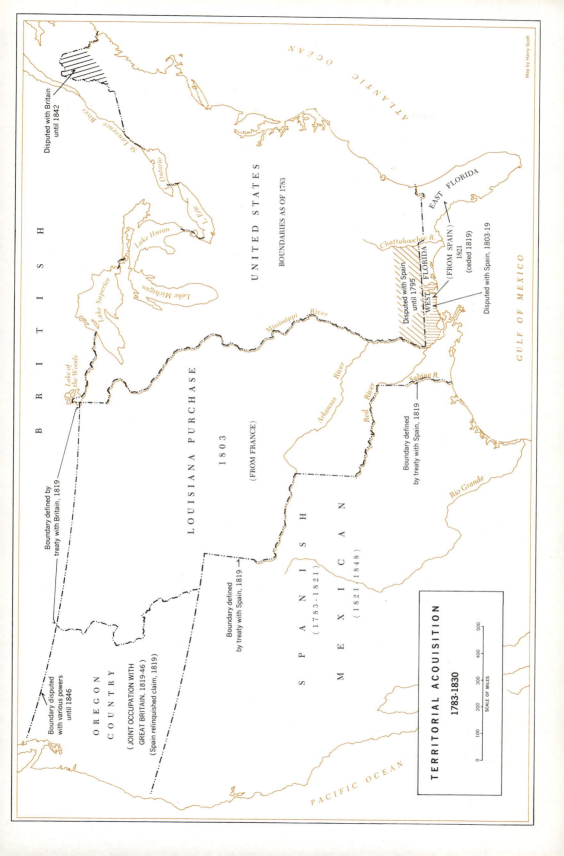

Map by Harry Scott

ATLANTIC OCEAN

Disputed with Britain
until 1842

St. Lawrence River

Lake Ontario

Lake Erie

Lake Huron

Lake Michigan

Lake Superior

UNITED STATES

BOUNDARIES AS OF 1783

EAST FLORIDA

Chattahoochee R.

EAST FLORIDA

(FROM SPAIN)
1821
(ceded 1819)

Disputed with Spain, 1803-19

WEST FLORIDA

Disputed with Spain
until 1795

Disputed with Spain, 1803-19

GULF OF MEXICO

B R I T I S H

Lake of
the Woods

Mississippi River

Arkansas River

Red River

Sabine R.

Boundary defined
by treaty with Spain, 1819

Rio Grande

LOUISIANA PURCHASE

1803

(FROM FRANCE)

Boundary defined by
treaty with Britain, 1819

Boundary defined
by treaty with Spain, 1819

S P A N I S H
(1783 - 1821)

M E X I C A N
(1821 - 1848)

Boundary disputed
with various powers
until 1846

OREGON
COUNTRY

(JOINT OCCUPATION WITH
GREAT BRITAIN, 1819-46)
(Spain relinquished claim, 1819)

PACIFIC OCEAN

TERRITORIAL ACQUISITION

1783-1830

0   100   200   300   400   500

SCALE OF MILES

Johnson of Connecticut; Luther Martin, from Maryland; and Elbridge Gerry of Massachusetts. Four outstanding national leaders were absent: Thomas Jefferson and John Adams were on diplomatic duty in Europe, and Patrick Henry and Samuel Adams refused to attend because they opposed the movement for a stronger National Government.

Despite the varied background and interests of the delegates, most of them shared a commitment to nationalism, economic conservatism, and practical politics. Perhaps only three or four would have acknowledged that they were "democrats," or believers in the ultimate wisdom of the general populace. On the other hand, Alexander Hamilton's purported dictum "the people are a great beast" would not have served as a representative opinion. To most of the group, the issue was not simply democracy versus aristocracy, but national union versus disintegration. They did not seek to impose a fixed political philosophy but to find a way to reconcile conflicting theories within a framework of stability and orderly growth. Some of the delegates stood to gain financially from the fiscal stability that was expected to follow the creation of a strong central government, but many stood to lose. On key issues, delegates often voted against their personal interests for what they believed to be the common good. If the Constitution was a conservative document, its underlying philosophy was potentially democratic.

The Constitutional Convention convened at Philadelphia on May 25, 1787, and lasted nearly 4 months. Because it was not open to the public, few Philadelphians were aware of exactly what was taking place inside the statehouse. Still, even some disinterested observers must have guessed that an important meeting was in session. Once a quorum had assembled, the delegates quickly went to work. They elected George Washington as President of the Convention and William Jackson as secretary. Jackson kept only sketchy minutes, but fortunately James Madison, who figured prominently in the Convention, maintained a comprehensive journal of the proceedings.

On the third day Gov. Edmund Randolph of Virginia introduced 15 resolutions that went far beyond mere amendment of the Articles of Confederation and proposed the creation of a sovereign National Government. The Virginia Plan, as the resolutions were called, proposed a separate executive, a system of Federal courts, and a two-house national legislature based on proportional representation. This alarmed advocates of State sovereignty. Virginia was the largest and most populous State.

In subsequent debates, delegates from the smaller States—New Jersey, Maryland, Delaware, Connecticut, and Georgia—voiced fears that adoption of the Virginia Plan, including the provision for proportional representation in the national legislature, would mean domination of the Government by the three most populous States: Virginia, Massachusetts, and Pennsylvania.

Two weeks after the introduction of the Virginia Plan, the smaller States countered with their own proposal. William Paterson offered the New Jersey Plan, which proposed to revise and strengthen the Articles. It would give the National Government power to collect taxes and regulate commerce, but would maintain the equality of individual States by creating a plural executive under their control. As under the Articles, equal representation would be preserved for each State in the national legislature.

The debates grew heated. In a speech lasting the greater part of 2 days, Luther Martin of Maryland argued that equality among the States was fundamental to the federal idea of government. In rebuttal Madison suggested that this issue was largely irrelevant. The danger that the three large States would pool their votes to dominate the Government

Departure of the Marquis de Lafayette from Mount Vernon in 1784. A French hero of the War for Independence, General Lafayette was well liked by Americans. From a lithograph by E. Farrell. Courtesy, Library of Congress.

was illusory. Their economic interests were too diverse. Virginia was a tobacco State, Pennsylvania depended heavily on flour, and Massachusetts relied on fishing. Both sides remained adamant. The Convention was deadlocked; unless the delegates resolved the issue of representation, it would dissolve.

In mid-July the "Great Compromise" broke the deadlock. Almost 1 month before, the Convention had rejected Roger Sherman's suggestion that representation in the national legislature should be proportional to population in the lower house and by State in the upper house. On July 5 a committee appointed 3 days earlier to seek a compromise recommended the adoption of Sherman's proposal. This proposal, plus provisions that money bills should originate in the lower house and that Senators could vote as individuals instead of by States in the upper house, formed the basis of the Great Compromise. The Convention accepted the compromise proposal after further refining it by the stipulation that representation in the lower house should be based on the total free population plus three-fifths of the slaves. For each 30,000 people, determined by this formula, one Representative might be elected. Madison was right about the large-small State issue. Later conflicts were most often along sectional lines. But acceptance of the Great Compromise had cleared the way for the Convention to proceed.

The Convention then drafted 23 articles that represented a preliminary version of the Constitution. During August and early September the delegates ironed out the details. They set the terms of office for Senators, Representatives, and the President. They gave Congress the power to regulate interstate commerce and foreign trade; and, in an early clash between opponents and defenders of slavery, they compromised by agreeing to take no action to halt the slave trade before 1808. By September 10 the debates were over. The Convention selected a committee to draft the final document. Gouverneur Morris of Pennsylvania was the chairman and William S. Johnson of Connecticut, Rufus King of Massachusetts, James Madison, and Alexander Hamilton rounded out the committee. They produced a final draft in 2 days. After 5 more days of deliberation, delegations from each of the 12 States represented signified their approval. Only 42 of the 55 delegates were present on September 17, the final day of the Convention. Of these, 39 signed the Constitution and then adjourned to the City Tavern for a farewell dinner.

A bundle of compromises that left many questions unanswered and many areas of sovereignty undefined, the Constitution was not a revolu-

tionary document. It contained no radical political ideas. The concept of
a government of checks and balances went back at least as far as the
mid-18th century, to the French political theorist Montesquieu. Most of
the specific provisions could be traced to English law as modified by the
American colonial experience, and to a lesser extent classical Greek and
Roman political ideas. Perhaps the only major innovation was the election of the President by an electoral college instead of the State legislatures. Yet the Constitution was a solid, practical document, and most of
the Convention delegates, though not fully satisfied with it, still regarded
it as a good summer's work. Now it was up to the people of the States to
accept it. Would they?

The Convention set up a procedure for making the Constitution the
law of the land. Each State could call a convention, whose delegates
would be elected by the voters. After nine State conventions adopted, or
ratified, the Constitution, the new Government could begin operation.
During the yearlong political struggle that ensued in the States, two distinct political factions emerged: the Federalists, supporters of the Constitution; and their opponents, called the Antifederalists. The composi-
tion of the two factions differed in every State. A host of geographical,
economic, social, and political factors entered into determining who was
for or against the Constitution. All rich merchants and planters did not
necessarily favor the Constitution nor the poor farmers and mechanics
oppose it. Nor was the eastern seaboard totally Federalist or the West
completely Antifederalist.

The Antifederalists had many objections to the Constitution. Patrick
Henry, who had declined to serve in the Convention because he "smelt a
rat," began his objections with the first three words of the Constitution.
Who, he wondered, were the Convention delegates to say "We, the people." They should have said "We, the states." Otherwise the Government would no longer be a compact among equal States but a "consoli-
dated, national government of the people of all the states." George
Mason feared that a remote National Government based on the Constitution would destroy the rights of the people. Possessed of such sweeping
powers unbridled by a bill of rights, the National Government would soon
revert to monarchy or corrupt aristocracy. Richard Henry Lee, in his
"Letters by a Federal Farmer" of 1787, presented a powerful statement of
the Antifederalist case. He argued that the Federalists were attempting to
rush the Constitution through, and, as he saw it, they were removing

power from the many to the few to prevent future political change and reform. Other Antifederalists expressed fears that the new Government would be more powerful and tyrannical than the British Government had been in 1776.

Federalist arguments stressed the need to amend the Articles. The Federalists accepted the charge that the Constitution was not perfect, but replied that it was superior to the Articles and that its imperfections could easily be purged by amendment. The most effective statement of the Federalist position was a series of 85 newspaper essays, *The Federalist Papers*, addressed to the people of the State of New York. The work of Alexander Hamilton, James Madison, and John Jay, these essays brilliantly and convincingly expounded virtually every reason why the Constitution should be adopted. More simple and direct in pleading the Federalist cause was the letter George Washington sent along with the Constitution when, as President of the Convention, he submitted it to the Continental Congress. Its purpose, he wrote, was "the consolidation of our Union, in which is involved our prosperity, felicity, safety, perhaps our national existence." Arguments were important, but the actual process of ratification in the States involved practical politics.

The contest for ratification revealed that some States, apparently less secure in their independence than others, were eager for a National Government. One of these, Delaware, leading the way on December 7, 1787, voted unanimously for ratification. Surprisingly, Pennsylvania, one of the most self-sufficient States, followed only 1 week later. Before the Antifederalists could organize the opposition, Pennsylvania Federalists had applied rough-and-tumble tactics to obtain ratification. Less than 1 month after Pennsylvania ratified, New Jersey, Georgia, and Connecticut joined the list of States that accepted the Constitution. In short order five States ratified. But people knew that the real test would come in three large States: New York, Virginia, and Massachusetts. Without their approval, the new Government would have little chance of success.

In the Massachusetts ratifying convention, Elbridge Gerry led a strong opposition to the Constitution. Only when John Hancock shifted his support to the Federalists in return for their promise to recommend a bill of rights did the Constitution win approval, by a vote of 187–168. By mid-June 1788 the requisite number of States had ratified. Maryland and South Carolina had acted in the spring and New Hampshire, the ninth, did so in June. Still, New York and Virginia remained undecided. In the Virginia convention Patrick Henry championed the Confederation faction against Madison's Federalists. On June 25, after a stiff fight, the Madisonians won. The Constitution, accompanied as in some of the other States by a recommendation for a bill of rights and additional amendments, passed the Virginia convention by a vote of 89–79.

Despite the influence of *The Federalist Papers,* the New York Antifederalists were clearly in the majority at the State convention. Alexander Hamilton, chief strategist of the New York Federalists, managed to postpone a final vote until the anticipated news arrived that Virginia and New Hampshire had ratified. When the news came from those two States, the balance of power swung to the Federalists. On July 26 New York became the 11th State to ratify. North Carolina would not join the Union until 1789 and Rhode Island until 1790, but the victory in New York gave advocates of the Constitution the opportunity to test it in action.

For all the passions generated by the State ratification battles, the Antifederalists accepted defeat gracefully. They would give the Constitution an opportunity to stand or fall on its own merits.

L A U N C H I N G   T H E   G O V E R N M E N T — C O N F L I C T I N G
I D E O L O G I E S   A N D   R O O T S   O F   P A R T Y   S C H I S M

When the Constitution went into effect in the spring of 1789, President Washington and the Congress faced the challenge of organizing and setting in motion administrative machinery, appointing competent officials, establishing procedures, and formulating policies. The accomplishments of Washington's administration were impressive. The Bill of Rights became a part of the Constitution. The Judiciary Act created the Federal court system. Secretary of the Treasury Alexander Hamilton's fiscal program placed Government finances on a sound basis and won for the Government the support of the influential businessmen. But Hamilton's fiscal program, together with the ramifications of the French Revolution, divided the Federalists. By 1796, when Washington retired from the Presidency, the political harmony of 1789 had given way to the dissonance of quarreling political factions.

Federalist John Adams, who succeeded Washington, was himself caught between elements of his own party and the Jeffersonians. His term, marked by bitter political feuding and an undeclared war with France, ended in the defeat of the Federalist Party and a sweeping victory for the Jeffersonians in the election of 1800. The Federalists would never

The inauguration of George Washington as President, at Federal Hall, New York, in 1789. From a drawing by H. A. Ogden, reproduced in *Harper's Weekly*, 1889. Courtesy, Library of Congress.

elect another President, but they had led the Nation through the first 12 years of Government under the Constitution.

On April 30, 1789, Chancellor Robert R. Livingston of New York State administered the oath of office to George Washington, the Nation's first President, at New York City's Federal Hall. Washington, who had built, led, and by the force of his example sustained the Army through the War for Independence, was now the leader of the Government. If integrity and respectability were important to winning the support of the people, Washington was a wise choice for the Presidency. To most Americans, he embodied the two qualities more than any other man.

The office of President was new. How should the Executive behave in public? The United States had 4 million people and a land area greater than that of most of the European powers. Kings governed large nations, but the United States was a republic, not a monarchy. Washington fostered the formal dignity of the Presidency but stopped short of the pomp and trappings of European monarchs. He held formal receptions on Tuesdays and rode about in an elegant coach emblazoned with the family coat of arms. Advocates of republican simplicity found both practices objectionable, and the formal appearance of the President in Congress touched off a spirited debate. Some supported the view that Congress should follow the procedure of the British Parliament when the King visited it. Others feared this would herald the return of monarchy.

If the trappings and demeanor of the Presidential office worried some exponents of representative government, one of the initial legislative acts of Congress and the President should have calmed their fears. The new Congress was strongly Federalist. Half the Senators had been delegates to the Constitutional Convention. Recognizing the need to confirm the confidence of the people, they moved quickly to meet the major criticism of the Constitution. In September 1789 they approved 12 amendments to the Constitution and sent them to the States for ratification. Based largely on George Mason's Virginia Declaration of Rights of 1776, the Bill of Rights, as the 10 amendments that the States adopted are known, made explicit the fundamental rights of citizens and pledged the U.S. Government to uphold them.

To make the Constitution work, administrative machinery had to be created. The Continental Congress bequeathed to Washington a tiny Government staff. It consisted of a foreign affairs office, manned by two Ministers, a supervisor, and two clerks; a Board of Treasury, which had no money; a department of war, without a real army; and an inadequate postal system. Furthermore, the national debt was large. The appointment of capable and dedicated officials, the establishment of new agencies, and the collection of ample revenues were vital to the launching of the Government.

Washington placed Federalists, friends of the Constitution, and men

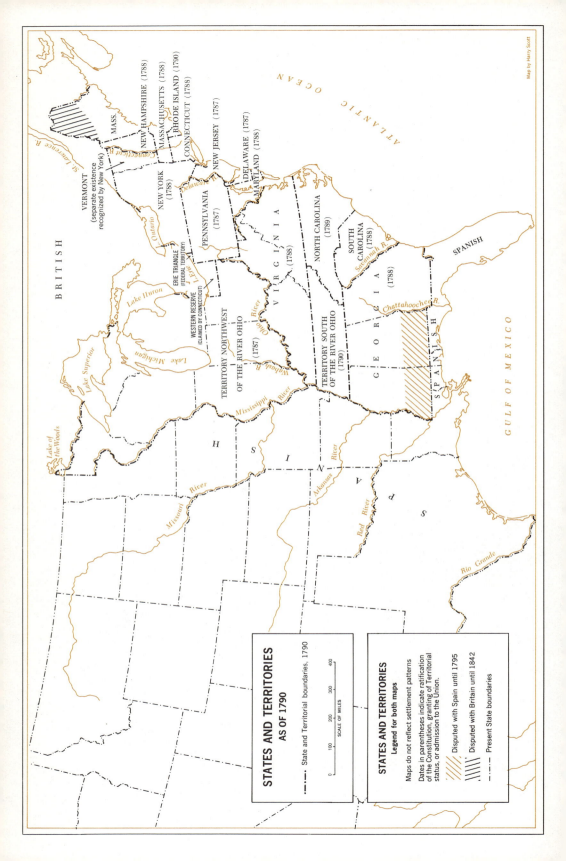

BRITISH

ATLANTIC OCEAN

Map by Harry Scott

VERMONT
(separate existence
recognized by New York)

St. Lawrence R.

L. Ontario

Lake Superior

Lake Huron

Lake Michigan

Lake of the Woods

MASS.

NEW HAMPSHIRE (1788)

MASSACHUSETTS (1788)

RHODE ISLAND (1790)

CONNECTICUT (1788)

Connecticut R.

NEW JERSEY (1787)

NEW YORK (1788)

PENNSYLVANIA (1787)

Delaware R.

DELAWARE (1787)

MARYLAND (1788)

VIRGINIA (1788)

NORTH CAROLINA (1789)

SOUTH CAROLINA (1788)

Savannah R.

G E O R G I A (1788)

Chattahoochee R.

ERIE TRIANGLE (FEDERAL TERRITORY)

WESTERN RESERVE (CLAIMED BY CONNECTICUT)

TERRITORY NORTHWEST OF THE RIVER OHIO (1787)

Ohio River

Wabash R.

TERRITORY SOUTH OF THE RIVER OHIO (1790)

Mississippi River

Missouri River

Arkansas River

Red River

Rio Grande

SPANISH

S P A N I S H

GULF OF MEXICO

I N D I A N S

STATES AND TERRITORIES
AS OF 1790

— · · — · · — State and Territorial boundaries, 1790

SCALE OF MILES
0   100   200   300   400

STATES AND TERRITORIES
Legend for both maps

Maps do not reflect settlement patterns

Dates in parentheses indicate ratification
of the Constitution, granting of Territorial
status, or admission to the Union.

/// Disputed with Spain until 1795

\\\ Disputed with Britain until 1842

— · · — Present State boundaries

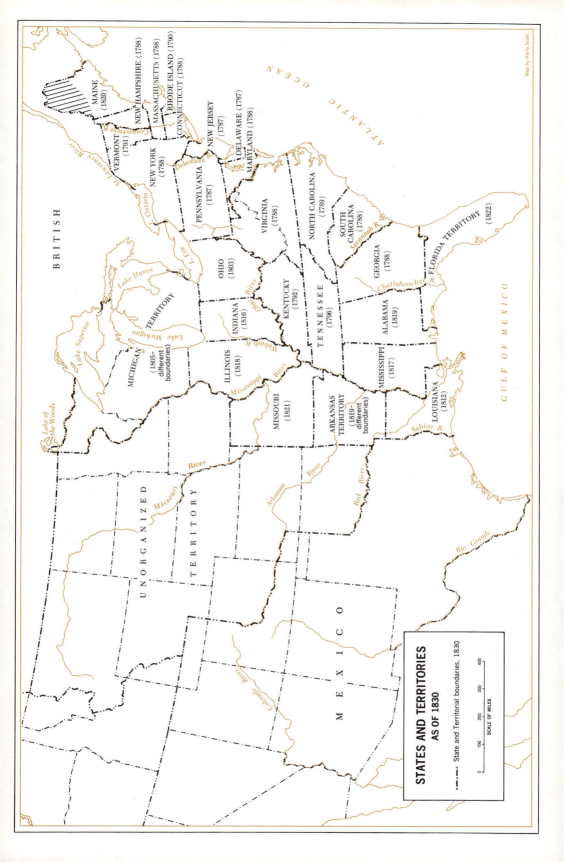

STATES AND TERRITORIES
AS OF 1830

▬·▬·▬ State and Territorial boundaries, 1830

SCALE OF MILES

0   100   200   300   400

Map by Harry Scott

ATLANTIC OCEAN

BRITISH

MAINE (1820)
NEW HAMPSHIRE (1788)
MASSACHUSETTS (1788)
RHODE ISLAND (1790)
CONNECTICUT (1788)
VERMONT (1791)
NEW YORK (1788)
NEW JERSEY (1787)
DELAWARE (1787)
MARYLAND (1788)
PENNSYLVANIA (1787)
VIRGINIA (1788)
NORTH CAROLINA (1789)
SOUTH CAROLINA (1788)
GEORGIA (1788)
FLORIDA TERRITORY (1822)
OHIO (1803)
INDIANA (1816)
KENTUCKY (1792)
TENNESSEE (1796)
ALABAMA (1819)
MISSISSIPPI (1817)
ILLINOIS (1818)
MICHIGAN TERRITORY (1805 – different boundaries)
MISSOURI (1821)
ARKANSAS TERRITORY (1819 – different boundaries)
LOUISIANA (1812)
UNORGANIZED TERRITORY

MEXICO

GULF OF MEXICO

St. Lawrence River
L. Ontario
L. Erie
Lake Huron
Lake Michigan
Lake Superior
Lake of the Woods
Connecticut R.
Delaware R.
Ohio River
Wabash R.
Mississippi River
Savannah R.
Chattahoochee R.
Sabine R.
Missouri River
Arkansas River
Red River
Colorado River
Rio Grande

of more than average ability in most of the major judicial and administrative posts. The Judiciary Act of 1789 created Federal legal machinery. Washington appointed John Jay as Chief Justice of the United States, and Edmund Randolph as Attorney General. Judgeships in district and circuit courts went to known supporters of the Constitution. The two key posts in the Executive Branch next to the Presidency were Secretary of the Treasury and Secretary of State. Washington called Thomas Jefferson home from his post as Minister to France to take over the State Department. After Robert Morris declined to serve as Secretary of the Treasury, Washington offered Alexander Hamilton the $3,500-a-year position. Sacrificing a $12,000 annual income from his law practice in New York, Hamilton accepted and became a dominant figure in the Washington administration.

A nationalist and an aristocrat, Hamilton believed that the country had little to fear from a well-administered central Government. In his view, powerful interests in the large States represented the major threat to the Union. He believed that the future of the country lay in commerce and manufacturing. If the Government were to survive, it must have the aid and support of the men of means: Merchants, bankers, and businessmen. What the Government must do first, he reasoned, was establish sound public credit and reliable sources of revenue. In a series of reports to Congress on credit and manufactures, during the period 1789–91, Hamilton articulated his program and saw it become national policy.

The Continental Congress bequeathed to the new Government a foreign and domestic debt of $54 million. Hamilton proposed that this national debt be funded and paid dollar for dollar. No one objected to the payment of the foreign part of the debt. But the domestic debt was mostly in the form of certificates that the Continental Congress had used to pay soldiers during the War for Independence; it promised to redeem them at a later date. For living expenses, many veterans had been forced to sell their certificates to speculators for as little as 12 cents on the dollar. Hamilton proposed to pay all certificate holders 100 cents on the dollar. The speculators would get rich and the original holders who had sold would never realize the full value of their certificates. Hamilton's erstwhile political friend, Madison, led the congressional faction opposing the funding, but Hamilton prevailed with his argument that the Government must establish a reputation for payment of its debts and that a distinction in payment between holders and former holders of certificates was clearly impossible.

To gain the support of financial interests for the Government and at the same time raise money to help pay the national debt, Hamilton recommended to Congress the sale of Government long-term interest-bearing bonds to individuals and the enactment of a tariff to protect U.S. manufactures. Congress later adopted the recommendation on bond sales, and the tariff of 1789 authorized collection of duties on 80 manufactures at points of entry to the United States.

Assumption by the Federal Government of the war debts of the States aroused strong opposition from representatives of those States, especially in the South, that had already paid most of their war debts. The measure passed Congress only after Hamilton struck a bargain with the opposition. Southern representatives supported it in return for Hamilton's support of the placement of the permanent Capital of the United States in a Southern locale. The site selected was a 10-mile tilted square straddling the Potomac River around Georgetown, Md., and Alexandria, Va. Further compromise was necessary to secure passage of the assumption measure. States with small war debts received credits from the Government to compensate for the burden lifted from States with heavy debts.

A national bank was another part of Hamilton's program. The bank, really a private bank affiliated with the Government, would serve as a depository and investment agent for money collected by the Treasury. By means of branch banks, it would carry on Government business throughout the Nation. State banking interests opposed the national bank. Although legislation for the bank had passed Congress, Washington, unsure if the measure was constitutional, hesitated to sign it. In a written opinion, Jefferson, in a "strict" interpretation of the Constitution, had argued that chartering of the bank was unconstitutional because it was not among the powers enumerated in the Constitution. In rebuttal, Hamilton, employing a "broad" interpretation of the Constitution, held that certain implied powers gave Congress the authority to do what was "necessary and proper" to accomplish ends not prohibited by the Constitution or inimical to the public good. Washington yielded to Hamilton's reasoning and signed the national bank bill, but both Jefferson's "strict construction" and Hamilton's doctrine of implied powers would have historical significance far beyond the bank controversy.

By 1792 Hamilton's leadership had pushed his program through Congress and carried the opposition before it. Hamilton's reports had been

Alexander Hamilton, first Secretary of the Treasury, sought to strengthen the Federal authority. From a painting by John Trumbull. Courtesy, Library of Congress.

brilliant and practical, but they had showed more concern for order than liberty, had valued property over human fulfillment, and had benefited the merchant and speculator at the expense of the common farmer. An opposition was rising. Thomas Jefferson would be its leader.

Jefferson was part practical politician and part political philosopher. On the philosophical side, he envisioned a nation of self-sufficient small "yeoman farmers" living in rustic simplicity, peace, and liberty amid the splendors of nature. These farmers would be informed, intelligent citizens who would govern themselves in small democratic units, and the troubles of Europe—crowded cities, oppressive institutions, and the rest—would be far away beyond the broad Atlantic.

On the practical side, Jefferson recognized that the reality must be less idyllic. Still, the United States *was* uncrowded and free of monarchy and hereditary aristocracy. Agriculture *was* the keystone of the economy. And the Atlantic did separate North America from Europe. As Hamilton's economic program unfolded, Jefferson saw in it the death of his dream. The fiscal program would destroy the yeoman farmer's independence, tax him into debt, and destroy local political power. The tariff would interrupt the free trade that was sacred to the farmer's economic independence. It would also encourage the growth of manufacturing, which meant the growth of cities and the rise of a moneyed aristocracy. As Jefferson saw it, Hamilton's program might bring material wealth to the United States, but it would not improve the *quality* of life.

Personal animosity compounded the ideological split between Jefferson and Hamilton. Hamilton regarded Jefferson as a dangerous radical out to destroy him and felt that he was always meddling in Treasury affairs. To Jefferson, it seemed that Hamilton had come to control the President and was trying to make him king in fact if not in name. By 1791 both Hamilton and Jefferson were making anonymous attacks on each other in the newspapers—Hamilton in John Fenno's *Gazette of the United States* and Jefferson in Philip Freneau's *National Gazette*.

Another source of dispute between Jefferson and Hamilton was the French Revolution. It had resulted in war between Great Britain and

The U.S. Capitol, from Pennsylvania Avenue, before the British burned it, in 1814. From a watercolor, drawn from memory, by Benjamin H. Latrobe, one of the architects of the Capitol. Courtesy, Library of Congress.

France, each of which vied for the support of the United States. President Washington issued a Proclamation of Neutrality in 1793. Like most U.S. statesmen of the time, he believed it vital to the independence of the Nation to stay out of European wars and avoid entangling alliances. But neither the Hamiltonians, or Federalists, nor the Jeffersonians, or Democratic-Republicans, were really neutral. The Hamiltonians strongly favored Great Britain because of the former colonial attachment, respect for English institutions, and the belief that Britain was the United States' best customer and protector of her commerce. Most Jeffersonians identified with France. They remembered that the French had aided the United States in the struggle for independence, and they respected the liberal principles of the Revolution.

The issue flared up in 1793 with the Citizen Genêt affair. Genêt, the French Minister to the United States, openly ignored Washington's Proclamation of Neutrality by attempting to recruit U.S. citizens for military expeditions against Louisiana, the Floridas, and Canada. His indiscretion was too much even for Jefferson. The United States demanded Genêt's recall. The incident, however, brought the issues of the French Revolution to the foreground in public affairs.

Two more events, the Whisky Rebellion and Jay's Treaty, further divided the dissident political forces. The rebellion came about because of Hamilton's attempt to raise national revenue by placing an excise tax on alcoholic spirits. The tax burden fell upon back-country farmers, who found it necessary to transport their bulky grain to market in liquid form. Convinced that the tax would destroy them, in 1794 a group of farmers in western Pennsylvania rebelled. An army of 16,000 men, commanded by Hamilton, easily put down the rebellion. The new Government thus demonstrated that it could act expeditiously in an emergency, but the Federalists won few friends in Western regions.

In 1795 John Jay returned from Great Britain with the draft of a treaty between the United States and Great Britain, negotiated in 1794. It created a furor. In return for a few commercial concessions and a promise that the British would finally evacuate their military posts in the Northwest Territory by 1796, Jay accepted restrictions on U.S. trade with neutral countries and promised that U.S. ports would not serve as bases for privateers or British enemies. Considering the relative power of the two countries, Jay had done about as well as he could, but the Jeffersonians argued that it was not good enough. In spite of hostile public opinion, the President and Congress accepted Jay's Treaty. But the treaty issue advanced the formation of political parties a step further. The Jeffersonians called a caucus, the first in U.S. history, and began to organize a disciplined and responsive political party.

One bright spot in diplomatic relations during the period was Thomas Pinckney's negotiations with Spain. In Pinckney's Treaty, or the Treaty of San Lorenzo (1796), the United States obtained the right of free navigation of the Mississippi, the right to unload goods at New Orleans, and a favorable settlement of the dispute over the northern boundary of Florida.

Washington, as he retired from the Presidency, knew that, though the country still faced difficult problems, the Government was underway.

LIBERTY AND AUTHORITY—OPPOSITION
OR SEDITION?

The Federalists nominated Vice President John Adams to succeed Washington and diplomatic hero Thomas Pinckney as his running mate. The Democratic-Republicans, the Jefferson-Madison party, backed Jefferson and Aaron Burr. Hamilton did not fully trust Adams, so he maneuvered to have certain Federalist electors vote for Pinckney but not Adams. Pinckney would become President and Adams would remain "buried" in the Vice-Presidency. The plan backfired when Adams' New England supporters discovered Hamilton's plan and withheld their votes from Pinckney. As a result, Adams won—by a mere three electoral votes—and Jefferson became the Vice President. Handicapped by a Cabinet that answered to Hamilton, a hostile Congress, and his political enemy Jefferson as Vice President, Adams pursued a lonely course for the next 4 years.

Foreign affairs were a major problem. The British and French were locked in the wars of the French Revolution. Great Britain was not particularly solicitous of the rights of American ships, but the major obstacle to peace was France. Its Government, angered by the Jay Treaty, demanded that U.S. ships discontinue carrying British goods and threatened to hang any U.S. seamen found serving on British warships. In 1798, by which time Franco-American relations had badly deteriorated, Adams sent C. C. Pinckney, Elbridge Gerry, and John Marshall to France to effect a reconciliation. The French Foreign Minister, Talleyrand, humiliated the United States by refusing to receive the delegation. Through agents known as "X," "Y," and "Z," he demanded a bribe of $250,000,

John Adams, first Vice President and second President of the United States. He was also the progenitor of a distinguished American family. From a lithograph by John Pendleton, after a painting by Gilbert Stuart. Courtesy, Library of Congress.

a \$12,000,000 loan, and a formal apology for Adams' public criticism of France. In return, he hinted at concessions, but promised nothing beyond acceptance of the delegates' credentials. In reply to Talleyrand's agents, Pinckney reportedly said "no, no, not a sixpence." When the President turned the negotiators' report over to Congress and the word of the XYZ affair spread, the public rallied to the defense of the Government and the President. "No, no, not a sixpence" became "Millions for defense, but not one cent for tribute!" War with France seemed imminent. Hamilton and most Federalists favored war as a way of uniting the country and building a strong Army and Navy. The Jeffersonians, controlling roughly half the votes in Congress, opposed war, as far as they dared, but public opinion was bellicose. If Adams had asked for a declaration of war, the antiwar party could not have stopped it.

Between 1798 and 1800 Franco-American relations further deteriorated. The United States, having an Army of only 3,500 men and a Navy of but 3 frigates, was not ready for war, but increasing depredations by French picaroons, or privateers, on U.S. merchant vessels caused Congress to enact a series of defensive measures. Though neither nation declared war, between 1798 and 1800 they fought a sea war in the Caribbean and off the South Atlantic coast. By 1800, 14 U.S. warships, under Secretary Benjamin Stoddert's 2-year-old Navy Department, augmented by hundreds of privateers, had cleared the French picaroons from U. S. waters. And, for the first time since the War for Independence, the United States had a naval hero. Capt. Thomas Truxtun, commanding the *Constellation,* had beaten one French frigate, *L'Insurgente,* and severely mauled another.

In 1798 Elbridge Gerry returned from France with the news that the French Directory wanted to explore the possibilities of peace. The French hoped to reoccupy Louisiana and to use U.S. shipping to counteract Britain's naval supremacy. War with the United States was thus inimical to French policy. In November 1799 Adams sent three Envoys to France. By the time they reached Paris, Napoleon had gained the ascendency and was anxious to make peace. By a convention signed in September 1800, France agreed to the abrogation of earlier treaties, notably the historic Franco-American alliance of 1778, and endorsed the principle "free ships, free goods." Congress ratified the convention in December 1800.

Bitter political frustrations found release in the Federalist Alien and Sedition Acts and in the Democratic-Republican response, the Kentucky Resolutions and the Virginia Resolutions. As the Democratic-Republicans continued to oppose war with the old ally in the War for Independence, France, and the Federalists drew closer to the old enemy, Great Britain, rational discussion of political differences between the two parties degenerated into an ever more shrill exchange of insults. The Democratic-Republicans caricatured the President as the "bald, toothless, querulous Adams," and Federalists called their opponents "the refuse, the sweepings of the most depraved part of mankind." Partly to silence opposition, partly to tighten controls over aliens in preparation for war with France, in 1798 Federalist legislators, without the active support of Adams or Hamilton, pushed the Alien and Sedition Acts through Congress. Three of the four acts dealt with immigration and the rights of aliens. Of these, one never went into effect; another was never enforced. The third, the Naturalization Act, extended the residence requirement for aliens seeking citizenship

"Congressional Pugilists" depicts Representatives Matthew Lyon, a Democratic-Republican, and Roger Griswold, a Federalist, clashing in Congress Hall in 1798. Griswold allegedly insulted Lyon's record during the War for Independence. This clash, though extreme, reveals the acrimony between the parties that prevailed at the time. From a cartoon by an unknown artist. Courtesy, Maryland Historical Society.

from 5 to 14 years. The fourth act, "An Act for the Punishment of Certain Crimes," was the notorious Sedition Act. It prohibited oral and written expressions of a "false, scandalous, and malicious" character respecting the Government or its officers on pain of fine and imprisonment.

In one minor sense the act was a victory for free speech. Where common law let the court decide whether a statement was or was not libelous, the Sedition Act required that malicious intent be proved and that the defense could win acquittal if it would prove the truth of "libel." The great injustice of the act was its application. Federalists used it to defend the Federalist President against unfair attack without extending its protection to the Democratic-Republican Vice President, the object of equal censure.

In the best known of the prosecutions of Democratic-Republicans under the act, Matthew Lyon, outspoken Congressman from Vermont, defended himself by challenging its constitutionality. Lyon lost his case and went to jail, where he became a popular hero and won reelection. In the meantime, Democratic-Republican leaders took up the matter of constitutionality in the Virginia Resolutions and the Kentucky Resolutions. James Madison drafted the Virginia Resolutions (1798), by which the Virginia legislature announced its belief in the unconstitutionality of the Alien and Sedition Acts. Jefferson, in the Kentucky Resolutions (1789–99), went further. He maintained that the acts were null and void *per se* and that a State should nullify or refuse to comply with them. The two resolutions had no legal effect, and the acts remained on the books.

Amid all the turmoil, in October of 1800 John Adams and the 132 Government officials and clerks packed up and the next month left the temporary Capital, Philadelphia, for the incomplete but permanent Capital on the Potomac. The Capitol was unfinished, and workmen's shacks sat near the "President's House." But at last the Government had a permanent home.

THE REVOLUTION OF 1800: ASCENDENCY OF THE JEFFERSONIANS

More than a decade of Federalist Government ended in 1800, when the Nation elected Jefferson to the Presidency. For the next 24 years, Virginians—Jefferson, Madison, and Monroe—would lead the United States, and the Democratic-Republican Party would guide the national destiny. Jefferson introduced a different political philosophy to the Executive Office. Economy, simplicity, informality, and noninvolvement in European affairs were its touchstones. But, for all his differences from his predecessors, his "Revolution of 1800" was less revolutionary than his followers boasted or the Federalists feared. Jefferson's greatest accomplishment was the Louisiana Purchase, his greatest disappointment the failure of the Embargo Act of 1807 during the Napoleonic Wars. James Madison, who succeeded Jefferson, inherited a political situation that was difficult to control. His efforts to keep the peace through diplomacy did not succeed, and, in 1812, the Nation found itself at war with Great Britain.

In 1800 John Adams stood a good chance of reelection. His handling of the dispute with France had made him popular. His defeat occurred in large measure because of disunity in the Federalist Party and because the Jeffersonians had created better party machinery and tighter party discipline. A national caucus, or meeting of party leaders, which directed the activities of local "Democratic" clubs and State committees, encouraged the election of State and National candidates pledged to support Jeffersonian principles. Party newspapers lauded Jefferson and his running mate Aaron Burr; and, in defiance of the Sedition Act, heaped scorn upon the Federalists. The Federalists' caucus, hopelessly divided, reflected the mutual enmity of the party leaders, Adams and Hamilton.

In the election the Jeffersonians won the Southern States and New York and the victory. They had elected a President, but whom? Jefferson and Burr were tied at 73 electoral votes each. By the rules of the electoral system, only the House of Representatives, voting by States, could break the tie. Democratic-Republican electors had intended that Jefferson should be President, but he had political enemies and Burr did not withdraw from the contest. Ironically, it fell to Federalist Party leader Alexander Hamilton to wield his influence to break a weeklong deadlock in the House and choose between two of his bitterest political enemies. He backed Jefferson as the lesser evil. Burr, irritated, had to settle for the Vice-Presidency.

On March 4, 1801, Thomas Jefferson became the first President of the United States to be inaugurated at the Capitol in Washington, D.C. The Federalists feared the worst from his ascendency. In the heat of the Presidential campaign, the philosophical differences between the two parties had been emphasized to a point where it seemed that the election of Jefferson would turn the country upside-down. Though the Jeffersonians made changes in national administration, they also continued many Federalist policies and never wavered from a basic commitment to the Constitution. The frequently quoted sentence from Jefferson's First Inaugural Address, "We are all Republicans, we are all Federalists," suggests that the political disagreements of the time took place within the framework of a basic faith in representative government. The Jeffersonians continued much of Hamilton's financial program, including the First Bank of the United States, funding, and assumption. They permitted some avowed Federalists to continue to hold administrative positions. Although Jefferson believed in an agricultural America, he encouraged commerce.

Yet Jefferson did bring new faces and ideas to the Government, and his Congress reversed some Federalist policies, particularly those concerning the Alien and Sedition Acts. James Madison, his friend and mainstay

Thomas Jefferson, Founding Father, first Secretary of State, and third President. From a painting by Thomas Sully. Courtesy, Library of Congress.

of the Democratic-Republican Party, became Secretary of State. Albert Gallatin, a Swiss emigré who shared Jefferson's economic views, took over the Treasury Department. Certainly Jefferson's appointments did not bear out the Federalist fear that he would fill the Government with inexperienced and undistinguished "democrats."

Jefferson stressed informality. He discontinued the weekly Presidential levees and abandoned the practice of delivering his messages to Congress in person. He often dressed in an informal fashion and disdained the niceties of diplomatic protocol. Refusing to use an ornate Presidential coach, he walked or rode about the Capital City on horseback. And, perhaps most important, he made himself accessible to the public. If a citizen had a grievance or a problem, the President was willing to discuss it.

The election of 1800 gave the Jeffersonians control of two branches of the Government—the executive and legislative—but the Federalist-sponsored Judiciary Act of 1800 had created a number of Federal judgeships, to which Adams in his last days as President had appointed staunch Federalists. Particularly alarming to Jefferson was the activity of one of these "midnight appointments," Jefferson's own distant cousin, Chief Justice John Marshall. In *Marbury v. Madison* (1803), he asserted the right of the Supreme Court to declare acts of Congress unconstitutional, though he did not actually challenge specific acts of Congress. Jefferson became convinced that the Court in the hands of Federalist judges would thwart the will of the people. In 1802 the Jeffersonian Congress had repealed the Judiciary Act of 1800 and thus abolished many Federalist-held judgeships. In March 1804 the Senate removed Federalist Judge John Pickering, but, after an attempt to impeach Associate Justice Samuel Chase failed, the Jeffersonians abandoned this method of removing political enemies from the Supreme Court. Instead, they relied on the slower process of filling vacancies as they occurred with Democratic-Republicans.

The fiscal policies of Jefferson and Secretary of the Treasury Gallatin included the reduction of Government expenditures and taxes, an attempt to retire the national debt, and the elimination of internal taxes. Jefferson believed that the United States should withdraw from European affairs, at least while the Napoleonic Wars raged. The State Department slashed expenses. Army strength dropped from 4,000 to 2,500 men; State militias would serve if the country were invaded; to provide for a cadre of trained officers to lead the militia in time of war, the U.S. Military Academy at West Point, N.Y., opened on July 4, 1802. The naval

Lt. Stephen Decatur, one of the first U.S. naval heroes, achieved fame for his daring attacks on the pirates of Barbary during the Tripolitan War (1801–5). His feats are memorialized in this print of a wood engraving by Whitney and Jocelyn, after F. O. C. Darley. Courtesy, Library of Congress.

buildup begun by Adams was halted. Ships were sold. Only coastal fortifications and a flotilla of inexpensive gunboats remained to repel invaders by sea.

In spite of his commitment to defensive warfare, Jefferson dispatched a naval force to the Mediterranean to end pirate raids on U.S. shipping along the Barbary coast. The Tripolitanian War, 1801–5, was inconclusive, but it produced a new naval hero, Lt. Stephen Decatur. Decatur's daring night raid, which destroyed the captured U.S. vessel *Philadelphia* under pirate guns in the harbor of Tripoli, brought him fame.

In another instance, Jefferson departed from the abstractions of his philosophy. Forswearing his "strict construction" of the Constitution, he supported the purchase of Louisiana. In 1800, in the Treaty of San Ildefonso, the Spanish King had secretly retroceded the vast but vaguely defined Territory of Louisiana to France. But Napoleon's dream of reestablishing a French empire in the North American West vanished with the lives of 50,000 of his soldiers who in 1800–1802 perished as a result of Toussaint L'Ouverture's uprising against French rule in Santo Domingo. By 1803 Napoleon, preparing for the next round of war with Great

Britain, recognized that Louisiana was a far too distant outpost to be held by France against the British Navy. In French hands, Louisiana might precipitate a U.S.-British alliance against France. Why not satisfy the United States and make a profit by selling Louisiana?

French plans to sell Louisiana were unknown to Jefferson, but he recognized that New Orleans and control of the Mississippi River were vital to Western trade. In 1802, after the Spanish Intendant of New Orleans revoked the U.S. right of deposit, or the right to unload goods, Jefferson dispatched James Monroe to assist the U.S. Envoy to France, Robert R. Livingston, in negotiating the purchase of New Orleans and possibly the Floridas. Florida was not for sale—it was not even French! But to the surprise of Monroe and Livingston the French offered instead New Orleans and a vast area west of the Mississippi River—some 828,000 square miles as it turned out.

The U.S. diplomats swallowed hard and exceeded their diplomatic instructions. In April 1803 they agreed that the United States would pay $15 million for the Louisiana Territory. According to Jefferson's interpretation of the Constitution, the Government had no authority to purchase Louisiana. A constitutional amendment was necessary to grant that power. But an amendment might take too long, and in the meantime Napoleon might renege on the agreement. Recognizing the immense practical importance of obtaining Louisiana, Jefferson won congressional acceptance of the terms of the purchase, New England dissenting, and in December 1803 the U.S. flag was raised over New Orleans.

If the flag were to keep flying over New Orleans and the rest of the West, Spanish intrigue and domestic conspiracy had to be punished. To do so, Jefferson in 1807 influenced the trial of Aaron Burr, his former Vice President. Burr was charged with treason. The judge was Chief Justice John Marshall. Much about Burr's "conspiracy" remains a mystery to this day. After Hamilton used his influence in 1804 to help defeat Burr's bid for the New York Governorship, Burr believed that once again Hamilton had thwarted his plans and challenged him to a duel. The ensuing duel, in which Burr killed Hamilton, wrecked Burr's political fortunes in the East. Like many another, he sought a new fortune in the West.

Burr later said that he had hoped to become Emperor of Mexico, but the charge against him was treason and stemmed from the belief held by many people that he had endeavored to separate the West from the rest of the United States. Whatever his true purpose, Burr spent much time during the years 1804–7 in conferring with westerners and Spanish and British officials and seeking money to finance his schemes. Finally, in 1807, U.S. authorities arrested Burr in the Southwest and returned him to Richmond, Va., for trial before a Federal court. The trial was rife with political overtones. Jefferson, in his zeal to see Burr convicted, virtually conducted the prosecution by proxy. But the presiding magistrate, Chief Justice Marshall—political enemy of Jefferson and known for his "broad" interpretation of the Constitution—chose a "strict" interpretation of treason in the Burr case. For conviction, the Constitution required two witnesses to the act of treason. The Government could not produce them. To Jefferson's disgust the verdict was "not guilty."

In 1804 Jefferson won reelection by a landslide of electoral votes. C. C. Pinckney, the Federalist candidate, won only Connecticut. The Federalist Party was no longer a serious contender for national political power. The continuing effort to avoid involvement in the Napoleonic Wars dominated Jefferson's second term. Neutrality was difficult to maintain because the agricultural United States needed overseas outlets and European manufactured goods. The world's second largest merchant fleet carried the U.S. flag to the centers of world trade, where U.S. neutral rights clashed with the military strategy of one or the other of the European powers. In 1806–7 Napoleon, whose armies controlled Europe, promulgated the Continental System in his Milan and Berlin decrees. They closed the ports of Europe to British trade. Great Britain retaliated with Orders in Council that forbade neutrals such as the United States to carry goods to Europe. As the powers attempted to strangle one another's commerce, U.S. shipping suffered. The Royal Navy seized and confiscated U.S. vessels bound for Europe or the French West Indies. French privateers did the same to ships carrying goods to British ports. Before the struggle ended, the French had confiscated about 500 U.S. ships, the British 1,000.

The British war effort depended heavily upon the Royal Navy, whose desertion rate was high because of harsh conditions. To maintain adequate crews, the British stopped, searched, and removed suspected British deserters from neutral ships, especially U.S. ships. This practice violated the sovereignty of the United States and inflamed public opinion against Great Britain. In 1807 a flagrant incident occurred. The *Leopard* of the Royal Navy accosted the U.S. Frigate *Chesapeake* in U.S. territorial waters. When the surprised *Chesapeake* ignored the *Leopard's* challenge, she received a deadly broadside. The British then boarded her and removed four crewmen, one of whom they later hanged as a deserter.

As word of the affair spread across the country, war appeared imminent. Jefferson immediately ordered British warships out of U.S. waters, and demanded an official apology and the return of the seamen. The apology and the return of the seamen would not be forthcoming for 5 years. But Jefferson did not call for war. Instead, he turned to economic sanctions to persuade both the British and French to abandon their maritime harassment. His Embargo Act of 1807 withdrew the Nation from world trade. Drawing strong protest from shippers, it prohibited the export of U.S. goods and denied ships the right to leave U.S. ports for foreign ports. Many New England shippers violated the embargo. Those who did not, as well as Southern export agriculturists, suffered economically. Once again some New Englanders talked of secession. In 1809 Jefferson acquiesced in the repeal of the embargo. It had averted war, but at a high cost to North-South relations and to U.S. trade.

Jefferson's two terms as President had been physically and mentally exhausting. Believing that a President should serve no more than two terms and preferring life at Monticello to a third term, Jefferson proposed James Madison as his successor. Eastern antiembargo Democratic-Republicans nominated George Clinton of New York for President. John Randolph of Roanoke and John Taylor of Caroline, leaders of the extreme Southern agrarian wing of the party, favored an unwilling James Monroe, who soon withdrew from the race. Despite Democratic-Republican Party dissidence, Madison easily defeated his competitors and Federalist C. C. Pinckney. In March of 1809 Madison began 8 difficult years as President.

Drifting toward war

James Madison, "Father of the Constitution" and cofounder with Jefferson of the Democratic-Republican Party, conceived his role as President to be that of a manager. By and large he left policymaking to Congress. Inevitably, for the British Orders in Council and French decrees were still in effect, foreign affairs dominated Madison's first term, as they had Jefferson's second. Madison's Cabinet was weak and for the most part its members had been forced upon him by political necessity.

Construction of the U.S. Frigate *Philadelphia*. Because a naval war between France and the United States seemed imminent, by 1800 the newly created Navy Department had built 14 warships. From a drawing and engraving by William Birch and Son. Courtesy, Library of Congress.

Congress was strong and growing stronger. Vigorous young men, a new generation, were beginning to assert themselves in the House.

Madison was of the older generation; he struggled to maintain peace through diplomacy. The Non-Intercourse Act of 1809 replaced the embargo. The new act permitted trade with all nations except Great Britain and France. U.S. shippers quickly took advantage of the act, and prosperity temporarily replaced the depression of the embargo period. The British, who had felt the loss of both the Continental and American trade during the embargo, offered trade concessions to the United States. During the negotiations, however, British representative David Erskine yielded too much, and the British Foreign Office repudiated the Erskine-Rufus King agreement. Anglo-American relations worsened.

Napoleon exploited the situation by taking advantage of a new U.S. policy. Expounded in Macon's Bill Number Two of 1810, it offered trade with France or Great Britain if either repealed their commercial restrictions. In a highly ambiguous diplomatic note, Napoleon apparently

convinced Madison that the decrees were no longer in effect toward the
United States. The President announced that trade with France would
resume in March 1811 but not with Britain until she repealed the Orders
in Council. Doubting that Napoleon had really rescinded the restrictions, the British hesitated to repeal the orders. Still, Great Britain did
not want another enemy at this time. Finally, on June 23, 1812, the
British did repeal the orders. But it was too late. Five days earlier the
United States, by a vote of 79–49 in the House and 19–13 in the Senate,
had declared war on Great Britain.

The U.S. Frigate *Constitution* defeats the British *Java,* off the coast of Brazil,
during the War of 1812. From an aquatint by Coquerel, after Garneray.
Courtesy, Library of Congress.

The War of 1812: Military Stalemate
and National Awakening

The recurring problem of neutrality on the seas, a new generation's wish to prove its independence of Great Britain, the expansionists' desire to acquire Canada—these and other factors' meshed in 1812 to produce the declaration of war. The Nation was unprepared for war, and more than 2 years of conflict produced little better than a stalemate. The United States failed to achieve its military objectives. Canada and the Floridas eluded capture, and at the end of the war the U.S. Navy was helplessly blockaded in its own ports. The British fared no better. Their attempts to invade the United States failed, and the Royal Navy was unable to drive the hundreds of U.S. commerce-raiding privateers from the sea. On the domestic front the war aggravated a discontent, particularly in New England, that approached disunion at the Hartford Con-

Captain Perry transferring his flag from the *Lawrence* to the *Niagara* during the Battle of Lake Erie (1813). This U.S. victory paved the way for William Henry Harrison's march into Canada. From an engraving of a painting by Thomas Birch. Courtesy, Library of Congress.

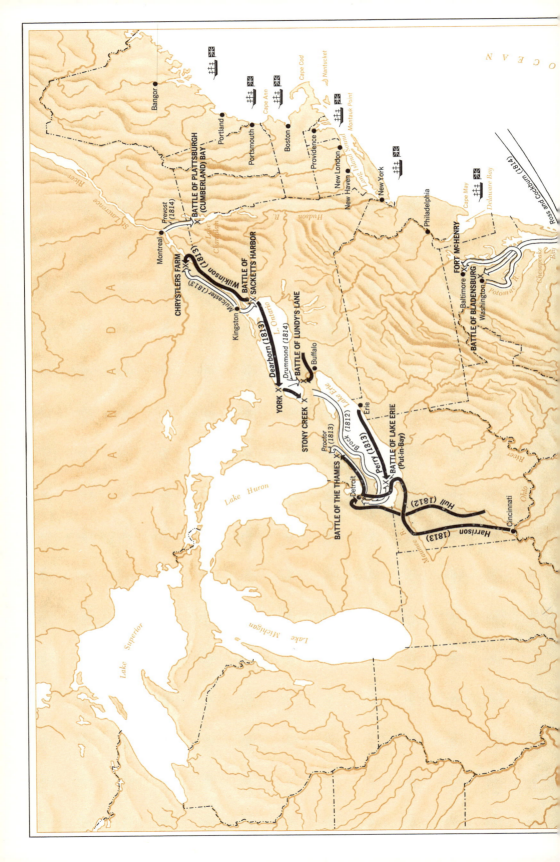

THE WAR OF 1812
MAJOR LAND AND SEA CAMPAIGNS

United States Forces
British Forces
X   MAJOR BATTLES
General location of British fleets
blockading the coast
Present State boundaries

SCALE OF MILES
0   100   200   300

ATLANTIC

Cape Hatteras
Cape Lookout
Cape Fear

Charleston
Savannah

BATTLE OF HORSESHOE BEND
(Creek War)

St. Marks

Huntsville
Jackson
(1813-14)

Tennessee R.
Tallapoosa R.
Alabama R.

Jackson (1813-14)

Nicholls (1814)

Pensacola

Fort Mims

Mobile

Jackson (1814-15)

Pakenham
survivors (1815)

Pakenham (1814-15)

Mississippi River

New Orleans
BATTLE OF
NEW ORLEANS

GULF OF MEXICO

Map by Harry Scott

vention. The peace treaty, the Treaty of Ghent, was inconclusive. Mentioning none of the causes of the war, it merely restored prewar conditions. Yet the war was important to the United States both as a preface to 19th-century nationalism and as a final chapter in the struggle for independence from Great Britain.

Neutrality on the seas and the "war hawks"

In his request to Congress for a declaration of war, President Madison listed as justification the violation of the flag on the high seas, the impressment of U.S. seamen, trade restrictions against U.S. commerce, and the frontiersmen's charge of British sponsorship of Indian attacks along the frontier. There were other factors. After 1811 a group of freshmen Congressmen from the South and West, all Democratic-Republicans, clamored for war against Britain. These "War Hawks" included Henry Clay and Richard M. Johnson of Kentucky; William Lowndes, John C. Calhoun, David R. Williams, and Langdon Cheeves of South Carolina; and Felix Grundy of Tennessee. They argued for an aggressive policy of territorial expansion and defense of the national honor. Expressing the sentiments of their supporters, they aimed to end Indian harassment of Western settlements, to conquer Canada and the Floridas, and to make the United States a fully independent power in North America. They chafed because the Embargo and the Non-Intercourse Acts had failed to force admission of Southern and Western goods to the European markets. To the "War Hawks," these had been acts of submission that had led to national humiliation and economic suffering in the West. Unlike most Federalists, they sought less diplomacy and more action.

Land campaigns — battle of the thames and the "rocket's red glare"

If the "War Hawks" and others wanted military action, they might have given thought to preparation for war. Its financing alone would be difficult. The Treasury was nearly empty, and Congress hesitated to enact new taxes. The First Bank of the United States had expired in 1811. Furthermore, the most prosperous section of the country, New England, opposed the war and would contribute as little as possible to its support.

In 1812 the Army consisted of 10 regiments, most of them on garrison duty in the West. Many of the ranking officers had seen no action since

Artist's version of the Battle of the Thames (October 5, 1813), Canada, one of the major battles of the War of 1812, in which the Shawnee chief Tecumseh died. From a lithograph by John Dorival. Courtesy, Library of Congress.

the War for Independence. To supplement the Regular Army, Congress authorized the recruitment of 25,000 5-year volunteers and 50,000 1-year militiamen. But the Army never achieved authorized strength, and for the most part it was inadequately supplied and poorly led.

During the 2½ years of the war, events seemed to conspire against the conquest of Canada by the United States. In 1812, before the United States could get an offensive underway, the British and their Indian supporters captured outposts at Detroit and Fort Dearborn (Chicago). The British had temporarily closed the western invasion route to Canada. To the eastward, the invasion of Canada went little better. Claiming that the terms of their enlistments did not require them to cross national boundaries, most State militiamen refused to join Regulars in thrusts across the Canadian border near Buffalo and over Lake Champlain toward Montreal.

The next year, 1813, gave the country some encouragement. William Henry Harrison, commander in the Northwest, with a small force endeavored to recapture Detroit, the gateway to western Canada. But he was unable to advance beyond Fort Meigs, near Toledo, as long as British ships controlled Lake Erie. Then, in September 1813, he received a message that began "We have met the enemy and they are ours." On September 10, 1813, a U.S. fleet commanded by the author of the message, 29-year-old Oliver Hazard Perry, had defeated a British squadron at the Battle of Lake Erie, near Put-in-Bay. Perry's victory forced the British to abandon Detroit and opened the way for Harrison's force to march into Canada.

Harrison moved quickly. His army pursued the retreating British and Indians 100 miles into Canada to the Thames River, where they made their stand. The Battle of the Thames, in October of 1813, was a decisive defeat for the British in the Northwest. Among the battlefield dead was Tecumseh, leader of the Indian resistance to the advance of the frontier. Harrison's men had destroyed the British strength in the old Northwest and opened the way to settlement of lower Michigan and Illinois country. Elsewhere in 1813 the land war was indecisive. Gen. James Wilkinson, a veteran of the War for Independence, failed in his effort to capture Montreal.

This cartoon, satirizing the Hartford Convention, depicts the Massachusetts delegate urging the Connecticut and Rhode Island representatives to leap into the arms of the King of England. At the Hartford Convention representatives of some of the New England States opposed U.S. participation in the War of 1812. From an etching by William Charles. Courtesy, Library of Congress.

James Madison, one of the authors of *The Federalist Papers* and fourth President. From a lithograph by John Pendleton, after a painting by Gilbert Stuart. Courtesy, Library of Congress.

In 1814 the impending defeat of Napoleon in Europe allowed the British to turn more attention and divert materiel to the war with the United States. Red-coated British veterans, fresh from European triumphs, boarded transports bound for North America. The British planned to take the offensive. They would invade the United States from Canada. One force would drive southward over the Lake Champlain route and another cross the Niagara River into western New York State. An amphibious force would also attack the east coast of the United States and later seize New Orleans to gain control of the mouth of the Mississippi River.

By 1814 more than 1 year of war had hardened and improved the U.S. Army and permitted several excellent officers to rise to positions of command. Two of these were Gen. Jacob Jennings Brown and young Gen. Winfield Scott. They showed courage and talent in stopping the

British invasion attempt in the Niagara region at the bloody Canadian battles of Chippewa and Lundy's Lane. To the east, the success of the British invasion over the Lake Champlain route required the capture of Plattsburgh, N.Y. There the 30-year-old Thomas Macdonough earned a place in the hall of naval heroes and the gratitude of the Nation by leading a hastily assembled flotilla of 14 ships against the British at the Battle of Plattsburgh (Cumberland) Bay, in September 1814. Macdonough's victory saved Plattsburgh and ruined the most promising opportunity of the British to invade the United States.

More spectacular, if less important to the outcome of the war, was the British diversionary raid in the Chesapeake Bay region of August and September 1814. By then ships of the Royal Navy were ranging along the entire east coast of the United States virtually at will. U.S. naval vessels, hopelessly outnumbered by the largest fleet in the world, remained helplessly blockaded in port.

In August the British repaid the Americans for the burning of York (Toronto), Canada, earlier in the war. A combined military and naval force entered Chesapeake Bay and sailed northeastward. The main force

"The Taking of the City of Washington in America," a British version of their attack on Washington (August 1814). The letters indicate key actions. From a wood engraving by an unknown artist, published by G. Thompson. Courtesy, Library of Congress.

of soldiers and marines under Gen. Robert Ross left their ships at the mouth of the Patuxent River and marched overland toward Washington, D.C. The defenses of the Capital were inadequate. The British raiding force, about 3,000 men, easily defeated a makeshift defensive force at the Battle of Bladensburg, August 24. Of the 7,000 defenders of the Capital, only a few were Regulars. The latter gave a good account of themselves, especially a force of several hundred sailors, under Commodore Joshua Barney, who stymied the British advance for half an hour. But the sailors finally yielded, and the redcoats entered Washington. They set fire to the Capitol, White House, and other Government buildings. The Government had fled. A sudden rainstorm helped douse the fires but not before they had caused more than $1 million in damage. Then the British moved on to attack Baltimore.

The situation was different at Baltimore. The U.S. militia stood firm behind earthwork defenses south of the city, and the British attempt to flank the militia by water was met by the garrison of Fort McHenry at the entrance to Baltimore harbor. For 24 hours, on September 13 and 14, the British poured shot, shell, and rockets into the fort. Watching the bombardment from a U.S. truce ship detained by the British was a young Maryland lawyer, Francis Scott Key. As he watched, the giant American flag continued to wave above the fort. The British could not conquer Fort McHenry, and the attack on Baltimore failed; they moved back down the Patuxent, toward the sea. The defense of Baltimore helped

The British bombardment of Fort McHenry. From an aquatint by John Bower. Courtesy, Library of Congress.

to soften the humiliation of the burning of the Capital, and the bombardment of Fort McHenry gave the Nation "The Star-Spangled Banner."

THE NAVAL WAR: VICTORIES BUT NOT VICTORY

The U.S. Navy entered the War of 1812 slightly better prepared than the Army. The undeclared naval war against France, the pirate wars on the Barbary Coast, and other skirmishes had provided invaluable experience and *esprit de corps*. But the task of the Navy in the War of 1812 was herculean. Its 16 warships must combat the largest fleet in the world. The British would have numerical superiority in virtually any situation. Considering the odds, the Navy did well, but inevitably it was swept from the seas.

The White House after the British attack on Washington, August 24, 1814. From a drawing by W. Strickland. Courtesy, Library of Congress.

At the beginning of the war, individual U.S. warships met and defeated individual British ships. Capt. Isaac Hull of the *Constitution* electrified the Nation in the summer of 1812 by outsailing a British squadron and then defeating the British frigate *Guerrière*. Not to be outdone were Commodore William Bainbridge, new commander of the *Constitution*, and Decatur, commanding the *United States*. In the course of 6 months they and supporting vessels managed to defeat three British frigates and two sloops-of-war. They lost but one ship, the *Wasp*. But U.S. naval ships were too few, and by 1814 only two frigates were at sea. The others lay blockaded in port.

U.S. privateers were more numerous and more successful. Privately financed and frankly committed to making money by attacking British merchant shipping, they carried the war to British waters. Lightly armed and schooner-rigged, they were strong enough to outfight a merchantman and fast enough to outsail British warships. During the war the privateers probably captured 1,300 British ships and cargoes worth $40 million. In spite of the danger, privateering was so lucrative that the Navy found it difficult to compete with the privateers in recruiting seamen. Ironically, most of the profit from privateering flowed to New England, which led the opposition to the war.

THE HOME FRONT—DIVISION AND THE THREAT OF DISUNION

In 1807, after the *Chesapeake-Leopard* affair, the people of the United States had been psychologically ready for war with Great Britain. In 1812 they were not. By then, British interference with U.S. shipping was an old story, and the Nation entered the war badly divided. Commercial shipping interests, particularly in New England and New York City, saw ruin in a war that would bring the wrath of the British Navy down upon them. In westward expansion and the possible acquisition of Canada, New Englanders could see an increase in the political power of Southern and Western agricultural interests. The privateers brought some profit to shipping, but the British blockade after 1813 was effective. In 1814 U.S. exports dropped to 90 percent below those of 1807. To finance the war, Congress doubled the tariff and enacted an excise tax, a stamp tax, and a direct tax on the States. The tax load fell heaviest on New England, possessor of much of the Nation's liquid capital.

Loyalty in the Northeast reached its nadir in the Hartford Convention of December 1814 and January 1815. Despite the extreme sentiments of some of the delegates, most of them followed a reasonable course. The moderates, led by George Cabot and Harrison Gray Otis, were able to resist a radical movement for secession from the United States. The convention's final report blamed the Democratic-Republicans for the evils of the time. It also asked for constitutional amendments prohibiting embargoes of more than 60 days, limiting the President to one term, and

Authorized infantry uniforms and equipment during the period 1802–10. Enlisted men in foreground and officers in background. Artillerymen wore similar uniforms. From a lithograph by G. H. Buek and Company, after H. A. Ogden. Courtesy, Library of Congress.

prohibiting the election of two successive Presidents from the same State. When the convention dissolved, it pledged to take its grievances to Washington. But New England's grievances disappeared amid the news that the war was over and that Jackson had won a resounding victory at the Battle of New Orleans.

PEACE AND THE VICTORY AT NEW ORLEANS

Almost since the beginning of the war, elements in both countries had talked of peace. Both sides had entered and fought the war halfheartedly. In August 1814 a U.S. peace commission began negotiations with the British at Ghent, in Belgium. The U.S. commissioners, John Quincy Adams, Albert Gallatin, Henry Clay, Jonathan Russell, and J. A. Bayard, had specific instructions. They were to demand an end to impressment, British adherence to international law in the enforcement of blockades, and payment for illegal seizure of U.S. ships.

The British wanted territorial concessions from the United States, notably portions of New York and Maine, surrender of U.S. control of the Great Lakes, and an Indian-occupied buffer state in the West. They also demanded navigation rights on the Mississippi River and restrictions on American fishing rights in the Newfoundland Banks. Both sides predicated their demands on anticipated military successes that never materialized. The U.S. invasion of Canada had failed and so had the British invasion of the United States. Merchants in both countries were eager to resume trading. Under the circumstances negotiators of both sides abandoned their diplomatic instructions. The Treaty of Ghent, signed on Christmas Eve 1814, ended the war by simply ignoring its causes. The treaty restored the *status quo ante bellum*—the way things were before the war. Yet it offered the promise of future solution to U.S.-Canadian boundary and Atlantic fishing disputes by providing for the establishment of an Anglo-American commission to seek their settlement.

In a time of slow communications, a major battle occurred before the news of the signing of the treaty reached the United States. The U.S. victory at the Battle of New Orleans could have no effect on the peace terms but would facilitate U.S. ratification, in February 1815. The war in the South had generally gone well for the United States. In 1813 the "Red Sticks" faction of the Creek Indians had taken advantage of U.S. involvement in the War of 1812 and mounted an attack along the Southwestern frontier. Tennessee and Kentucky militiamen under Gen. Andrew Jackson responded. The climax of the Creek War came in March 1814, at the Battle of Horseshoe Bend, where Jackson's army killed 900 braves and captured 500 women and children. The Treaty of Fort Jackson wrested from the Creeks most of what is today southeastern Alabama. In short order, Jackson moved on to invade Spanish Florida and seize the port of Pensacola, where the British, with Spanish acquiescence, had created a base from which to attack Mobile.

Upon his return to Mobile late in 1814, Jackson learned that a British amphibious force that had attacked Washington and Baltimore was at Jamaica, West Indies, refitting for another expedition, presumably against New Orleans. In December he hurried to New Orleans and, before the British arrived, managed to assemble a colorful, if motley, army. The army consisted mainly of militia that lacked the necessary

A panoramic version of the Battle of New Orleans (January 8, 1815), a major U.S. victory and last significant battle in the War of 1812. From a lithograph by P. S. Duval. Courtesy, Library of Congress.

training and discipline for face-to-face combat against Regulars in the open field but that might do well behind fortifications.

After weak U.S. reconnaissance permitted the British to advance to within 7 miles of New Orleans from the east—attack had been expected from the west—Jackson reacted quickly. When a surprise attack on the British camp failed on December 23 and 24, 1814, his men threw up earthworks between a cypress swamp and the Mississippi, 5 miles from New Orleans, to block the British advance. As time passed and the defenders of Fort St. Philip on the Mississippi prevented the British fleet from moving into position to flank Jackson's earthworks, Gen. Sir Edward Pakenham, the British commander, decided to make a frontal assault against the entrenched forces. On the morning of January 8, 1815, thousands of British soldiers, tightly massed, marched across the plain toward Jackson's line. Twenty-five minutes later hundreds of them were dead, including Pakenham, and many hundreds more were wounded or prisoners. Jackson's forces suffered only light casualties. The British withdrew. New Orleans was safe. The Mississippi remained open.

Even though the U.S. victory at New Orleans was won after the signing of the peace treaty, it was important. Had the British won, they might have held New Orleans and with it control of the Mississippi, peace treaty or no. Coming as it did with the news of peace, the victory at New Orleans brought the inconclusive war to an end on a note of triumph. And Jackson, hero of New Orleans, took a long stride toward the White House.

An Emergent Nationalism, 1815–1828

The War of 1812 proved to a fresh generation of Americans that theirs was a free and independent Nation. It had stood up to the world's strongest power and come away unbowed. Isolationist nationalism, territorial expansion, and intensifying sectionalism characterized the postwar years 1815–28. The ardent new nationalism was expressed in Madison's fiscal program, in the "Era of Good Feelings," and in a diplomacy that sought to isolate the country from Europe and extend the national domain westward.

To keep pace with the westward movement, new roads, canals, and even rudimentary railroads came into being. The application of steampower and waterpower to the manufacturing process, inventions, and ready capital signaled the beginnings of industrialization. Expanding markets, additional lands, and technical innovations revolutionized Southern agriculture and made cotton king of the exports. Competition— North against South—for Western lands, markets, and political support intensified sectional disharmonies. Statesmen of the period worked to control the forces of sectionalism by bolstering those of nationalism.

"Democracy" was another increasingly powerful movement with which statesmen had to reckon after the War of 1812. The interplay of emergent public attitudes—the romance of frontier individualism and self-reliance, an optimistic faith in progress, and new humanitarian and social ideas—helped bring about institutional reforms, the extension of suffrage, and the rise of the common man.

DOMESTIC PROGRAMS AND PROBLEMS

The nationalism that swept over the United States after the war found political expression in the program that President Madison outlined in his Seventh Annual Message to Congress, December 1815. It was a Hamiltonian program. The war had exposed patches and tears in the national fabric that needed mending: In the armed services, banking, transportation, and manufacturing. Congressmen were well aware of the situation. Were they not meeting in the Patent Office Building, the only suitable one in the Nation's Capital that the British raiders had spared in 1814? To avoid the repetition of raids on the Capital, and protect the country as a whole, Madison proposed to strengthen the land and naval forces. Congress authorized a standing Army of 10,000, only half the number recommended. It revised the militia system and strengthened the Military Academy at West Point. It also authorized more ships and better facilities for the Navy, the strongest barrier to European interference in U.S. affairs.

To strengthen the national financial structure, Madison proposed the revival of the United States Bank. After the expiration of the charter of the first bank in 1811, State banks had proliferated. They often lacked adequate gold and silver reserves to back their notes, the paper money of the time. The result was inflation. As a bewildering variety of paper notes and certificates flooded the country, both the Government and private individuals found it difficult to conduct business effectively. Few denied the need for corrective measures. Congressional leaders, including Clay and Calhoun as well as Jeffersonians who had once opposed a national bank on principle, supported the bank measure, and in 1816 the Second Bank of the United States received a 20-year charter. The bank was expected to strengthen the national financial structure by helping to curb inflation and speculation and by providing a safe depository for Federal funds.

Because the War of 1812 had drastically reduced foreign sources of manufactured goods, domestic industries had sprung up—$40 million worth—in New England and the Middle States. After the war, British merchants attempted to destroy U.S. industry by flooding the country with cheap manufactured goods. To encourage national self-sufficiency by protecting the war-born domestic industries, Madison asked Congress for a protective tariff on foreign manufactures. Congress responded by enacting the Tariff of 1816—a mild measure but one that represented a departure from the traditional Jeffersonian belief in free trade.

On one question, the matter of Federal authority over internal improvements, Madison remained a prewar orthodox Jeffersonian. To help unite the country and provide for the expeditious movement of troops and supplies in time of war, Congress, led by John C. Calhoun, passed the Bonus Bill of 1817. It provided for the use of Federal funds to finance the building of roads and canals. Madison, though a strong advocate of internal improvements, vetoed the Bonus Bill. He believed that the Constitution did not grant to the National Government the power to finance directly the construction of roads and canals.

Except on this key issue, Madison's postwar program and the congressional response to it showed that the party of Jefferson, in less than a decade, had moved from a philosophy of Federal restraint to one of Federal action in the Hamiltonian tradition. The third branch of the Federal Government, the judiciary, had to make no such change. It had been ardently nationalistic since John Marshall had been appointed as Chief Justice of the Supreme Court in 1801.

Chief Justice of the Supreme Court John Marshall. During his long term (1801–35), the Court asserted its power and handed down decisions of far-reaching importance that established fundamental principles of constitutional interpretation. From an engraving by W. G. Jackman. Courtesy, Library of Congress.

From then until 1835 Marshall dominated the nationalistic Court. It set many major precedents, particularly in fields where the Constitution required elaboration and further definition. It tended to interpret Federal powers broadly, and promulgated a body of doctrine that was essentially Hamiltonian. In so doing it confounded Hamilton's prediction that the judiciary would be the weakest of the three branches of Government. In several landmark cases, Marshall and the Court progressively broadened the constitutional powers of the Federal Government, especially in the nationalistic period that followed the War of 1812.

In 1810, in the case of *Fletcher v. Peck,* the Court had annulled a law of the Georgia Legislature and thus asserted the Constitution's superiority to the powers of State legislatures. In 1816, in *Martin v. Hunter's Lessee,* the Court extended this doctrine to include State courts by overruling a Virginia court decision. Two decisions in 1819 further strengthened Federal authority under the Constitution. In the Dartmouth College case, the Court denied the right of a State legislature to pass a law violating the constitutional guarantee of the sanctity of contracts. In a test of the constitutionality of the Second Bank of the United States, *McCulloch v. Maryland,* it denied the right of the State of Maryland to tax a branch of the bank. This decision affirmed the right of the Federal Government to maintain national institutions within State boundaries without State interference. In 1824 the Court further enhanced the edifice of national supremacy in the case of *Gibbons v. Ogden.* Its decision cost Robert Fulton and Robert Livingston their Hudson River steamboat monopoly, but it established the U.S. Government as arbiter of interstate navigation and opened the way to Federal activity in the area of interstate commerce.

After two terms, Madison retired from the Presidency and recommended another Virginian, James Monroe, as his successor. In 1816 the Nation was prosperous, and Monroe, a member of the party in power, won the election easily. Rufus King, the Federalist candidate, carried only Connecticut, Delaware, and Massachusetts. Indeed, it seemed that the Federalist opposition to Monroe was a mere formality. In 1817, when Monroe toured the old Federalist stronghold, New England, he was cordially received. Boston's Federalist *Columbian Centinel* alluded to the "good feelings" that accompanied his visit. Taking their cue from the *Centinel,* many have called Monroe's 8 years in the White House the "Era of Good Feelings." Recent scholarship has cast doubt on this interpretation. From 1817 to 1819 there was apparent national harmony and prosperity. But the Panic of 1819 and the growing sectional tensions, exemplified by the Missouri debates of 1819–21, are strong indicators that serious political disharmony existed during Monroe's final 6 years as President.

POWER DIPLOMACY—CONTINENTAL DEFINITION
AND HEMISPHERIC SECURITY

During the years 1815–28 the United States showed more self-confidence in foreign affairs. Diplomats and soldiers added Spanish Florida to the national domain. Treaties settled a portion of the United States-Canadian boundary dispute and partially cleared the way for a U.S. foothold in the Pacific Northwest. In support of the Latin American independence movement, President Monroe warned European nations to stay out of the Western Hemisphere. To consolidate the "good feelings" that greeted his election, he selected a Cabinet representative of the Nation's major geographical sections. A New England member of the Cabinet was Secretary of State John Quincy Adams, the son of President John Adams. The younger Adams proved most able.

The first diplomatic success of the Monroe administration was the Rush-Bagot Agreement of 1817. Monroe as Secretary of State and Adams as Minister to Great Britain, both under Madison, had laid the groundwork for the agreement. It reduced armaments on the Great Lakes to a minimum. Although complete border disarmament did not come about until the Treaty of Washington (1871), the Rush-Bagot Agreement was an important precedent.

The Oregon question was more difficult. The United States, Great Britain, Spain, and Russia all claimed that ill-defined region. By negotiation, Adams succeeded in persuading Russia and Spain to renounce their claims. But both Great Britain and the United States claimed discovery of the region and fur traders from both countries were operating there. The decision, in 1818, was to postpone solution. The two nations agreed to occupy the Oregon country jointly for a decade, and in 1827 joint occupancy was extended for an additional decade.

In the South, Adams capitalized on Spain's colonial difficulties and Andrew Jackson's aggressive military activities to add Spanish Florida to the United States. After the Napoleonic Wars the Spanish colonial empire was tottering. Uprisings in Spain's vast South American domain required all the military effort she could muster. She had little capability to defend a minor and strategically exposed colony such as Florida. The Spanish knew that the United States wanted to acquire Florida. They probably expected to lose it, but they wanted something in return.

To Don Luis de Onís, Spanish Minister to the United States, fell the task of negotiating the Florida issue. In 1815 he demanded U.S. repudiation of the Louisiana Purchase and acceptance of the Mississippi as the western boundary in exchange for Florida. As Spain's situation

John Quincy Adams. An experienced diplomat, he became Secretary of State and then President. From a lithograph by D. W. Kellogg and Company. Courtesy, Library of Congress.

worsened, in 1817 Onís abandoned his demands for repudiation of the Louisiana Purchase and moved the proposed southwestern boundary west to a north-south line in central Louisiana between the Mermentau and Calcasieu Rivers. He would not concede any territory beyond this line. Adams held out for the Colorado River of Texas as the southwestern boundary of the United States. The negotiations were deadlocked.

In 1818 Andrew Jackson broke the stalemate by action. Under orders from Washington, he led a military force from Fort Scott, Ga., into Spanish Florida to punish the Seminole Indians and runaway slaves for their continuing assaults on Georgia settlers. After making only minor

St. John's Episcopal Church, in 1816, shortly after its construction. The White House, in the background, is in the process of being renovated following its burning by the British, in 1814. From a drawing by Benjamin H. Latrobe, architect of the church.

contact with the Seminoles, Jackson determined to exceed his orders. He led his army across northern Florida, during which time he executed several Seminoles and two British subjects. The high points of the expedition were the seizures of the Spanish forts at St. Marks and Pensacola.

When the news of the exploit reached Washington, Jackson was again the hero of the hour. Although his violation of Spanish sovereignty was embarrassing to the United States, at the same time it strengthened Adams' hand in his negotiations with Onís, for Jackson had demonstrated the weakness of Spain's grip on Florida. The Adams-Onís, or Transcontinental, Treaty of 1819 followed shortly thereafter. Spain ceded Florida to the United States, and the Sabine River—a portion of the present Texas-Louisiana border—became the Southwestern boundary of the United States. The Western boundary continued then generally northwest along the Red River to the 100th meridian, north along the 100th meridian to the Arkansas River, west on the Arkansas to the Sangre de Cristo Mountains, north to the 42d parallel, and thence west to the Pacific. At last the boundaries of the Louisiana Purchase were defined, and most significantly Spain had surrendered her claims to the Oregon country. In return, the United States agreed to pay $5 million in claims of U.S. citizens in the acquired territory against Spain. It was a good treaty for the United States.

One after another, between 1811 and 1825 Spanish and Portuguese colonies in South and Central America declared political independence, as Simon Bolivar and José San Martín flashed across the pages of history. Spain's only hope of recovering her colonies, and it was a slim one, depended upon aid from other European nations. In 1815 the rulers of France, Russia, and Prussia joined Ferdinand VII of Spain in the Holy Alliance. Its purpose was preservation of the old regimes of Europe against a growing wave of antimonarchist sentiment. The alliance was too busy with European problems to intervene actively in Latin America, but it did show disapproval of the newly independent nations by refusing them diplomatic recognition.

In the United States sentiment was strong for recognition of and assistance to the struggling peoples. Were not the Latin Americans rebelling against colonialism and injustice just as the United States had in 1776? Despite the promptings of Henry Clay and other leaders for recognition, Monroe and Adams hesitated to do so until the Florida negotiations with Spain were completed. So it was only after the Adams-Onís Treaty that the United States moved toward support of the new nations, and in 1822 she officially recognized them. Belated though the recognition was, it was the first to be made by non-Latin American countries.

Prompted by the revolutionary struggle, a British proposal for an Anglo-American alliance to prevent European intervention in the affairs of the Western Hemisphere brought about the Monroe Doctrine. In the beginning, it was not a "doctrine" but a declaration incorporated in President Monroe's Sixth Annual Message to Congress, in 1823. Monroe, with the concurrence of the elder statesmen Madison and Jefferson, had inclined toward acceptance of the British proposal for a joint Anglo-American policy of opposition to European encroachment. But John Quincy Adams was determined to avoid entangling alliances—especially one that might embarrass future U.S. efforts to annex Cuba and Texas. Adams was adamant, and Monroe concurred in his reasoning. The Monroe Doctrine was the result. It promised that the United States would not interfere in purely European affairs, nor in the affairs of "existing colonies or dependencies" in the Western Hemisphere. It warned that the United States would consider as unfriendly action any European intervention in the affairs of independent hemispheric nations that were recognized by the United States. Lastly, it declared that Europe should consider the Western Hemisphere "out of bounds" for further colonization.

Great Britain reacted with irritation to the declaration. After all, if any nation in 1823 had the power to enforce Monroe's declaration, it was Great Britain. The U.S. public applauded Monroe's words, then soon forgot them. But future American statesmen would remember them. In 1845 President Polk would reaffirm the declaration in connection with the Oregon boundary dispute with Great Britain. From the time of the Civil War, it would become an active and vital diplomatic policy. In 1823, however, it was not an expression of national power. Rather it was an exposition of basic principles of U.S. foreign policy as they had evolved since 1776.

Economic expansion and sectionalism

While nationalistic sentiment increased in the United States after the War of 1812, so did sectional economic specialization and sectional feeling. In the South, each year more bolls of upland cotton waved over the

Vice President John C. Calhoun. A prominent advocate of States rights, he also served as Representative, Senator, Secretary of War, and Secretary of State. From an engraving by James B. Longacre, after a painting by C. B. King. Courtesy, Library of Congress.

rich soil of Alabama and Mississippi; they represented the resurgence of the plantation system. In the West, corn, wheat, and livestock production burgeoned to help feed Europe and the Eastern States. In the East, increased commercial activity, the beginnings of industrialization, and advancing urbanization registered economic health.

Ominously, during the years 1815–28 residents of the three economically and socially different regions became more aware of their differences. The Missouri debates of 1819–21 brought the sectional issue to the surface of politics, and the Missouri Compromises of 1820 and 1821 laid it aside again without solution. In 1828 John C. Calhoun's "South Carolina Exposition and Protest" once again returned the issues of sectionalism and States rights to the political foreground. As the years passed, they would return again and again.

In 1828 agriculture remained the basis of the economy, but since 1783 it had undergone significant changes. Europe's industrial evolution, which had been accelerating since the 18th century, had created new demands for foodstuffs and agricultural raw materials. Planters in the South and farmers in the Midwest were quick to take advantage of the demands.

Since colonial times, Southern planters had utilized the plantation system to provide tobacco, rice, indigo, and other staples for the export market. The plantation was a practical solution to the problem of abundant land and scarce labor. Then, toward the close of the 18th century, it had seemed that the South would have to modify its economy in order to grow. In eastern Maryland, Virginia, and the Carolinas, good land was scarce. Much of the soil was worn out. Southern interest in the application of new agricultural techniques and more diversified production seemed to many to bode the end of the plantation system and the eventual abandonment of the institution of slavery. But this was not to be. The industrialization of the British textile industry, the opening of Western lands and waterways to the Gulf of Mexico after the War of 1812, and the widespread adoption of the cotton gin provided the stimulus required to bring about the revitalization of plantation agriculture.

Before 1800 a few Southern coastal planters had reaped large profits from the production of "sea island" cotton for export. Without much difficulty the seeds could be separated from the lint. But this cotton demanded a maritime climate. Upland cotton, which would grow well inland, required so much labor to separate the lint from the seeds as to make its commercial production unprofitable. In 1793 Eli Whitney, of

Artist's rendition of the first trip, in 1807, of Robert Fulton's steamboat, the *Clermont*, from New York to Albany. Soon after the *Clermont's* success, steamboat travel began to flourish. From an etching by an unknown artist, probably S. Hollyer, copyrighted in 1907. Courtesy, Library of Congress.

Connecticut, constructed a simple device that quickly and efficiently separated upland cotton bolls into lint and seeds. Whitney's cotton gin saved hours of labor and constituted an agricultural breakthrough of foremost importance.

The spread in use of the gin and the British mills' insatiable demands for cotton caused production to increase by leaps and bounds. After the War of 1812 cotton was on its way to becoming "king." The wholesale price of cotton—and production—rose continuously until 1837. In 1801 U.S. production totaled 100,000 bales. In 1810 it rose to 171,000 bales. In the next 20 years, as cotton production spread through most of Georgia, Alabama, Mississippi, Louisiana, and north into Tennessee, the annual crop more than quadrupled, reaching 731,000 bales in 1830. The economic importance of cotton would have national political repercussions.

But not everyone in the South was a cotton planter. Tobacco, rice, sugar, hemp, peas, beans, livestock, and wheat were also widely grown products. Less than 1 percent of all southerners owned more than 50 slaves, and most Southern farmers owned no slaves at all. On the other hand, most farmers aspired to own slaves and become large planters. The economic importance of cotton as a way to financial success would be significant in giving conscious identification to the South as a political entity.

The Ohio Valley States, too, were emerging as a self-conscious region and had special economic problems. The regional specialty was agriculture—but of a different sort than in the South. The climate north of Tennessee was unsuited to cotton production, and slavery was prohibited by law north of the Ohio. Intensive cultivation, utilizing crop rotation and fertilizers, was the rule. Tobacco and corn were the principal products of Kentucky, southern Ohio, Indiana, and Illinois. In the northern regions of Ohio, Indiana, and Illinois and in lower Michigan, wheat was the major crop. The land was rich and it produced a salable surplus. The West could grow rich—if only it could get the surplus to market.

Transportation was the problem. The Ohio-Mississippi River system flowed eventually to New Orleans, which seemed the most likely outlet for Western agricultural produce. The region's trade with New Orleans was considerable and led to the development of Western river ports, where produce was gathered for shipment downriver. Louisville, at the fall line of the Ohio, was one such port; Cincinnati, called "Porkopolis"

James Monroe, fifth President and author of the Monroe Doctrine. From a lithograph by John Pendleton, after a painting by Gilbert Stuart. Courtesy, Library of Congress.

after the local specialty, was another. But the river system was not wholly satisfactory as an outlet for Western goods. The trip downriver was long and slow. Furthermore, the shallowness of the rivers during much of the year often forced farmers to send their surplus downriver during the spring and fall floods. The dumping of so much produce at New Orleans at the same time glutted the market and depressed wholesale prices.

In addition, New Orleans' western location raised the cost of manu-factured goods—the shoes, clothes, and household goods upon which westerners were coming to depend—to prohibitive levels. Store goods usually had to come by wagon over the mountains from the East. This circuitous counterclockwise trade was a hardship to westerners. So, too, was the section's helplessness against the fluctuations of the European grain market. The depression known as the Panic of 1819 struck the Western States particularly hard and helped to make them conscious of their geographic isolation and economic dependence on Europe, the East, and an inadequate transportation system. National political power was the West's best weapon against isolation. As the conflict between Northeast and South deepened, both sections would woo Western political support—the Northeast by improving roads and build-ing canals and railroads and the South by improving the river transpor-tation system, developing the colorful river steamboats and, less success-fully, building its own canals and railroads toward the West.

During the period 1815–28 the economy of the Northeastern States grew further apart from that of the South. Most easterners continued to be small farmers, but many of them—significant beyond their mere numbers—grew rich in mercantile and industrial pursuits. After the War of 1812 the shipping industry, depressed by the embargo, the wartime dislocation of the European trade, and the British blockade, had come to life again. Ships from New England, New York, and Philadelphia ranged the North American coast and ventured to Europe, the Indies, and even China in search of profit. An ever-increasing number of U.S. ships cleared Eastern ports, particularly New Bedford, Mass., to challenge Great Britain's supremacy in the pursuit of the whale. On land, industrialization gathered speed.

As early as the 1790's Samuel Slater had smuggled the secrets of British textile manufacture to the United States. In 1800 Eli Whitney had demonstrated in the manufacture of muskets for the U.S. Army the basic principle of interchangeable parts that was so important to the mass production process. Little came of either development as long as more advanced British industry could undersell struggling U.S. manufacturers. The period 1807–12 gave U.S. industry the chance to take root. To prevent the British from uprooting it after the War of 1812 with a flood of cheap manufactured goods, Congress enacted the protective tariff of 1816.

Woolen- and cotton-textile mills using water or steampower proliferated in New England. In 1814, at Waltham, Mass., Francis Cabot Lowell opened a textile mill in which a single power source provided all the power necessary to operate the whole clothmaking process. In 1826 the township of Lowell came into being. Located at the falls of the Merrimack River in Massachusetts, it would become a 19th-century industrial center. Within 14 years, it would contain nine textile mills and the Nation's largest machine shop.

After the war the manufacture of iron, a basic ingredient of the industrial revolution, flourished in Pennsylvania. Production increased slowly, but after 1817 and the introduction of new processes for ore separation using coal instead of charcoal, the iron furnaces could leave the forests and come to the cities. Philadelphia, Scranton, and, to a lesser degree, Pittsburgh would become iron manufacturing centers.

The growth of trade, the burgeoning of cities such as New York, Philadelphia, Boston, and Baltimore, and industrial stirrings characterized the East. In spite of the diversity and internal competition, easterners came to share a broad cluster of common political ideas that sometimes conflicted with those of the West and frequently with those of the South.

"View of Boston and the south Boston Bridge." Lithographed by Deroy, figures by V. Adams, from the drawing by Jacques G. Milbert. Courtesy, Library of Congress.

Slavery had been a source of debate in the country since the 17th century. At the Constitutional Convention of 1787, it had been the subject of extended discussion. As early as 1786 some people were helping runaway slaves to escape to Canada. The Fugitive Slave Law of 1793 was unpopular in the Northeast, and the law of 1808 prohibiting importation of slaves into the United States irritated some Southern planters. Yet for a decade after 1808, slavery seemed a dead issue, but it suddenly awakened after Missouri petitioned for statehood in 1817.

Missouri was to be a State in which slavery was legal, and her admission would give the slave States a 24–22 vote majority in the Senate. The majority might affect legislation on sectional issues—the tariff and internal improvements—but only temporarily. It was known that Maine would soon seek admission as a free State and restore the balance. But in 1819, as Congress considered Missouri statehood, an amendment to the Missouri Enabling Act, submitted by Representative James Tallmadge of New York, came as a political bombshell. The Tallmadge Amendment proposed that admission be contingent upon an end to the importation of slaves into Missouri and the gradual emancipation of those already there. The amendment passed the House of Representatives by virtue of the Northern majority, but Southern votes rejected it in the Senate.

The deadlock between the two branches of Congress occasioned a prolonged and heated debate. Proponents of the amendment claimed that the framers of the Constitution had intended that slavery wither away—that it was a temporary institution. Their opponents argued that new States, like older States, had the constitutional right to determine their own internal arrangements. These were significant expositions of conflicting interpretations of the Constitution. But ominously, as the debates grew heated, legislators on both sides of the issue abandoned constitutional argument for emotional appeals based on the moral aspects of slavery. So long as emotionalism prevailed, no compromise was possible.

Eventually, for a time, reason won out. Enough Congressmen were able to put the preservation of the Union above sectional interests to produce the Missouri Compromise of March 1820. It made possible the admittance of Maine as a free State and Missouri as a slave State, but it excluded slavery from the Louisiana Purchase north of 36° 30′ and west of Missouri. Still, the issue would not die. Late in 1820 a defiant Missouri Legislature drafted a State constitution that barred free Negroes from the State and thus outraged antislavery members of Congress. The anti-

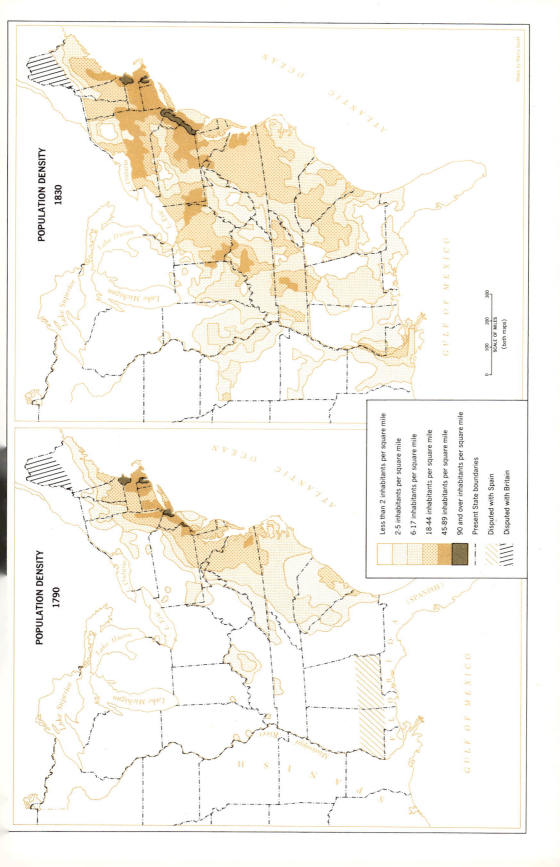

POPULATION DENSITY
1830

POPULATION DENSITY
1790

Less than 2 inhabitants per square mile
2-5 inhabitants per square mile
6-17 inhabitants per square mile
18-44 inhabitants per square mile
45-89 inhabitants per square mile
90 and over inhabitants per square mile

Present State boundaries

Disputed with Spain
Disputed with Britain

SCALE OF MILES
(both maps)
0   100   200   300

Maps by Harry Scott

ATLANTIC OCEAN

GULF OF MEXICO

Lake Superior
Lake Huron
Lake Michigan
Lake Ontario
Lake Erie

FLORIDA
(SPANISH)

Mississippi River

slavery forces had the power to prevent the final admission of Missouri, and so a second Missouri Compromise became necessary. Formulated by Henry Clay of Kentucky, the second compromise passed Congress in March 1821. It provided that Missouri could gain final admission only when her legislature acknowledged that the controversial State constitutional clause did not sanction the right to passage of any law that abridged the rights of U.S. citizens. With qualifications, the legislature finally accepted the limitation in June 1821. In August Missouri became the 24th State.

The Missouri Compromise banished slavery from the forefront of politics for a time, but the issue remained. The Missouri debates sounded to Jefferson like a "fire bell in the night." He feared disunion. But, for the time being, the bonds of nationalism were too strong to yield to the pull of sectionalism. In the 1820's Americans were much more excited about the rise of democracy.

JOHN QUINCY ADAMS AND THE RISE OF THE JACKSONIAN OPPOSITION

By the close of Monroe's second term, 24 years of political supremacy over a steadily dwindling Federalist opposition had severely weakened Democratic-Republican Party discipline. In the presidential election of 1824, it became apparent that the Federalists would not even offer a candidate. In the absence of opposition candidates, no fewer than five second-generation leaders of the party of Jefferson vied to succeed Monroe. Secretary of the Treasury William H. Crawford won the nomination in the "official" party caucus. But various other factions supported their own candidates: John Quincy Adams, Henry Clay, John C. Calhoun, and Andrew Jackson. Before the election, Calhoun withdrew from the presidential race to become the unopposed candidate for Vice President, but the other four candidates remained in the running.

The election was inconclusive. Jackson won 99 electoral votes, a plurality but not the required majority. Adams had 84, Crawford 41, and Clay 37. Because none of the candidates had a majority, it became the responsibility of the House of Representatives, voting by States, to choose the next President from among the top three candidates. A paralytic stroke practically removed Crawford from consideration. The choice was between Jackson and Adams. Henry Clay, by swinging his support to one candidate or the other, could choose the next President. Clay and Adams saw nearly eye-to-eye on domestic matters. Both were ardent nationalists and supporters of high tariffs and Government-financed internal improvements. Clay and Jackson were Western political rivals, and Jackson op-

In 1806 Henry Clay, the "Great Compromiser," began a distinguished congressional career. During the War of 1812 he was one of the "War Hawks." From a lithograph by Charles Fenderich. Courtesy, Library of Congress.

posed Clay on the issues of the tariff and internal improvements. Thus, Clay supported Adams, who became President. Subsequently, after Adams appointed Clay as Secretary of State, Jackson's supporters—but not Jackson himself—charged that Clay and Adams had stolen the election from the hero of New Orleans by a "corrupt bargain." Soon after the election, Jackson resigned from the Senate and returned to Tennessee to begin his long campaign for the Presidency in 1828. The troubles of Adams' administration would aid Jackson's bid for the Presidency.

President John Quincy Adams tried to be a President above party, but his lack of tact, intraparty warfare, and the fact that his political enemies occupied many governmental positions hampered his effectiveness. Much of the opposition stemmed from Adams' political program, which called for the National Government to take a strong and positive role in domestic affairs. The program helped to bring about a division and realinement of political parties. The Adams-Clay element, calling themselves the National Republicans, would become the Whig Party in 1834; their opponents, the Jacksonians, would keep the name Democratic-Republicans.

In foreign affairs solid accomplishments could be expected of the Adams administration. Adams had long diplomatic experience and an outstanding record as Secretary of State. Yet in two matters where his administration might have achieved striking success, it did not. Negotiations to open the lucrative British West Indian trade to U.S. merchants failed. Adams' proposal that the United States participate in the 1826 Panama Conference of Hemispheric Nations engendered an acrimonious debate. Though Congress reluctantly appointed delegates to the Conference, they did not attend, mainly because of the controversy engendered.

Adams' domestic policy was even less successful. In his First Annual Message to Congress, Adams proposed that the Government participate in building roads and canals. He called for a national astronomical observatory and a national university. He asked for funds to send explorers into the unknown areas of the West and Pacific Northwest. He appealed for Federal aid to literature and the arts and sciences and recommended legislation to encourage agriculture and industry. He called for the creation of a Department of the Interior. To many, especially Southern advocates of States rights, the Adams program seemed too sweeping and not sufficiently cognizant of each State's right to work out its own destiny.

Little of Adams' legislative program became law. Of that which did, the irony of two instances is striking. Adams favored a protective tariff, but the Jacksonians did not. In 1828 antiadministration Congressmen helped to pass a tariff act that openly discriminated against Southern planters— a much stronger measure than Adams had recommended. The bill was a political device. If Adams vetoed it, he would defeat a portion of his own legislative program. If he signed it, he would give the Jacksonians a major issue in the presidential campaign of 1828. Adams signed it, and the "Tariff of Abominations" became a Jacksonian rallying cry and an inspiration for Calhoun's famous "South Carolina Exposition and Protest," a trenchant defense of States rights.

Adams' handling of Indian relations further estranged him from the South and West. In showing concern for Indian rights by refusing to adhere to a patently unfair treaty with the Creek Indians, he offended land-hungry westerners and southerners. His threat to use military force to keep Georgia settlers from taking advantage of the repudiated treaty angered States rights proponents.

Maj. Gen. Andrew Jackson. His victories at Horseshoe Bend and New Orleans brought him national popularity and helped him become President. From an engraving by James B. Longacre, after a painting by Thomas Sully. Courtesy, Library of Congress.

Federal participation in the building of roads and canals was another important facet of the National Republican program. After much opposition, Congress passed a bill to aid Maryland, various municipalities, and private investors in financing the construction of the Chesapeake and Ohio Canal. On July 4, 1828, Adams journeyed several miles up the Potomac River from Washington to turn the first spade of earth for the joint Federal, State, and local project. The success of the canal might have proved the wisdom of Adams' policy of national financing of internal improvements. But the canal never reached Pittsburgh, its projected terminus, and Adams' policy of direct Federal aid for roads, canals, and railroads was to be set aside. Private individuals and the States would finance such projects after the rise of Jackson and "democracy."

The presidential campaign of 1828 was one of the most heated in history. The opposing candidates were the incumbent Adams and Andrew Jackson. The issues were the tariff, financing of internal improvements, the national bank, and States rights. But personalities played the major role. In an appeal for mass support, Jacksonian publicists and stump speakers emphasized Old Hickory's military exploits and his identification with the West and the frontier. They characterized him as the champion of the common man against the patrician Adams, the "corrupt bargainer," and his Eastern backers. Adams' supporters retorted in kind. They attacked Jackson as an uncouth and dangerous frontier savage whose election would bring the reign of the mob. But Jackson won. He had 647,231 popular votes, and Adams 509,097.

The South, the West, New York, and Pennsylvania supported Jackson. Western farmers, Southern planters, and Eastern city mechanics, tradesmen, and small farmers had backed him strongly. His election was a landmark in the political evolution and national growth of the United States. He was the first President from the West and the first from a State other than the Original Thirteen. Jackson was no "common man," nor a frontier barbarian. He had been a soldier, a lawyer, a Governor of Tennessee, and a U.S. Senator. He was a rich and successful planter and slaveowner who had a fine estate, the Hermitage. Reserved and formal at large gatherings, he was warm and sympathetic with family and friends. Scholars still debate whether his political philosophy was radical and forward-looking or conservative and rooted in the past. But multitudes of common men, voting in a presidential election for the first time in 1828, chose Jackson—the symbol of the new political democracy. It did not spring up overnight. It was the product of the gradual rise of a democratic and humanitarian faith in response to changed ideas and conditions. In part it reflected Jeffersonian ideals; in part it recognized social realities of the 1820's.

RISE OF DEMOCRACY—BROADENING CONCEPTS OF PROGRESS AND MANKIND

The 19th-century democratic faith in the United States grew out of a cluster of diverse ideas and impulses, some imported and others derived from the national experience. Its elements included a belief in progress, fundamental law and natural rights, and the worth and dignity of the individual. A widespread belief in a national mission to settle the continent and make it the best place in the world to live was a source of the dynamism that translated the ideals and impulses into action. The democratic faith was many-sided and expressed in many forms. The movement toward a more democratic political structure, symbolized by the election of Jackson, was one such expression. Another was the urge for a more humane and enlightened society, manifest in educational and cultural strivings and in the growth of reform movements.

The most prominent feature of the political democracy was the movement in the States to extend the right to vote to all white males 21 years of age and older. The movement to reduce property qualifications for voting had been underway since the War for Independence. The movement to eliminate them completely had begun before the War of 1812. New Jersey and Maryland had removed them entirely in 1807 and 1810, respectively. After the War of 1812 new States—Indiana, Illinois, and Alabama—entered the Union with universal white male suffrage already in their constitutions. Pressure in the same direction was mounting in the older States. Between 1818 and 1821 Connecticut, Massachusetts, and New York discarded property qualifications. Religious voting qualifications still prevailed in a few States, but they were tending toward a more liberal policy. Many States were also making efforts to reapportion representation to keep pace with shifting population balance. By 1828 all of the 24 United States except Delaware and South Carolina had withdrawn the right to choose presidential electors from the State legislature and placed it in the hands of the voters, and the common man could believe that he had helped elect Jackson. Thus did the democratic faith affect politics. In other areas of American life, it was influential, too.

Parallel to the rise of political democracy was the movement for social improvement and reform. To a growing number of Americans, it seemed that many 18th-century social institutions must be modified to keep pace with 19th-century ideals, for many did not share directly in the democratization of the political structure. By the time of Jackson's election in 1828, individuals and associations were hard at work to broaden the opportunities of the disadvantaged and handicapped. Pennsylvania and New York had established model prisons. Many States had revised harsh laws requiring imprisonment for failure to pay small debts.

The founding of four "asylums" between 1817 and 1830 signaled society's recognition that the "insane" were not criminals to be thrown in jail or chained in attics. Individual reformers dedicated their lives to

Norfolk, from Gosport, Virginia. From an aquatint by J. Hill. Courtesy, Library of Congress.

aiding the physically handicapped. An example was Thomas Hopkins Gallaudet, who in 1817 became headmaster of the country's first free public school for deaf mutes, the American Asylum at Hartford, Conn. The movement for free public education was well underway. A number of model public school systems—the most famous being New York City's Public School Society—attracted attention, but the public school would not become anything like "universal" until after the Civil War.

Many movements were in the early stages of development. Among them were antislavery, women's rights, temperance, trade unions, and Utopian experiments. Some of the proposed multitude of reforms soon faded into oblivion. Others did not, but had to struggle against centuries of prejudice and habit to achieve their ends. But whatever the cause, whatever the outcome, the social ferment that brought later changes began bubbling in the nationalistic fervor that followed the War of 1812.

The pursuit of a national culture was another expression of nationalist feeling. Until the 1830's U.S. literary ambitions far exceeded accomplishments, though a few poets and novelists achieved memorable success. Washington Irving's tales of life and legend in New York State were notable. So, too, were the works of William Cullen Bryant, author of the poem "Thanatopsis" (1817). And James Fenimore Cooper's frontier

Francis Scott Key's original draft of "The Star-Spangled Banner," first known as "Defense of Fort McHenry." In 1931 Congress officially designated it as our national anthem. Courtesy, Maryland Historical Society.

novels of the 1820's, *The Pioneers, The Last of the Mohicans* and *The Prairie,* had considerable influence. To his generation, and many after, Cooper's tales offered an escape from routine to the adventure and romance of the West—to the world of the noble savage and the self-reliant frontiersman. In Irving, Bryant, and Cooper, the United States found the promise of a mature national literature.

Excellent architects were at work in the United States between 1783 and 1828. Charles Bulfinch designed splendid public and private buildings in New England and elsewhere. Benjamin Henry Latrobe left his architectural stamp on Baltimore, Philadelphia, and Washington. Thomas Jefferson made major contributions and helped to inspire the Greek Revival. But it is difficult to describe the works of these architects as uniquely American. Ancient Greek and Roman buildings were their models. In borrowing from the Greeks and Romans, the architects of the early 19th century were consciously trying to express democratic and republican ideals. The domes and columns of the great public buildings were to serve as visual reminders of the purposes of the Nation. But a uniquely "American" architecture would emerge only later.

Artists in other fields sought to express the ideals and nationality of the United States. Painters produced battle scenes and portraits. Some— such as Gilbert Stuart, the Peales, John Trumbull, and Samuel F. B. Morse—achieved competence and fame but little originality. In music and the theater, little was created that was enduring. Most Americans looked to Europe for cultural models. For many generations to come, U.S. artists, struggling for originality, would also have to strive for recognition. The heavy emphasis on material success and a dispersed agricultural population nurtured a climate essentially indifferent to the needs and problems of artists. Much work had to be done to build the country. Leisure and contemplation would have to wait. First, Americans must settle the West.

Toward the Setting Sun—The Westward Movement, 1783–1828

At the end of the War for Independence, the West was the land between the Appalachian Mountains and the Mississippi River. To the south and southwest of the United States the flag of Spain fluttered over long-established posts and settlements in Florida, New Orleans, Texas, and the Far West. In the forests of the Ohio country, which the British had not yet abandoned, scattered stockades displayed the Union Jack. The few thousand Indians, trappers, traders, and subsistence farmers living in the West in 1783 made little imprint on the land. It was still mostly wilderness.

During the next two generations, the Spanish, the British, the Indians, the forests—all retreated before waves of emigrating Americans. In 1803 the Louisiana Purchase doubled the size of the Nation. By 1830 the population west of the Appalachians was nearly equal to that of the entire United States in 1783. Most of the wilderness east of the Mississippi had been carved into States. Turnpikes and canals linked many of the cities. Towns and prosperous farms dotted the landscape. In less than half a century, the "West" had come into being and changed the character and political balance of the Nation. A political power in its own right, it was wooed by North and South. It also provided the base for the further westward thrust toward the Pacific.

The settler's desire for land was insatiable. By 1828 the frontier had reached the Mississippi River, and in the Missouri region it had pushed far beyond. Settlers were moving into Arkansas and Texas. Before long they would cross the "Great American Desert" on their way to Oregon and California. The fur traders and trappers led the way. In search of beaver, they explored parts of the Southwest, the Rockies, the Dakotas, and as far west as the Pacific coast. They opened new trails, and gathered important information on geography, flora and fauna, and the native peoples. Yet the days of the far western migration still lay ahead.

The precise influence of the West on national institutions is difficult to define. To some, the frontier—the successive zones where civilization and wilderness met—symbolized self-reliance, individualism, and democracy. To others, it epitomized savagery and lawlessness. The truth lies somewhere between these extremes. The frontiersman certainly learned to be self-reliant or he did not survive, but he also learned something about getting along with his neighbors. The impact of the West on the growth of democracy is debatable. Frontier conditions tended to blur social distinctions and demand that a man be judged by what he could do rather than by who he was. The constitutions of each new State seemed more democratic. Yet democratic ideas were not unique to the West. That they found reflection in Western State constitutions occurred in part because the westerners could start fresh when they wrote their constitutions—though usually they copied in large measure those of the older States, where entrenched interests were well equipped to resist change.

DREAMS, OPPORTUNITIES, AND REALITIES

Who were the people who went West? Where did they come from— and why? Some were immigrants from Europe. The first wave of German and Irish immigration began in the 1820's. But the majority of the

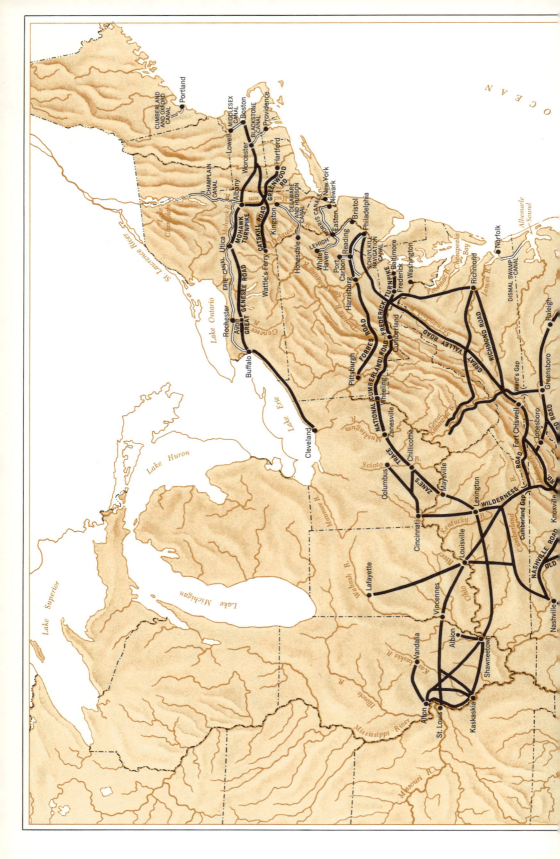

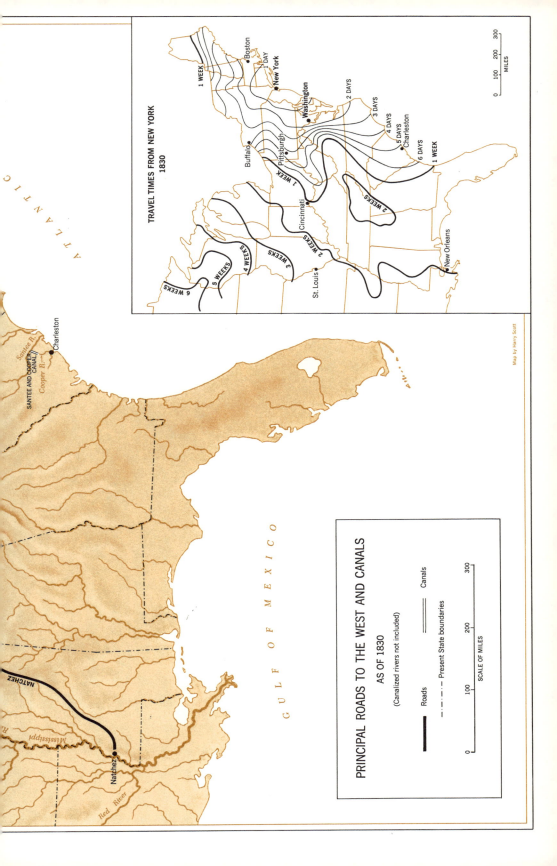

ATLANTIC

TRAVEL TIMES FROM NEW YORK
1830

1 WEEK
Boston
1 DAY
New York
Washington
2 DAYS
3 DAYS
4 DAYS
Charleston
5 DAYS
6 DAYS
1 WEEK
Buffalo
Pittsburgh
1 WEEK
2 WEEKS
2 WEEKS
Cincinnati
2 WEEKS
St. Louis
3 WEEKS
4 WEEKS
5 WEEKS
6 WEEKS
New Orleans

MILES
0   100   200   300

Map by Harry Scott

Charleston
Santee R.
SANTEE AND COOPER
CANAL
Cooper R.

GULF OF MEXICO

NATCHEZ
Natchez
Mississippi R.
Red River

PRINCIPAL ROADS TO THE WEST AND CANALS
AS OF 1830
(Canalized rivers not included)

Roads
Canals
—·—·— Present State boundaries

SCALE OF MILES
0   100   200   300

emigrants were farmers, planters, and agricultural workers from the Eastern States. For a time after the War of 1812, the exodus even decreased the population of some States, such as Connecticut and Maryland.

No single factor explains the westward migration, nor was it an organized, coherent movement. Each migrant had his own reasons for making the journey. Cheap land was a magnet. Land prices in the East, particularly in New England after the War of 1812, were rising and good land was becoming scarce. In the South, soil exhaustion—from the repeated planting of crops such as tobacco—caused the uprooting of planters and farmers.

Frustrations—political, social, religious, and economic—and the desire for adventure motivated some to risk the uncertainty of life in a different environment. Others were misfits—outcasts from civilization—and some were fleeing debts in the East. But most were ordinary citizens. For all, except the slaves, who had no choice in the matter, the westward journey was in some way a fresh start, a chance to begin again, and perhaps to do better.

Ways westward—roads and canals

In the 1780's the journey westward was difficult. New England, the Middle States, and the South each had a road system that carried settlers and goods across the Appalachian Mountains on the first leg of the journey to the interior. The major route from New England crossed New York from Albany to Utica over the Mohawk Turnpike and on to Avon over the Great Genesee Road. This was the least mountainous route. In the Middle States, Forbes' Road from Philadelphia and Braddock's Road from Baltimore converged at Pittsburgh and the Forks of the Ohio. In the South, the Great Valley Road, from Philadelphia, and the Richmond Road converged at Cumberland Gap, and the Jonesboro Road provided a way for Carolinians to reach the transmontane country. Further south, numerous traces served the pioneer.

Natural waterways could not carry pioneers across the mountains, but they could often be used for the second leg of the journey. Pittsburgh, where the Allegheny and Monongahela Rivers join to form the Ohio, was the starting point for thousands of settlers traveling downriver to the Northwest Territory or Kentucky.

Between the 1780's and the 1830's the road system improved consid-

The Erie Canal, crossing nearly the entire State of New York, was a major 19th-century engineering accomplishment and provided a new outlet for Western goods. The passengers not only included westward-bound emigrants but also gentry living along the route, who sometimes took sightseeing trips. From a diorama-painting, probably prepared by the Public Roads Administration. Courtesy, Library of Congress.

erably. A turnpike boom began in the 1790's that transformed the main east-west routes from stump-filled dirt paths that forded streams into graveled or paved roads replete with bridges and toll stations. The most impressive of the new roads was the Government-built National (Cumberland) Road, which followed in part the route of Braddock's Road. Macadamized pavement on some sections and sturdy bridges made it the best road of its time. Begun in 1811 at Cumberland, Md., it was projected to join the East and the Mississippi River. Technical and financial difficulties delayed its construction, however, and it was completed only to Vandalia, Ill., in 1852. After the War of 1812 it was the most popular and heavily traveled road. Pack trains, Conestoga wagons, and a variety of colorful stagecoaches crowded the right-of-way. Inns for freighters and stagehouses for travelers sprang up to provide hospitality and entertainment.

As time went on, water transportation to the West also improved. The Erie Canal, which opened in 1825 from Albany to Buffalo, N.Y., provided a connection that linked the Great Lakes and the Atlantic Ocean. The Erie proved so popular and successful that it created a canal-building "fever" that by 1850 had produced more than 4,000 miles of canals. Canals offered cheap and smooth two-way transportation—an improvement over one-way river transportation.

Traveling together for protection, or risking danger alone, individuals, families, and occasionally whole communities moved into the wilderness. They carried their possessions in Conestoga wagons or on packhorses. They often drove livestock, perhaps a cow and some swine. Women and children sometimes rode, but often they walked. The journey itself was only the beginning of hardship. Living in isolation on uncleared land, the settler's work was backbreaking, and loneliness the bane of his womenfolk. Using gun, ax, and hoe, the frontiersman had to hunt for meat, clear the land, and plant crops. His first crop was most probably corn. It would feed both man and beast; in liquid form it could take the chill off the night or fetch profit in distant markets. As soon as the settler was able, he would plant fruit trees and flax, add chickens and sheep to his livestock, and if all went well become prosperous.

TRAILS AND CLEARINGS—TOWARD THE MISSISSIPPI

Just after the War for Independence, the first major wave of settlers crossed the mountains, where they had to compete with the Indians, Spanish, and British for control of the land. Other obstacles to settlement were the uncertain authority of the National Government, and a primitive transportation system. In two decades, military victories and treaties and the pressure of numbers had driven back the Indians and their allies. Growing Western political power had helped to elect Jefferson and resulted in national legislation beneficial to the region. The transportation system was incomplete but improving. Above all, the Nation at large had caught the spirit of the West and was coming to recognize that the future lay over the mountains.

During the years 1783–1803 the frontier pushed northwestward from the Ohio River into the old Northwest and southwestward from bases in Tennessee, South Carolina, and Georgia into the Mississippi-Alabama area. In both regions the Indians defended their lands with the help of European allies.

The Federal Ordinances of 1785 and 1787 had created the Northwest Territory and a legal process by which it was to progress in orderly stages from wilderness to statehood. The system had flaws. Prior to settlement, Government surveyors were to mark off the land into townships. The thousands of would-be settlers, waiting to enter the virgin lands north of the Ohio River, felt that the surveying took too long. To the Indians, who were unwilling to see their hunting grounds become farmlands and who resisted the settler's encroachment, it moved too fast. Yet Marietta, Ohio's first permanent settlement, did not come into being until 1788, a full 3 years after the Ordinance of 1785.

In the 1780's the Federal Government tried to maintain order by sending military forces to the Northwest. At the same time, Government representatives tried to accommodate Western interests by negotiating a series of treaties with the Indians that gradually opened the land to settlement. In the second treaty of Fort Stanwix (1786), the once-powerful Iroquois ceded their claims to Ohio lands. But the Ohio tribes did not subscribe to the treaty and resolved to drive the Americans back to the Ohio River. In 1791 Gen. Arthur St. Clair tried in vain to conquer the Indians. His defeat encouraged them to undertake extensive raids along the frontier in the winter of 1791–92. In 1793 the Army moved against the Indians once again, this time under Gen. "Mad Anthony" Wayne.

After almost 1 year in the wilderness, Wayne's forces met and defeated an Indian army at the Battle of Fallen Timbers. The battle crippled the

Fort Harmar, Ohio, in 1790. One of the first frontier outposts in the old Northwest, it protected U.S. surveyors and frontiersmen. Lithographed in 1842 from a drawing by Joseph Gilman. Courtesy, Library of Congress.

spirit of the Indians. Their British allies had not helped them, and they themselves had not been able to unite in common cause against the Americans. The following year, in the Treaty of Greenville (1795), the Indians ceded to the United States most of the present State of Ohio. Ratification of Jay's Treaty (November 1794) that same year dealt them a further blow. By its terms the British would withdraw from their north-western posts by 1796 and leave the demoralized Indians to fend for themselves.

In the old Southwest the Indians were better organized to resist the advance of the frontier and had Spanish support. Spain's control of the mouths of Southern rivers—water highways of the time—gave her eco-nomic leverage against U.S. settlers to the north of Florida. The allegiance of 14,000 Indian warriors also gave her military power. But her willing-ness to use her power was qualified by the knowledge that its intemperate use might drive the United States and Great Britain into alliance against her. The strength of the British Navy could place Spain's vast American colonial empire in danger. Under the circumstances Spain hesitated to go too far, but intrigued to detach the West from the United States. Her officials pensioned and cajoled dissident westerners. By threatening to close the port of New Orleans to U.S. goods, she stirred up considerable Western unrest, especially in 1786. At the culmination of the fruitless Jay-Gardoqui negotiations that year, it appeared to westerners that the Government was willing to trade free navigation of the Mississippi for a commercial treaty with Spain.

A major point of conflict between Spain and the United States in the 1780's and 1790's was the Yazoo strip—today's southern Alabama and Mississippi. Both Spain and the United States claimed the region. To preserve a buffer there against the pressure from American settlers, Spain favored an independent Creek Indian State and maintained forces to support it. But the Creeks and the Spanish were no match for the land-hungry Americans. By the Treaty of Augusta (1783), an element of the Creek Nation angered the rest by surrendering the lands in northern Georgia, as far west as the Oconee River, to the Americans. Hoping that a strong leader could unite them against further American encroach-ments, the Creeks appointed the able Scotch-French-Creek Alexander McGillivray as their "king." By playing off the Spanish against the Americans, he was able to resist temporarily the tide of American settle-ment. But in 1793 he died and the divided Creeks were driven back.

In the next decade, despite speculators, legal confusion resulting from the Yazoo land fraud of 1795, and economic unrest created by the Whisky Tax of 1791, settlers moved into the Yazoo strip. The Indians fell back before the weight of numbers. In 1798, recognizing the hopelessness of the situation, Spain abandoned her Yazoo strip forts, and the same year the region became a part of the newly created Mississippi Territory, which Congress extended in 1802 to include all of present Alabama and Mississippi. By 1800 a growing but temporary rapprochement between Great Britain and the United States helped to convince Spain that Louisiana was indefensible. In that year, by the Treaty of San Ildefonso, she ceded Louisiana to France. Three years later France would sell the Louisiana Territory to the United States. In the meantime the Government and the settlers were finding it difficult to arrive at a fair and efficient means of developing the lands east of the Mississippi.

The problem was particularly acute in the Northwest Territory. The difficulty was that most settlers had no ready cash for the purchase of land. Speculators became active. They bought the land from the Government, often on credit, in large lots and then resold it to settlers in small lots, also often on credit. The system had its inequities, and westerners sought, by political action, to eliminate these middlemen and force the Government to sell at lower prices and in smaller lots. By 1800 the westerners had acquired sufficient voice in Congress to liberalize somewhat the sale of land.

One of the most vocal of the Western Congressmen was William Henry Harrison, representing the Ohio Territory, who was instrumental in the passage of the Land Act of 1800. One of a series of attempts to establish a workable system for distributing lands to settlers, it halved the minimum required purchase stipulated in the Land Act of 1796 to 320 acres, but maintained the official price of $2 per acre. This attempt to broaden the sale of land failed. Few could raise $640 to buy a wilderness farmsite, even with 4 years to pay. As a result many who took up lands could not pay for them, and at the end of the War of 1812 half the lands sold by the Government remained unpaid for. The Land Act of 1820—the basic land law until the Homestead Act of 1862—abolished the credit system. But it revised purchase regulations to make it possible for anyone with $100 to buy an 80-acre tract.

The price was still beyond the reach of thousands of debt-ridden farmers, so they simply squatted where they chose without title to the land. The Western pressure for preemption rights, expressed as early as the

Campus Martius in 1791. The thriving town of Marietta, Ohio, grew up around this fort, the first settlement in the Northwest Territory. From a wood engraving by Munson, published in 1842. Courtesy, Library of Congress.

debates over the Land Act of 1800, finally resulted in a general preemption law of 1841 that gave settlers the right to purchase the land on which they had squatted at the minimum price. Behind the legal and political struggle lay, on the one side, the Government's need for revenue, the desire to promote orderly, progressive settlement of the West, and pressure groups of speculators and profiteers. On the other side were the settlers' chronic indebtedness and lack of hard cash and the belief expressed by many that the squatters and pioneer farmers were doing a national service by clearing the land and extending the area of civilization and thus deserved to own their land for their labor.

Whatever the cost or the hardships, settlers continued to set out. The largest of the Western cities in 1800 was Frankfort, Ky., whose population was only 1,795. But 220,000 people were residing in Kentucky, and it had been a State since 1793. Since 1796 Tennessee, too, had been a State. By 1803 the Northwest Territory had been divided, and a portion of it became Ohio, the 17th State, in that year. At the same time, the Indiana Territory was being rapidly occupied. So, too, was the Mississippi Territory. But even before the occupation of the area between the Appalachians and the Mississippi was complete, the Louisiana Purchase had doubled the Nation's size, and made the Mississippi an American river from its source to the gulf.

THE CHALLENGE OF EMPIRE

During the period 1803–14 Americans became increasingly interested in the trans-Mississippi West. The Louisiana Purchase and the expeditions of Lewis and Clark and of Zebulon Pike helped to arouse public interest. Trappers and mountain men then penetrated the region and began to gather detailed knowledge of it. East of the Mississippi, settlement of the Great Lakes region and the Gulf Plains continued, and new States gained admission to the Union. Settlement in Kentucky and Tennessee approached the Mississippi River and would soon spill over into Missouri and Arkansas. The press of westward expansion continued to bring clashes with the Indians and Spanish. The War of 1812 slowed the movement temporarily, but it removed obstacles to settlement. The result was a postwar wave of migration. The American people were fast developing the spirit that would carry them to the Pacific.

The Louisiana Purchase of 1803 provided awesome challenge and immense promise. For across the Mississippi was a rich and varied land. Immediately west of the river were the familiar forests. But west of the 98th meridian, the land became arid and treeless. Settlers would have to learn new ways to live with the land and the climate before the Plains country could fulfill its promise. This would take time. Explorers and mountain men would pave the way.

Hardly a person in the United States had a deeper interest in the West than Thomas Jefferson. As early as 1786 he had encouraged John Ledyard of Connecticut to attempt an exploratory west-east journey on foot from Paris across Siberia, Alaska, and the Pacific Northwest to the United States. Ledyard failed when the Czarina of Russia stopped his trek, but Jefferson's fascination with the unknown reaches of the continent persisted. In January 1803—before the consummation of the Louisiana Purchase—Jefferson secretly asked Congress for $2,500 to send a Government military expedition to develop trade with the trans-Mississippi Indian tribes, and to explore "even to the Western Ocean." He hoped that the expedition would bring back detailed information about the geography, geology, and flora and fauna. Congress authorized the funds, even though the expedition would undoubtedly trespass on Spanish territory.

To lead the expedition, Jefferson chose his personal secretary, 32-year-old Meriwether Lewis. To share the leadership, Lewis, with Jefferson's permission, invited along William Clark, brother of frontier fighter George Rogers Clark. On May 14, 1804, the two men and their party set out from the mouth of the Missouri River. After many adventures and hardships, on November 7, in 1805, they finally reached the Pacific, at the mouth of the Columbia River. They built winter quarters nearby and named them Fort Clatsop, for the local Indian tribe. The men began the return trip in the spring of 1806 and arrived at St. Louis on September 23. [The Lewis and Clark Expedition, including the sites involved, will be treated in detail in the volume of this series dealing with the great explorers of the West and the mountain men.]

The journey of Lewis and Clark is an exciting story of adventure and courage. Hearing it, Americans, young and old, were fired with the desire to see for themselves this land of tall mountains and wide plains and rushing water. The private publication of the journals of Lewis and Clark in 1814 was a significant event in the history of westward expansion.

Even before Lewis and Clark had returned from their journey, other explorers set out under Jefferson's aegis. In 1804 and again in 1806, expeditions sought the source of the Red River. In 1805–6, 26-year-old Lt. Zebulon Pike reached Leech Lake, Minn., in his search for the source of the Mississippi River. A second expedition, in 1806–7, took him into the Colorado country, where he discovered the peak that bears his name, and the Southwest. Continuing his exploration, he and his companions fell into the hands of the Spanish authorities. Before releasing him, in Chihuahua, the Spaniards confiscated his papers, but Pike was able to write a report of his expedition from memory. Published in 1810, it stimulated interest in the Southwest. Jefferson said that the purpose of these explorations was to gather scientific data. Unquestionably they did so. But they often violated Spanish territorial claims. Spanish diplomats remonstrated, but to no avail. Spanish colonial Governors tried their best to intercept or halt the expeditions. Except in the case of Pike, they had little success.

As Lewis and Clark made their way back down the Missouri River toward St. Louis in 1806, they encountered American fur traders headed upriver. Individualistic and daring men such as these—the traders, trappers, and mountain men—were also explorers of the West. In their search for profit and adventure, they blazed the trails, wandered into the remote byways, lived among the Indians, and accumulated a priceless store of detailed information about remote regions. Often the trappers banded together in small groups to market their furs or worked for other men. Some of the leaders of the companies were themselves mountain men. One was Manuel Lisa, the Spaniard who during the period 1808–12 led the St. Louis Missouri Fur Co. in its efforts to found the fur trade along the upper reaches of the Missouri. Other leaders were Eastern entrepreneurs. One of the most influential was John Jacob Astor. In 1810 the Pacific Fur Co., subsidiary of Astor's American Fur Co., sent groups of traders overland from St. Louis and by sea around Cape Horn to set up a far western headquarters. In 1811 they founded a base at Astoria, near the mouth of the Columbia River, a few miles from the site of Fort Clatsop. But the War of 1812 made supply and defense of such a remote post untenable, and in 1813 the British North West Co. took over Astoria. In much of the West, during the War of 1812, British influence over the Indians made it difficult and dangerous for American fur traders to operate. After the war the trade would revive.

During the years 1803–14, while soldiers, trappers, and mountain men explored the trans-Mississippi West, farmers continued to move into the vacant lands east of the Mississippi. In 1805 the Indiana Territory had sufficient population to elect a Territorial legislature. In 1809 Illinois became a Territory. Caught between the advancing settlers and aggressive Sioux and the Chippewas, the Ohio country tribes made a major effort to save their hunting grounds. Two half-brothers, Tecumseh and "The Prophet," were northern Indian leaders. Tecumseh dreamed of a confederation of tribes from the Great Lakes to the Gulf of Mexico

William Henry Harrison, as Governor of Indiana Territory. In 1811 he and his army fought the Battle of Tippecanoe, which won him national recognition and influenced his election to the Presidency. From a lithograph by N. Currier. Courtesy, Library of Congress.

that would stand together, with British help, against the settlers. In 1810 Tecumseh visited William Henry Harrison, Governor of Indiana Territory, at Grouseland to protest the Treaty of Fort Wayne (1809), by which other Indian leaders had surrendered 3 million acres of land for less than 1 cent per acre. The protest fell on deaf ears. Tecumseh wanted to avoid all-out war with the whites, but the dispute flared into a border war along the Northwest frontier in the winter of 1810. The next year, Tecumseh traveled to the South to try to persuade the Creeks to join his confederation. While he was gone, Harrison advanced into the disputed territory. At the Battle of Tippecanoe, in November 1811, Harrison's men drove the Indians off and destroyed "Prophet's Town." It was a crucial but not decisive victory for the settlers. After Tecumseh's return from the South, the Indians sent out raiding parties that caused remotely situated settlers to seek the protection of the stockades, but the Americans had the initiative. The Western phase of the War of 1812 brought the end of Tecumseh and the defeat of his British allies.

Settlement in the old Southwest continued. Spain still held Florida and control of the mouths of rivers that many Southwestern settlers depended upon to market their crops. The extended legal controversy over the sale of lands in the Yazoo strip dragged on. As usual, international boundaries had little significance to the pioneers when it came to finding good land. By 1810 enough Americans had settled in West Florida, where Spanish rule was weak, that President Madison gave the U.S. Governor of Louisiana Territory permission to seize Florida as far east as the Pearl River. The Spanish could no more than protest; they were losing their hold in North America.

R O A D S   A N D   F A R M S — C I V I L I Z I N G   T H E   O L D   W E S T

The second major wave of westward emigration, a surge of nationalism, and unprecedented economic growth marked the period 1815–28. In the years between the end of the War of 1812 and the election of Jackson, settlement moved across the Mississippi and added States to the Union. The new States west of the Appalachians moved toward economic and social maturity and sent national leaders to Congress. By 1828 the political power of the West rivaled that of the older Northeast and South.

"Old America seems to be breaking up and moving westward," wrote Morris Birkbeck, who traveled the National Road in 1817. In 1810 about 1 million people lived in the West. Two decades later 1 million resided

Scene at the Fairview Inn, just outside of Baltimore, along the Frederick Pike, in 1827. The Frederick Pike ran from Baltimore to Cumberland. Inns provided accommodations for turnpike travelers. From a watercolor by Thomas Ruckle. Courtesy, Maryland Historical Society.

in Ohio alone and, according to the 1830 census, 3,672,069 west of the Alleghenies. This figure was about 28 percent of the total population of the United States and almost equal to the total population in 1783. In 1810 Kentucky, Tennessee, and Ohio were the only States west of the Appalachians. By 1830 Mississippi, Indiana, Louisiana, Illinois, Missouri, and Alabama had joined the Union.

Many factors helped to bring about this transformation. After the war, rapid economic changes—industrialization and sheep raising in New England and the revitalized plantation system in the South—drove many small farmers to seek virgin lands. Improved transportation facilities made the journey easier. The Indian menace seemed less frightening after Harrison's and Jackson's victories, and the Army was making its presence felt. Congress authorized a standing Army of 10,000 men and began the construction of a chain of forts in the first tier of States beyond the Mississippi as well as in the Michigan and Wisconsin country.

After the war of 1812, for the first time, the Government embarked on a policy frankly committed to the removal of the Indians from lands that were desired by whites. The settlers' urge to drive the Indians out was not new, but the open Federal commitment to it was. In 1825 President Monroe endorsed removal as a national policy. That same year treaties signed at Prairie du Chien laid the groundwork by dividing the lands of the Indians in the region into tribal areas. This division would facilitate later treaties that would separate the Indians from their lands. In 1827 the Creeks of Georgia were forced to begin migrating from their ancestral lands. In 1830 the removal became official. The Removal Bill of that year authorized the President to relocate Eastern tribes across the Mississippi. The Cherokees, the immediate object of the bill, fought in the courts, but to no avail. In 1834 they were forced to embark on the "Trail of Tears." In the course of time other tribes would have the same experience. The Indian way of life yielded to another.

By 1828 major roads and canals linked the growing cities and multiplying farms. Steamboats plied the rivers. Agriculture continued to dominate the Western economy as it dominated the national economy. Corn, wheat, tobacco, cotton, and livestock were major products. Rich deposits of coal and salt provided income for some. As the West matured, gristmills, sawmills, fulling mills, papermills, and linseed oil mills appeared. Meatpacking became an important industry.

The growing West helped to instill the optimism and faith in progress that are characteristics of the people of the United States. It allowed

West Point about 1810. The remodeled steamboat *Clermont*, shown in the foreground, is en route from New York to Albany. From a lithograph by F. Berthaux of Dijon. Courtesy, New York Public Library (Phelps Stokes Collection).

Americans to measure in quantitative terms how their country, population, and economy grew, census by census. In this bright picture of abundance—the coming of civilization and the fulfillment of the hopes of thousands of settlers—are a few dark shadows. The way of life of the Indian was the victim of "progress." So, too, was there tragedy in the stories of the many whose dreams did not find fulfillment in the West and those who died on the journey or in the Indian wars. Few noticed the shadows. For most, they were insignificant in comparison with the substance of abundance. Already, before 1830, the West had proved to be of immense consequence in the history of the United States.

Epilogue—Traditions and Ideals

During the period of history treated in this volume, some of our greatest men—Washington, Jefferson, Hamilton, Madison, John Adams, and Marshall—helped to shape the basic form and function of the Union and see the new Government through its crucial formative years. The Constitution, a timeless document, remains as relevant today as when it was written. Especially after the War of 1812, themes and trends emerged that shaped the later history of the Nation. Nationalism and sectionalism collided in the Civil War. The industrial revolution accelerated until it triumphed after 1865. The philosophy underlying the Monroe Doctrine guided national foreign policy into the 20th century. Westward expansion and the spirit of the frontier were vital forces until almost the end of the 19th century. Humanitarian concerns and the reform spirit remain active today. Above all, the preservation of individual liberty through representative government and the firm commitment to the democratic ideal have continued at the heart of the American political tradition.

Profound changes—political, economic, and scientific—separate us from the crucial and experimental years just after our Nation achieved independence. We live in another century, in another age. But, engrossed though we are in the perplexing problems of our own time, we must remember that our richest traditions and ideals were created by the wisdom of the Founders and the courage and hardihood of the early Frontiersmen.

PART II

Founders and Frontiersmen:

Survey of Historic

Sites and Buildings

T HE PHASES OF HISTORY treated in this volume—political
and military affairs and westward expansion during the
period 1783–1828—are well represented by surviving
sites and buildings. Illustrating settlement of the national
domain and the development of national institutions during those years,
they are located in the Eastern United States—ranging from the Atlantic
seaboard through roughly the first tier of States west of the Mississippi.
Many are maintained and administered by the Federal Government,
through the National Park Service, but a large number have been preserved by State, local, municipal, and private groups.

Only a few major sites and buildings illustrating political affairs are
located in the region west of the Appalachians. That region was still
largely frontier in character, and the arena of political decision was in
the more populous East. Among the more notable sites are those located
in the first three Capitals under the Constitution: New York, Philadelphia, and Washington. Of particular interest are Federal Hall National
Memorial, in New York, and Independence National Historical Park, in
Philadelphia, both administered by the National Park Service. Sites and
buildings are numerous in Washington, D.C. To provide special assist-

[99

ance to visitors, the National Park Service maintains a Visitor Information Center, located in East Potomac Park at the tip of Hains Point, and a number of information kiosks in the Mall-Memorial area. Three structures that are particularly pertinent to the political affairs during the early Federal period are the Capitol, the Washington Monument, and the Thomas Jefferson Memorial. They are described individually in this volume. Two areas are especially interesting: Pennsylvania Avenue and Lafayette Square.

On September 30, 1965, President Lyndon B. Johnson recognized the historical significance of Pennsylvania Avenue by approving Secretary of the Interior Stewart L. Udall's designation of it as a national historic site. For more than a century and a half, the segment of Pennsylvania Avenue between the White House and the Capitol has symbolized the majesty and power of the Republic and the triumphs and tragedies of its people. Along this truly national thoroughfare have traveled the newly inaugurated Presidents; the funerals of six Presidents and many national leaders; victory processions signaling the end of four major wars; and parades acclaiming military, civil, and scientific heroes. Along adjacent streets, at the hotels, boardinghouses, and restaurants, statesmen lodged, dined, debated the issues of the day, and planned courses of action that influenced the Nation's destiny. In the theaters, hostelries, and places of amusement, they sought release from the cares of office. In the markets and shops, they bought the necessities of life. And, in the area, assassins' bullets struck down two Presidents, Lincoln and Garfield.

Lafayette Square, originally known as President's Park, also has rich historical associations. On its south side stands the White House, residence of every President but George Washington. In the other buildings and houses that surrounded the square, much history has been made; still standing today are St. John's Episcopal Church, "Church of Presidents"; Decatur House; Dolley Madison House; and the Benjamin Ogle Tayloe House. Across the square itself have passed the Nation's political leaders, statesmen, diplomats, and military leaders. During the summer months, National Park Service historians conduct guided tours of the area, which begin at the Jackson Statue in Lafayette Park. Visitors may also separately tour the White House.

Most of the other remaining sites and buildings of major importance in political affairs of the period, in Washington and elsewhere, are in public or private ownership. In Virginia, home of a large number of the outstanding political leaders, many residences have been preserved, including those of Washington, Jefferson, Marshall, Madison, Monroe, and Mason. Most of these are in rural or semirural areas and have been spared the destruction or extensive alteration that has occurred in more populous and intensively developed regions. The Association for the Preservation of Virginia Antiquities has contributed much to preserving and maintaining the State's fine houses.

In other States, especially in the Northeast, the lack of historic private homes is attributable to the explosive spread of modern urbanization that has often swept away relics of the past. Most of the few top-ranking public buildings of the period that remain intact have survived because of continued active use by State and municipal governments. Most notable examples of these are the Massachusetts and Maryland State Houses and New York City Hall. Connecticut's Old State House has survived for much the same reason, although its function as a center of State and city government ceased a number of years ago, by which time its significance as a historic and architectural landmark was very well recognized.

Virtually every decisive military action undertaken by the United States on the frontier against the Indians and in the War of 1812 is preserved at one or more sites. Most of these are located in the trans-Appalachian West, where U.S. military effort was then concentrated. War of 1812 sites in the National Park System include Fort McHenry National Monument and Historic Shrine, Md., Chalmette National Historical Park, La., and Perry's Victory and International Peace Memorial National Monument, Ohio.

The States of Ohio, Indiana, and Michigan administer several sites and buildings associated with the military conquest of the old Northwest. The battlefields of Fallen Timbers, Ohio, and Tippecanoe, Ind., are in State ownership, as is the group of well-preserved buildings at Fort Mackinac, Mackinac Island, Mich. Indiana also maintains the First Territorial Capitol Building of Indiana Territory, at Vincennes, and Ohio has preserved the sites of a number of frontier forts, notably Forts Meigs and Recovery. The Anthony Wayne Parkway Board of Ohio has undertaken a comprehensive program to mark and interpret sites and travel routes related to key military campaigns.

Many of the historic places that marked the frontier advance during the period 1783–1828 have disappeared beneath cities and farms. Few of the earliest pioneer structures survive; their construction had few elements of permanence. More common, however, are the substantial dwellings and other buildings that sprang up as the frontier matured. Few towns cannot boast the home of an early settler. Almost without number are the sites of Indian fights and treaties, forts, trading posts, and early industries. Still visible are traces of the trails, roads, and canals that carried the Nation west.

The theme of frontier advance is represented in the National Park System by Jefferson National Expansion Memorial, Mo.; Cumberland Gap National Historical Park, Ky.-Tenn.-Va.; Natchez Trace Parkway, Ala.-Miss.-Tenn.; and Horseshoe Bend National Military Park, Ala. Chicago Portage National Historic Site, Ill., which also illustrates the westward movement, is in non-Federal ownership. The growth of interest in State and local history, both by private initiative and on every level of public administration, has prevented the mutilation or destruction of many frontier relics. Many of these are eligible for the Registry of National Historic Landmarks.

Unfortunately, there is a darker side. Many of the most significant frontier sites and structures have been irretrievably buried beneath the steel and concrete of cities, obliterated by the plow, consumed by fire, eroded by flood, or laid waste by age and neglect. At the same time, there are some heartening examples of restoration and preservation. One of the most striking examples is the clearing of the site of Fort Pitt at the Forks of the Ohio, Pittsburgh, Pa. A few years ago the site was buried beneath commercial structures and railroad yards. Today, it is being developed as a State park.

Many of the sites and buildings associated with political and military affairs and the westward movement during the years 1783–1828 are described in the following pages. They are arranged alphabetically by State within the following five categories: Units of the National Park System; National Historic Sites in non-Federal ownership; sites eligible for the Registry of National Historic Landmarks; Historic Districts eligible for the Registry; and sites of sufficient importance to merit attention but which are not considered nationally significant when measured and evaluated by the special Landmark criteria.

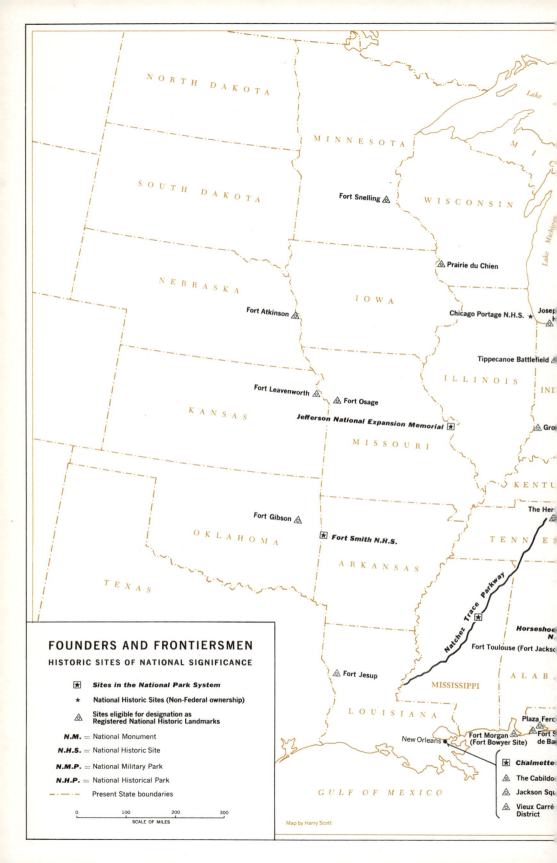

FOUNDERS AND FRONTIERSMEN

HISTORIC SITES OF NATIONAL SIGNIFICANCE

- ⊞   *Sites in the National Park System*
- ★   National Historic Sites (Non-Federal ownership)
- ⚠   Sites eligible for designation as Registered National Historic Landmarks

N.M. = National Monument
N.H.S. = National Historic Site
N.M.P. = National Military Park
N.H.P. = National Historical Park
—·—   Present State boundaries

| 0 | 100 | 200 | 300 |
SCALE OF MILES

Map by Harry Scott

NORTH DAKOTA

SOUTH DAKOTA

MINNESOTA

WISCONSIN

Fort Snelling ⚠

Prairie du Chien ⚠

NEBRASKA

IOWA

Chicago Portage N.H.S. ★

Jose⟨p⟩

Fort Atkinson ⚠

Tippecanoe Battlefield ⚠

ILLINOIS

INI

Fort Leavenworth ⚠   ⚠ Fort Osage

Jefferson National Expansion Memorial ⊞

⚠ Gro

KANSAS

MISSOURI

KENTU

Fort Gibson ⚠

The Her

Fort Smith N.H.S. ⊞

TENNE⟨SSEE⟩

OKLAHOMA

ARKANSAS

TEXAS

Natchez Trace Parkway

⊞

Horseshoe N.

Fort Toulouse (Fort Jackso⟨n⟩)

ALAB⟨AMA⟩

Fort Jesup ⚠

MISSISSIPPI

Plaza Fer⟨dinand⟩ ⚠

LOUISIANA

Fort Morgan ⚠   Fort S de Ba⟨rrancas⟩
(Fort Bowyer Site)

New Orleans ●

- ⊞ *Chalmette*
- ⚠ The Cabildo
- ⚠ Jackson Squ⟨are⟩
- ⚠ Vieux Carré District

GULF OF MEXICO

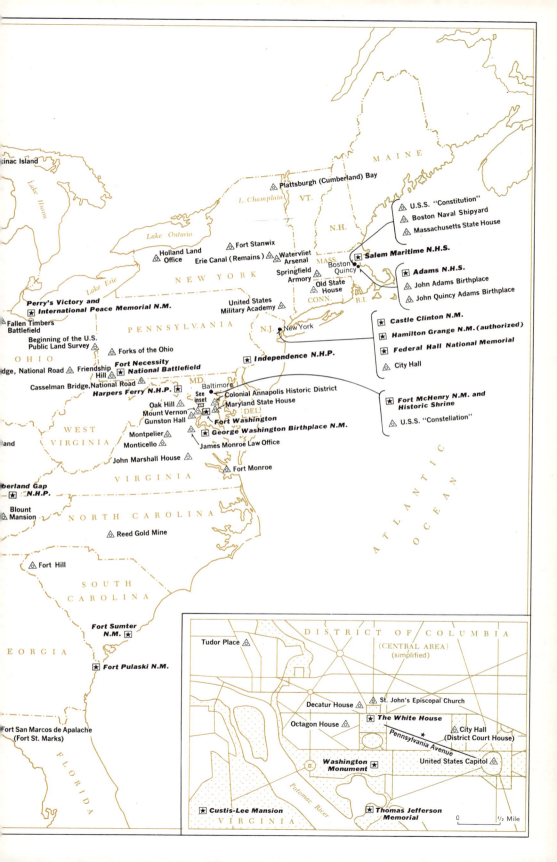

kinac Island

Plattsburgh (Cumberland) Bay

MAINE

VT.

L. Champlain

N.H.

△ U.S.S. "Constitution"
△ Boston Naval Shipyard
△ Massachusetts State House

Lake Ontario

△ Fort Stanwix

★ Salem Maritime N.H.S.

Holland Land
△ Office

Erie Canal (Remains) △△ Watervliet
Arsenal

△ Fort Stanwix

MASS.

Boston

NEW YORK

Springfield
Armory

Quincy

★ Adams N.H.S.

Old State
△ House

John Adams Birthplace

Lake Erie

CONN.

John Quincy Adams Birthplace

Perry's Victory and
★ International Peace Memorial N.M.

United States
△ Military Academy

R.I.

PENNSYLVANIA

N.J. ● New York

★ Castle Clinton N.M.

△ Fallen Timbers
Battlefield

★ Hamilton Grange N.M. (authorized)

Beginning of the U.S.
Public Land Survey △

★ Federal Hall National Memorial

OHIO

△ Forks of the Ohio

△ City Hall

dge, National Road △ Friendship
Fort Necessity
Hill △ ★ National Battlefield

★ Independence N.H.P.

Casselman Bridge, National Road
Harpers Ferry N.H.P. ★

MD.
Baltimore ●

★ Fort McHenry N.M. and
Historic Shrine

DEL.

See
inset

Colonial Annapolis Historic District

WEST
VIRGINIA

Oak Hill △
Mount Vernon △△△
Gunston Hall △

Maryland State House

△ U.S.S. "Constellation"

Fort Washington

Montpelier △
Monticello △

★ George Washington Birthplace N.M.

James Monroe Law Office

John Marshall House △

VIRGINIA

land

△ Fort Monroe

berland Gap
★ N.H.P.

A T L A N T I C

Blount
△ Mansion

NORTH CAROLINA

O C E A N

△ Reed Gold Mine

△ Fort Hill

SOUTH
CAROLINA

Fort Sumter
N.M. ★

E O R G I A

★ Fort Pulaski N.M.

Fort San Marcos de Apalache
(Fort St. Marks)

D I S T R I C T   O F   C O L U M B I A

Tudor Place △

(CENTRAL AREA)
(simplified)

Decatur House △   △ St. John's Episcopal Church

Octagon House △

★ The White House

△ City Hall
(District Court House)

Pennsylvania Avenue

Washington
Monument ★

United States Capitol △

F L O R I D A

Potomac River

★ Custis-Lee Mansion

VIRGINIA

★ Thomas Jefferson
Memorial

0   ½ Mile

A. Sites in the National Park System

The principal aim of the National Survey of Historic Sites and Buildings is to identify nationally important historic sites that are not units of the National Park System, but no such survey would be complete without mention of sites in the system. The sites described below are those administered by the National Park Service that have primary or secondary associations with the phases of history treated in this volume. Further information about a particular site may be obtained by writing directly to the superintendent at the address indicated.

Horseshoe Bend National Military Park, Alabama

Location: Tallapoosa County, on Ala. 49, about 12 miles north of Dadeville; address: P.O. Box 608, Dadeville, Ala. 36853.

At the Battle of Horseshoe Bend, commemorated in this park, Andrew Jackson in 1814 decisively defeated the warring faction of the Creek Nation and brought an end to the Creek War. The battle, which climaxed his determined campaign against the Creeks through central Alabama, dealt a severe blow to the Creek Nation; opened Alabama and other parts of the old Southwest to white settlement; and was the first step along the road that soon brought Jackson national fame for his military exploits and eventually led to the Presidency.

If the Battle of Horseshoe Bend did not involve a feat of generalship, it was at least a victory of will and determination that gained Jackson a reputation as a military leader and Indian fighter. Because of his success at Horseshoe Bend, where he served as a major general in the Tennessee Militia, 2 months later he obtained a commission as major general in the U.S. Army, and 7 months thereafter commanded the U.S. forces at the Battle of New Orleans, where his brilliant defeat of a numerically superior British force made him a national hero.

The Creek War (1813–14) occurred during the War of 1812. Because the U.S. Army was occupied in the clash with Britain, defense of the Southern frontier rested primarily with State militia. When Upper Creeks plunged their tribe first into civil war and then into war against the whites, the surrounding States quickly dispatched militia to quell the Indians. Among the five volunteer generals who took the field was Andrew Jackson, a talented and enterprising Tennessee politician.

In 1813 the Creeks occupied large areas of present Georgia and Alabama. The Lower Creeks resided along the Chattahoochee River in Georgia; the Upper Creeks, or "Red Sticks," along the Coosa and Tallapoosa Rivers in Alabama. Since 1790, when a treaty with the United States set the boundaries of the Creek Nation, the Indians had been at peace with the frontiersmen. Because the Lower Creeks, who lived closer to the whites, continued to strengthen bonds with them, the friction that had always existed between the two factions of the Creeks intensified. Tribal punishments for Creek attacks on white settlers broadened the gulf. The rebellious Upper Creeks, particularly the religious leaders, or "prophets," were also influenced by Tecumseh, an eminent Shawnee chief, who came south in 1811 to form a league with the Choctaws and Creeks. Supported by the Spanish in Florida, the Upper Creeks gained strength as white encroachment increased.

In February and July 1813 minor clashes between the frontiersmen and the Red Sticks led to a tribal civil war. Finally, in August, war broke out with the United States, when the Red Sticks massacred hundreds of white settlers and their wives and children at Fort Mims, on Tensaw Lake, 20 miles north of Mobile. The massacre aroused the frontier bordering the Creek country. Militia from Georgia and Mississippi Territory mounted drives against the hostile Indians, but it was Andrew Jackson, supported by thousands of Tennessee volunteers, Creek and Cherokee allies, and a regiment of U.S. infantry, who sustained the all-out, conclusive campaign against the Red Sticks.

During Jackson's first campaign, between October and December 1813, he marched southward from Fayetteville, Tenn.; united his forces with those of Gen. John Coffee, his chief subordinate; set up a supply base in Creek country; and scored a few minor victories. In January 1814, after reinforcements arrived, Jackson began his second campaign. Driving back two Creek assaults, he inflicted more damage than he suffered. In March his army once more began crossing the 52 miles of wilderness between the Coosa and Tallapoosa. Its destination was Horseshoe Bend, a 100-acre peninsula formed by a large loop in the Tallapoosa. A log wall, 5 to 8 feet high and pierced with a double row of loopholes, zigzagged across the narrow neck. Within this stronghold—called Tohopeka ("the fort") by the Creeks—were drawn up a thousand warriors, led by Monahee, their principal prophet, and Menewa, "the great warrior."

On March 27 Jackson made a frontal attack on Tohopeka, while General Coffee surrounded the peninsula to cut off any retreat over the Tallapoosa. The Creeks, heartened by Menewa's example, fought desperately but in vain. Hundreds of Creeks met death, though Menewa escaped. Jackson had few casualties. One of those wounded was Sam Houston, of later Texas fame, who at the time was a young ensign.

In late April, after turning over control of the Creek country to forces from Georgia, Jackson led his troops triumphantly home. On May 22 he obtained a commission as major general in the U.S. Army, and then assumed command of the 7th Military District, whose headquarters was in Mobile. One of his first tasks as military commander for Tennessee, Louisiana, and Mississippi Territory was to negotiate a treaty with the defeated Creeks. In August 1814, at Fort Jackson, second-rank chiefs of the Creeks agreed to cede 20 million acres in southern Georgia and central and southern Alabama—more than half the territory of the Creek Nation. This cession opened to U.S. settlement a vast and rich domain and separated the Creeks from Spanish influences in Florida.

Horseshoe Bend National Military Park was established in 1959. No identifiable remains are associated with the battle. Tohopeka and the Indian huts in the vicinity were destroyed by fire during and after the battle. In 1918 Congress erected a stone monument overlooking the battlefield. The visitor center contains interpretive exhibits and maps, and a tour road passes through the battlefield and connects key sites.

Natchez Trace Parkway, Alabama-Mississippi-Tennessee

Location: Traverses the States of Miss., Ala., and Tenn., from Natchez to Nashville; address: P.O. Box 948, Tupelo, Miss. 38802.

The Natchez Trace has important prehistorical and historical associations that antedate by many centuries the period of history treated in this volume. Early inland explorers and settlers in the Southeastern part of the present United States discovered a network of animal trails and Indian paths that formed a wilderness road between present Natchez and Nashville. During the 18th century Frenchmen, Englishmen, Spaniards, and Americans used the road. French explorers, missionaries, soldiers, and traders called it a "trace," a French word for "trail." Shortly after arriving at the gulf coast in 1699, the French first explored the trace area; in 1716 they established Fort Rosalie at the site of Natchez. In 1763 the French ceded the region to the English, who occupied it until 1779. The English, who used the trace mainly to trade with the Natchez, Choctaw, and Chickasaw tribes, called it the "Path to the Choctaw Nation."

At the end of the War for Independence, in 1783, Spain claimed the territory between the Mississippi and Chattahoochee Rivers, as far north as Memphis, as a reward for her aid to the colonies during the war. This territory included Natchez, at the southern end of the trace, which remained under Spanish control until it passed to the United States in

Natchez Trace Parkway, a scenic and historical route, generally follows the route of the old Natchez Trace. Dating from prehistoric times, the trace was later used by the Spanish, French, British, and Americans. For several centuries it was an important trade and emigrant road in the old Southwest.

1798, though in the interim the population had remained predominantly English-speaking. The United States immediately organized the Mississippi Territory. At the northern end of the trace, as early as 1780, American settlers had begun to populate Nashville. "Kaintucks," Kentucky traders and other Ohio Valley frontiersmen, rafted their cattle, produce, and furs down the rivers to the Mississippi and thence to Natchez or New Orleans, where they exchanged them for Spanish silver. Unwilling or unable to row upstream against the river current on the return trip, they trekked the bandit-infested trace—which they sometimes called the Chickasaw Trace—to Nashville and then proceeded to their homes in the Ohio Valley. Some rode horses bought in Natchez but most walked. By 1800 about a thousand made the trip each year, and mail service was initiated along the trace.

From 1800 to 1820 the trace was the most traveled road in the old Southwest. Over it passed a variety of colorful frontier characters: Missionaries, boatmen, Indian hunting parties, mounted postmen, and U.S. soldiers. A vital economic and social artery, the trace bound the old Southwest to the rest of the Nation. It was used for frontier defense in the "cold war" with Spain, until she abandoned all claims to Florida in 1819, and it became a valuable military and post road. At the beginning of the War of 1812 Andrew Jackson and his force of Tennessee Militia used it to travel to Natchez, and after the war they returned over it in triumph.

By 1820 the trace was no longer needed for frontier defense. Rivalries with Spain and England had ended, and the Indians were being forced westward. The new steamboat traffic, which moved both up and down the Mississippi, robbed the trace of much of its usefulness and traffic. As the States of Alabama, Mississippi, and Tennessee became more populous, sections of the trace were abandoned and other sections incorporated into local road systems. The trace had lost its frontier character.

The Natchez Trace Parkway is still under construction and follows roughly—crossing, recrossing, and at times paralleling—the route of the old trace. When completed, it will make possible a leisurely 450-mile drive through a protected zone of forest, meadow, and field that is rich in prehistorical and historical associations. Evidences of the aboriginal Indian inhabitants abound along the trace. Historic sites are indicated by markers, and interpretive exhibits point out their significance. The main visitor center is at Tupelo, Miss.

Fort Smith National Historic Site, Arkansas

Location: Sebastian County, on Rogers Avenue between Second and Third Streets, in downtown Fort Smith; address: P.O. Box 1406, Fort Smith, Ark. 72902.

Fort Smith was one of the first U.S. military posts in Louisiana Territory. For nearly fourscore years, from 1817 to 1890—first as a military post and then as seat of a Federal district court—it was a center of law and order for a vast expanse of untamed Western frontier. At the fort, soldier, Indian, lawman, and outlaw played their part in the drama that changed the face of the Indian country; blue-clad troopers marched out to carry the U.S. flag westward; and U.S. deputy marshals, the men who "rode for Judge Parker," crossed the Arkansas River to bring justice to the lawless lands beyond. At the site are preserved the remains of the small first Fort Smith (1817–39), the enlarged second fort (1838–71), and the building that housed the Federal district court (1871–90)—all reminders of the day when civilization and security ended on the banks of the Arkansas River and when men were pushing back the frontier to carve the Nation out of the wilderness.

At the end of the War of 1812, late in 1814, the normal pattern of westward expansion resumed. To protect the settlers, control the Indians, and promote the development of the fur trade, the Federal Government decided to found a series of forts along the Western frontier. In 1817 the War Department appointed Maj. William Bradford and Maj. Stephen H. Long of the Topographical Engineers in St. Louis as cocommanders of an expedition to construct a post just east of the Osage boundary line. Major Long, who performed the reconnaissance, chose a site in Missouri Territory on a rocky bluff at Belle Point—which French traders had named La Belle Pointe—at the juncture of the Poteau and Arkansas Rivers. In December Bradford arrived at the site from Arkansas Post and, using Long's plans, set his 70 men to work constructing a simple wooden fort, measuring 132 feet square, with two 2-story blockhouses and a number of wooden buildings. The unimposing fort was named Cantonment Smith (later Fort Smith) for Gen. Thomas A. Smith, commander of U.S. forces west of the Mississippi. Construction proceeded slowly and did not reach the final stages until late in 1822.

The fort's main mission was to keep peace between the Osage and

Cherokee tribes and to prevent white men from encroaching on Indian lands. In 1809 restless Cherokees had begun crossing the Mississippi River and were moving into northwestern Arkansas. Their penetration of the Osage hunting grounds produced the constant threat of war, but the Fort Smith troops were able to control the situation. In 1824, by which time the frontier had shifted farther westward, the garrison moved some 80 miles up the Arkansas River to the mouth of the Verdigris River, near the site of Muskogee, Okla., where it founded Fort Gibson. Only small detachments returned sporadically to Fort Smith until 1839, when the Army completely abandoned it. The fort rapidly deteriorated. Not until 1958, when archeologists uncovered its foundations, was its exact location rediscovered.

Demands from inhabitants of western Arkansas for protection against possible Indian uprisings caused Congress to authorize the War Department to reestablish Fort Smith in 1838. Plans called for an impressive installation to be located near the earlier fort. Work began in 1839, but the fort was never completed as first envisioned. By 1841 the danger of uprisings had faded. Col. Zachary Taylor, the newly appointed departmental commander, who later became President, ordered work stopped on the partially completed fort. Instead of following the 1838 plan, the Government modified its facilities to serve as a supply depot. Occupied by troops in May 1846, the second fort, during the remainder of its active military life, served to equip and provision other forts being founded deeper in the Indian Territory. During the Civil War both the North and the South used its supply and hospital facilities, but the second fort's days as a military post were almost over. In 1871 the War Department abandoned it.

That same year the U.S. Court for the Western District of Arkansas, which had been organized at Van Buren in 1854, moved to Fort Smith and occupied the barracks building. Thus for two decades Fort Smith would continue to maintain law and order on the frontier. The court had jurisdiction over some 74,000 square miles in Arkansas and Indian Territory. Though its jurisdiction included a part of Arkansas, State courts shared its sphere of authority concurrently. The court's influence and authority, therefore, was felt mainly in the Indian country. An unknown writer aptly described the chaotic conditions in this region when he wrote: "No Sunday West of St. Louis—No God West of Fort Smith." The eastern half of the old "Indian Country," in what is now Oklahoma, belonged to the "Five Civilized Tribes" or "Nations": Cherokees, Choc-

taws, Chickasaws, Creeks, and Seminoles. They had been forcibly removed from their ancestral homes in the Southeastern United States some
30 years earlier. The rest of the territory was the home of various other
tribes. In this vast area no system of law, as we know it today, existed.
Indians were subject to their own tribal courts, but these had no jurisdiction over white men. The most desperate class of criminals from all over
the United States found sanctuary from arrest or extradition in the region.
gion. Disorder ruled, and reputable men—white and Indian—called
upon the Federal Government for relief.

Headed by corrupt and inept judges, the court did not provide such
relief until 1875. In that year President Ulysses S. Grant appointed the
youthful and vigorous Isaac C. Parker to the judgeship. Parker approached his task with unparalleled zeal. For 21 years the court at Fort
Smith dispensed rapid justice from dawn to dusk throughout the year.
No appeals from the judge's decisions were possible during his first 14
years. Of some 13,400 cases docketed, 12,000 were criminal in nature—
ranging from theft to murder. Three hundred and forty-four men stood
before Parker accused of major crimes; 160 were convicted and 79
hanged. Some 65 of Parker's 200 deputy marshals were gunned down.
Gradually, however, more and more of the Indian country was opened
to white settlement, and the settlers demanded their own courts. Each
new court whittled away portions of Judge Parker's jurisdiction. In 1896,
some 6 years after Judge Parker moved his court to new quarters a short
distance from the fort, his court was dissolved and he died within 2
months.

Fort Smith National Historic Site, established in 1964, consists of 14
acres, most of which are in non-Federal ownership. No surface remains
of the first Fort Smith are extant, though archeological excavation has
revealed stone foundations believed to be those of the walls. Visible at
Belle Point are the quarries that were the source of stone for the second
fort. The only significant remains of this fort are the old stone commissary building and the altered barracks building that later housed the Federal district court and is now the Fort Smith Visitor Center. The former,
used by the Army until 1871 and now housing a museum, was built
between 1839 and 1846. Originally intended as the north bastion of the
fort, before completion it was converted into a commissary. Except for
minor alterations, it appears much as it originally did. Soldiers erected
half of the second building in the early 1850's for a barracks, on the
foundations of a larger barracks building that had been destroyed by

fire in 1849. In 1871 the Federal district court occupied it. The other half
of the two-story brick building is a later addition. Of special interest is
Judge Parker's courtroom, which has been restored to its original appearance. In the nearby Fort Smith National Cemetery, established soon after
the first fort, rest a number of Federal and Confederate dead from Civil
War battlefields of northwestern Arkansas, as well as the remains of
Judge Parker himself.

The White House, District of Columbia

*Location: 1600 Pennsylvania Avenue NW., opposite Lafayette
Square, in downtown Washington; address: Regional Director,
National Capital Region, National Park Service, 1100 Ohio Drive
SW., Washington, D.C. 20242.*

Since 1800, late in second President John Adams' administration, the
White House has been the official residence of our Nation's Presidents.
A national shrine that symbolizes the honor and dignity of the highest
office in the land, it has been the scene of many historic events and brilliant social affairs. Like the Nation itself, it bears the influences of successive Chief Executives. Although now rebuilt and modernized, it retains
the simplicity, charm, and dignity of its original appearance.

President George Washington approved the plans for the White House,

The White House, on historic Pennsylvania Avenue, has been the official
residence of every President of the United States except George Washington.

drawn by Irish-born James Hoban, who had won the prize competition. Maj. Pierre Charles L'Enfant, the French artist-engineer, located the mansion in his plan of the Federal City, in which it and the Capitol were the first public buildings erected. The cornerstone was laid on October 13, 1792. Workmen used light gray sandstone from the Aquia Creek Quarries, in Virginia, for the exterior walls, as well as those of the Capitol. During the course of construction or soon thereafter, workmen apparently painted them white. The building was thus unofficially termed the "White House" from an early date, but for many years it was usually referred to as the "President's House" or the "President's Palace."

In the Palladian style of architecture, the main facade of the White House resembles the Duke of Leinster's mansion in Dublin. Hoban probably derived the details of other faces and the interior arrangement from various contemporary British and European mansions. He supervised the original construction; the rebuilding after the burning by British forces, in 1814; and the erection of the north and south porticoes, some years later. Over the course of time, however, various architects modified Hoban's original plans, notably Latrobe during and after the Jefferson administration.

President and Mrs. John Adams were the first occupants, in November 1800, when the Government moved from Philadelphia to Washington. Some of the interior had not yet been completed, and Mrs. Adams used the unfinished East Room to dry the family wash. During Jefferson's administration the east and west terraces were constructed. Jefferson, who practiced democratic simplicity in his social life, opened the mansion each morning to all arrivals. In 1809, when James Madison became President, his wife, Dolley, introduced some of the brilliance and glitter of Old World courts into the social life of the White House.

In August 1814, during the War of 1812, British forces captured the city and set the torch to the White House, the Capitol, and other Government buildings in retaliation for the destruction by U.S. troops of some public buildings in Canada. Before Mrs. Madison fled to the Dumbarton House in Georgetown for temporary refuge, she managed to remove many valuable documents and the Gilbert Stuart portrait of George Washington that now hangs in the East Room. Only the partially damaged exterior walls and interior brickwork remained in the spring of 1815 when reconstruction began. The Madisons lived out his term of office in the Octagon House and the "Seven Buildings." In December 1817 the recently elected President, James Monroe, was able to occupy the White

House. In 1824 builders erected the south portico, the dominant architectural feature on that side; and in 1829 the large north portico over the entrance and driveway.

Since that time the White House has been extensively renovated and modernized on various occasions. However, the old sandstone walls have been retained, and the aim has been to retain the original atmosphere while providing a more livable home for the President and his family.

Furnishings and decorations on the first floor are predominantly 19th-century styles; earlier items are being acquired. Portraits of several Presidents and First Ladies hang in the lobby, main corridor, and rooms of the first floor. Six classic columns separate the lobby from the main corridor. The columns and the pilasters spaced along the walls are of vari-colored Vermont marble; floors are of gray and pink Tennessee marble. The seals of the Thirteen Original States are carved on the marble-faced opening of the stairway.

Located on the first floor are the East Room, the Green Room, the Blue Room, the Red Room, the State Dining Room, and the Family Dining Room. The East Room, the largest in the White House, is used for state receptions and balls. It has been the scene of several weddings, including those of Nellie Grant and Alice Roosevelt. In this room funeral services were conducted for Presidents William Henry Harrison, Zachary Taylor, Abraham Lincoln, Warren G. Harding, and Franklin D. Roosevelt. The bodies of Presidents William McKinley and John F. Kennedy lay in repose in this room. On the east wall is the most notable portrait in the White House, Gilbert Stuart's full-length rendition of George Washington.

The Green Room, used for informal receptions, has been restored as a Federal parlor of about 1800. The furniture is of American design, based on English styles. Known for its elliptical shape, the Blue Room is usually considered the most beautiful in the White House. In this room, where hang portraits of the first seven Presidents, the President receives guests at state dinners and receptions. It has been redecorated to represent the period of President Monroe. Grover Cleveland and Frances Folsom were married in this room in 1886, the only wedding of a President to take place in the White House. The Red Room, completely redecorated in 1961 as an American Empire parlor, is used as an informal reception room by the First Lady. In March 1877 Rutherford B. Hayes took his oath of office in this room. Among the furnishings are sofas that once belonged to Dolley Madison and Nelly Custis. Exceeded in size only by

The Blue Room, perhaps the most beautiful in the White House, is elliptical in shape and decorated to represent the period of James Monroe. There the President receives guests at state dinners and receptions.

the East Room, the State Dining Room can easily accommodate 100 guests at large dinners or luncheons. The Family Dining Room was refurnished in 1961 in the late 18th-century motif.

The second and third floors are reserved for the presidential family and guests. The Lincoln bedroom, in which stands his massive 8-foot bed, is furnished in Victorian style. The adjoining room—the Cabinet Room from about 1865 to 1902—has been restored as a conference room and is known as the Treaty Room. Many of its furnishings were purchased during the Grant administration. The Rose Guest Room (Queens' Bedroom) is furnished as an elegant lady's bedchamber of the early 19th century.

A corridor with vaulted ceiling and varicolored Vermont marble walls gives access to the rooms on the ground floor. The china room and cloakrooms are paneled in pine recovered from the old beams of the White House. The oval Diplomatic Reception Room was refurnished in 1960 with classical revival furniture and a rug with seals of the 50 States. The library, redesigned in 1961–62, contains a suite of rare Duncan Phyfe furniture. In 1952 the original kitchen, equipped with the old sandstone fireplaces, was restored. Adjoining it is a modern electric kitchen.

The simple dignity of the White House is enhanced by the natural beauty of its informal but carefully landscaped grounds. Many of the trees and shrubs are of historical interest, such as the magnolias planted by President Andrew Jackson. The flower gardens and well-kept lawns form an appropriate setting for the President's home.

The White House is open to visitors throughout the year on a special schedule.

Thomas Jefferson Memorial, District of Columbia

Location: Directly south of the White House and the Washington Monument, on the southeast edge of the Tidal Basin, Washington; address: Regional Director, National Capital Region, National Park Service, 1100 Ohio Drive SW., Washington, D.C. 20242.

This memorial, a circular colonnaded structure in the classic style associated with Jefferson in this country, appropriately honors his contributions to the founding and growth of the Republic. Author of the Declaration of Independence and the Virginia Statute of Religious Freedom, the Nation's third President, and apostle of democratic government and freedoms, Jefferson served with distinction in many high offices. An opponent of tyranny and proponent of personal liberty, he believed in a simple democratic form of government, freedom of the press, freedom of speech, education of the populace, and the dignity of the common man.

The reflections of the memorial in the Tidal Basin enhance its beauty. Factors of far greater significance than the purely esthetic, however, influenced selection of the site. Jefferson's position in the Nation's history demanded a memorial site of prominence in the central plan of the Capital and in relation to the other national memorials already built. The Capitol, the White House, and the Mall had been located in accordance with the famous L'Enfant Plan. The subsequent erection of the Washington Monument and Lincoln Memorial on the approximate west axis of the Capitol established the cardinal points of the city's plan. The lone remaining site in this cross-like scheme was the one selected for the Jefferson Memorial south of the Tidal Basin on a line with the south axis of the White House.

The significance of the classic architectural scheme of the memorial is apparent to even the casual student of Jefferson. One of the best-known characteristics of this genius was his many-sided ability and the remarkable practical application of his vast knowledge to many fields of activity. His outstanding ability as an architect can be seen in the design of the Virginia State Capitol, which was essentially his. His designs of the Rotunda at the University of Virginia and his home, Monticello, further indicate his preference for classical architecture.

The entrance to the memorial is from the plaza on the north, or Tidal Basin, side. The sculpture group above the entranceway, the work of Adolph A. Weinman of New York City, depicts Jefferson standing among the committee appointed by the Continental Congress to write the Declaration of Independence. To his left, as.viewed from the steps, are Benjamin Franklin and John Adams, and seated on his right are Roger Sherman and Robert R. Livingston.

The interior of the memorial is dominated by a heroic statue of Jefferson. Rudulph Evans, the sculptor, was chosen from more than 100 who participated in a nationwide competition conducted by the Thomas Jefferson Memorial Commission. The statue is 19 feet high and stands in the center of the memorial room upon a 6-foot pedestal of black Minnesota granite. The statue of Jefferson, together with the wall inscriptions executed in bronze, is in pleasant contrast with the white Georgia marble of the interior, and the Indiana limestone of the dome, approximately 67 feet above the head of the statue. Through the four colonnaded openings of the memorial—two on the east-west axis and two on the north-south—the statue may be viewed from many angles and with varying lights and shadows.

The exterior walls and dome of Danby Imperial Vermont marble

The Thomas Jefferson Memorial, on the south side of the Tidal Basin in the District of Columbia, is a fitting tribute to the brilliant American statesman and third President.

reach approximately 96 feet above the entrance. In early spring, usually in April, when the hundreds of Japanese flowering cherry trees bordering the Tidal Basin are in bloom, the memorial appears in its most beautiful setting. During this period, the annual Cherry Blossom Festival is staged near the Tidal Basin.

In 1934 Congress passed the act that provided for the building of an appropriate permanent memorial to Jefferson in the Capital City. The Thomas Jefferson Memorial Commission, created by this act, assumed responsibility for the planning and supervision of the memorial. John Russell Pope, Otto R. Eggers, and Daniel P. Higgins designed the structure. Ground-breaking ceremonies were held on December 15, 1938, and the cornerstone officially laid on November 15, 1939. On both of these occasions President Roosevelt and the members of the Commission took part. The memorial was dedicated on April 13, 1943, the 200th anniversary of the birth of Jefferson.

Washington Monument, District of Columbia

Location: On the Mall, between the Capitol and the Lincoln Memorial, to the south of the White House, in downtown Washington; address: Regional Director, National Capital Region, National Park Service, 1100 Ohio Drive SW., Washington, D.C. 20242.

This towering 555-foot-high obelisk, a striking monument to the "Father of Our Country" and one of the most famous in the world, is the dominating feature of the Capital. Built between 1848 and 1885 with funds from public subscriptions and Federal appropriations, it commemorates the achievements and unselfish devotion to public duty of our first President—peerless military leader of the War for Independence and wise statesman of the Republic.

In 1783 the Continental Congress first considered a monument in honor of Washington, but by 1833 Congress had still not taken any action on additional proposals. In the latter year, influential citizens of the Capital organized the Washington National Monument Society. Progress was slow at first, but, by 1847, $70,000 had been collected by popular subscription. A design submitted by Robert Mills, a well-known architect, was selected but later substantially revised. On January 31, 1848, Congress granted authority for the erection of the monument. About 5 months later, on July 4, the cornerstone was laid, using the trowel employed by Washington at the laying of the cornerstone of the Capitol in 1793.

Work continued until 1854, when the building of the monument became involved in a political quarrel. Many citizens became dissatisfied with the work; the collection of funds lagged; and, because of the growing disagreement between the North and South, which resulted in the Civil War, construction soon came to a halt. For almost 25 years the monument stood incomplete at the height of about 153 feet. Finally, in 1876, President Grant approved an act calling for the Federal Government to complete the monument. The Engineer Corps of the War Department took over direction of construction.

In 1880 work resumed on the shaft. Practically all the marble with which the remainder of the monument is faced was obtained from the same vein as the stone used for the lower part. Because it came from a different stratum, however, and has weathered to a slightly different tone, a "ring" is noticeable on the shaft. The walls of the memorial reached the height of 500 feet on August 9, 1884. The capstone was set in place on December 6, 1884. The monument was dedicated on February 21, 1885, and opened to the public on October 9, 1888. Its total cost was $1,187,710.

The monument, a hollow shaft of Maryland marble, without decoration or embellishment, which contains a few courses of Massachusetts marble, has little in common with Mills' original elaborate plan. The plan provided for a decorated obelisk 600 feet high and 70 feet at the base. It was to rise from a circular colonnaded building 100 feet high and 250 feet in diameter, surrounded by 30 columns, each 12 feet in diameter and 45 feet high. This temple was to be an American pantheon, a repository for statues of Presidents and national heroes, containing a colossal statue of George Washington. The proportions of Mills' shaft, at variance with traditional dimensions of obelisks, were altered to conform to the classic conception. The result was an obelisk unexcelled in grace and delicacy of outline.

The top may be reached by elevator or a stairway. The iron stairway consists of 50 landings and 898 steps. Inserted into the interior walls or otherwise displayed are 190 carved stones presented by individuals, societies, cities, Territories, States, and nations of the world, including a stone from the ruins of ancient Carthage. The observation platform at the top of the monument affords a majestic view of the central buildings and monuments in Washington. To the east, at the end of the wide vista of the Mall, is the Capitol. To the north is the White House; to the

The Washington Monument, rising from near the center of the Mall and towering majestically over the Capital City, is an imposing memorial to George Washington—revered statesman, military leader, and first President. The reflecting pool is in the foreground and the Capitol in the background.

west, the Lincoln Memorial; to the south, the Thomas Jefferson Memorial. These memorials, along with the Washington Monument, are a national tribute to those figures in our history who have made vital contributions to our independence, the preservation of the Union, and the concepts of liberty and democracy.

Fort Pulaski National Monument, Georgia

Location: Chatham County, entrance on McQueens Island, along U.S. 80, about 17 miles east of Savannah; address: P.O. Box 98, Savannah Beach, Ga. 31328.

This superb example of an early 19th-century fort, equipped with a moat and drawbridge, is typical of the fortifications constructed by the Government after the War of 1812 to bolster coastal defenses. It also represents the end of a distinct chapter in military science. Its massive walls, in which patient masons placed approximately 25 million bricks over a period of nearly 20 years, still bear the historic scars of a 30-hour bombardment by Federal artillerymen in 1862. The bombardment demonstrated to the world for the first time the tremendous battering power of the new rifled cannon. Surrender of the "impregnable" fortress by the Confederates, who had seized it at the outbreak of the Civil War, gave notice to military engineers that the day of brick citadels had passed forever.

The fort is strategically situated on Cockspur Island, a small marsh island in the mouth of the Savannah River on which two earlier forts had been constructed. In 1761, to defend Savannah Harbor and enforce customs and quarantine laws, the Georgia colonial government began the erection of Fort George, a palisaded log blockhouse and earthen fortification. In 1776 the colonists dismantled this fort, already partially destroyed by storms, as a British fleet approached. After the War for Independence, new defenses were needed for the Savannah River. In 1794–95 the Federal Government erected Fort Greene on the island, but the great equinoctial gale of 1804 demolished its battery and barracks. A quarter of a century then elapsed before the island was again selected as the site of a fortification to defend the south Atlantic coast and the Savannah River Valley.

During the War of 1812 U.S. coastal defenses proved to be seriously weak. In 1816 Congress created a military Board of Engineers for

Fort Pulaski, Georgia, was one of a series of coastal fortifications erected by the U.S. Government soon after the War of 1812. Built of brick and surrounded by a moat, it was considered impregnable until Union forces bombarded it in 1862.

Seacoast Fortifications, which undertook to devise a scheme of national defense that would consist largely of the erection of brick fortifications along the exposed coastlines. As a part of this plan, in the early 1820's the board chose Cockspur Island as the site of a fort. Brig. Gen. [courtesy title] Simon Bernard, who had been a famed military engineer under Napoleon and for a while his aide-de-camp, and who was associated with the board, prepared preliminary plans for the Cockspur fort, and work began 2 years later under the direction of Maj. Samuel Babcock. Robert E. Lee's first assignment after he graduated from West Point, in 1829, was to Cockspur Island, where he assisted with the work on the fort until 1831. Early that same year Lt. J. K. F. Mansfield replaced Major Babcock. Mansfield revised Bernard's plans for the fort, and completed most of the structure during the 14 years he served there. In 1833 the new fort was named Pulaski in honor of Count Casimir Pulaski, Polish friend of the United States during the War for Independence who fell in 1779 at the Siege of Savannah. From 1829 to 1847 construction continued. It was an enormous project, involving nearly $1 million and large quantities of lumber, lime, lead, iron, and other building supplies. In one respect it was never finished. Its armament was to include about 140 cannon, but at the beginning of the Civil War only 20 cannon had been mounted, and even these were not in a serviceable condition. [Activities at Fort Pulaski during the Civil War will be treated in the volume of this series dealing with that period.]

Fort Pulaski National Monument, established in 1924, consists of more than 5,364 acres on McQueens and Cockspur Islands, almost all of which are in Federal ownership. The fort, on Cockspur Island, is surrounded by marsh and woods, where an array of birds and semitropical plants is found. Comprehensive exhibits reveal the history of the fort, most parts of which visitors may view. Interpretive markers indicate special points of interest.

Cumberland Gap National Historical Park, Ky.-Tenn.-Va.

Location: Between Middlesboro, Ky., and Cumberland Gap, Tenn., extending northeast into Virginia, accessible by U.S. 25–E or U.S. 58, visitor center just south of Middlesboro; address: P.O. Box 840, Middlesboro, Ky. 40965.

This park commemorates a vital early phase in the westward movement and the indomitable courage of the first overland emigrants, whose descendants only a few decades later pushed on to the shores of the Pacific. Through Cumberland Gap, a natural passage through the forbidding Allegheny Mountains, passed the Wilderness Road. Hacked out in 1775 into Kentucky by a party under Daniel Boone, this road was one of the main arteries used by the settlers who occupied the region between the Appalachians and the Mississippi River.

Long before white men entered "Ken-ta-ke," it had been a magic word among the Indians. Its fertile grazing lands teemed with vast herds of buffalo, deer, and smaller game. Cherokee hunters from the south often visited the region and vied for its rich prizes with the Shawnees and other tribes from north of the Ohio River. Bloody clashes frequently occurred. One of the trails much used by war and hunting parties was "Warriors' Path," which crossed the mountain barrier into present southeastern Kentucky at Cumberland Gap.

English settlers east of the Alleghenies were unaware of the gap until 1750, when Dr. Thomas Walker, a surveyor, discovered it and named it "Cave Gap." He was leading an exploring expedition, which had set

Pinnacle Overlook at Cumberland Gap National Historical Park provides a breathtaking view of the historical gap and the adjacent area in several States. Through the gap once passed the Wilderness Road, a route hacked out by a party under Daniel Boone that thousands of westward-wending emigrants later used.

out from Albemarle County, in Virginia. The Loyal Land Co., which sponsored the expedition, was seeking an 800,000-acre land grant in the region. After discovering the gap, Walker followed the "Warriors' Path" for about 10 miles northwest to the Cumberland River, which he also discovered and named. Near the river the party built a log cabin, one of the first in Kentucky. After spending 2 months vainly exploring the hills of eastern Kentucky in search of the storied Bluegrass region of central Kentucky, the party crossed the mountains north of Cumberland Gap and returned home.

The French and Indian War (1754–63) and Pontiac's Rebellion (1763–65) prevented for awhile any attempt by other explorers to follow Walker's lead. When peace returned, however, small parties of hunters began passing through Cumberland Gap. The best known of this group was Daniel Boone, a native Pennsylvanian who was living in North Carolina at the time. In 1769 John Finley, Boone's fellow campaigner in the French and Indian War who had visited the Bluegrass region several years before, convinced Boone that it could be reached through Cumberland Gap. Following the "Warriors' Path," they and four companions moved northward until they came to a branch of the Kentucky River. Completely alone much of the time in hostile Indian country, Boone spent nearly 2 years exploring the rich and beautiful country. In September 1773 he led an unsuccessful attempt to settle in the region. Early in 1774, during the Indian uprising known as Lord Dunmore's War, he passed through Cumberland Gap and in 2 months' time covered 800 miles of Kentucky wilderness to warn white men of the danger.

The defeat of the Indians, in October, paved the way for an ambitious scheme to settle Kentucky. The following year, under the terms of the Treaty of Sycamore Shoals, Judge Richard Henderson purchased for his Transylvania Co. the Cherokee claim to 20 million acres south of the Kentucky River. To open the region for a private new colony, Transylvania, he engaged Daniel Boone to blaze a trail through Cumberland Gap; thus the Wilderness Road was born. Starting from Long Island of the Holston, now Kingsport, Tenn., in March of 1775 Boone led 30 axmen in cutting the road. Hacking its way across mountain and through swamp and canebrake, within 1 month's time the party reached the Kentucky River, 208 miles from its starting point. There the men erected a fort and named it Boonesborough, the only white settlement in the region except Harrodsburg, founded the previous year about 30 miles to the southwest by a party that had moved down the Ohio River. Soon Henderson arrived with reinforcements for the Boonesborough garrison.

The opening of the road attracted many pioneers, and other "Kentucky stations" began to spring up. When Henderson tried to assert authority over the new settlements, the individualistic backwoodsmen rebelled. In 1776 Virginia, at the request of the Kentucky settlers, formally organized Kentucky as its westernmost county. This action squelched Henderson's plans for a private colony, but his Wilderness Road guaranteed the permanence of white settlement in Kentucky. During the War for Independence (1775–83), the westward movement slowed to a trickle. The gap was frequently closed because of the threat from British-backed northern Indians; when open, it was used mainly to bring troops and supplies to the hard-pressed settlements. The tide turned in 1778–79, when a Kentucky and Virginia force under George Rogers Clark crossed the Ohio River and captured the important British posts at Kaskaskia, Cahokia, and Vincennes.

After the war, though sporadic Indian attacks continued, a flood of westward traffic passed over the Wilderness Road. By 1783 some 12,000 settlers had entered Kentucky, most of them through Cumberland Gap. At the time Kentucky entered the Union, in 1792, its population was 100,000; by 1800 it was 220,000. In 1796 the Wilderness Road was widened and improved for wagon traffic. Eventually, however, more direct routes across the mountains and the final defeat of the northern Indians diverted most of the traffic from the road. By 1825 it consisted mostly of livestock en route to Eastern markets. During the Civil War both Union and Confederate troops sought to control the gap, a strategic position for the invasion of enemy territory. It passed from one side to the other until the Union army finally captured it in September 1863.

Cumberland Gap National Historical Park, established in 1955, consists of 20,189 acres, or almost 32 square miles, in three States. Besides the gap itself, it contains about 2 miles of the Wilderness Road; the ruins of an early iron furnace; Civil War fortifications; Tri-State Peak, where Kentucky, Tennessee, and Virginia meet; the Pinnacle, from where parts of several States may be seen.

Chalmette National Historical Park, Louisiana

Location: St. Bernard Parish, at the eastern edge of New Orleans, on La. 39; address: P.O. Box 125, Arabi, La. 70032.

The Battle of New Orleans, fought at Chalmette Plantation, was the

This 100-foot-high monument at Chalmette National Historical Park, Louisiana, commemorates the Battle of New Orleans, the last major battle in the War of 1812. Gen. Andrew Jackson's brilliant victory over the British at this site on January 8, 1815, strengthened U.S. prestige internationally and made Jackson a popular hero.

last major battle of the War of 1812 and a brilliant U.S. land victory. Although it occurred after the signing of the Treaty of Ghent in December 1814, a fact not known in the United States at the time, hostilities with England had not ceased and the treaty had not been ratified. Ratification, in February 1815, was undoubtedly hastened by the U.S. triumph. The victory was a critical one, for a foreign power controlling the mouth of the Mississippi River would have seriously threatened the economic well-being of the entire Mississippi Valley and hampered U.S. expansion across the Mississippi. The Battle of New Orleans also enhanced U.S. confidence in its military prowess, increased its prestige in world affairs, fostered the growth of national unity, and helped make a popular hero of Andrew Jackson.

A major part of Britain's war plan was to capture New Orleans and gain control of the Mississippi Valley. In December 1814 a combined British force, consisting of fresh troops from England and the expeditionary force that had withdrawn after marching into Washington and attacking Fort McHenry in Baltimore, approached New Orleans from Jamaica, West Indies, by way of Lake Borgne, a shallow arm of the Gulf of Mexico. After British ships captured five U.S. gunboats that guarded the entrance to New Orleans, a land force made its way upriver over swampy land to the outskirts of the city, where it camped at various plantations along the way. The city had no organized line of defense against an attack from this direction, and if the British troops had advanced immediately they would likely have been victorious.

Gen. Andrew Jackson, in command of the military district that included New Orleans, had arrived in the city only a few weeks earlier. He immediately had recruited a motley force of volunteers to support his handful of Regulars and Tennessee Militia. The army numbered about 4,000. Receiving news that the British force was on the outskirts of town, Jackson moved toward the British lines. In a fierce night attack, he caught the British off guard, but darkness and confusion forced him to retreat to Rodriguez Canal, an abandoned millrace some 15 feet wide between the Chalmette and Macarty plantations, situated on a neck of dry land between the Mississippi River and an impassable swamp. He ordered his men to build a mile-long defensive rampart consisting of fence rails, posts, wooden kegs, and mud.

On December 28 Gen. Sir Edward M. Pakenham, the newly arrived British commander, attacked. He divided his crack troops, which numbered perhaps 5,400, into two columns, and deployed one near the river and one near the swamp. The flat, open canefields of Chalmette, however, afforded little cover, and the stubble made footing difficult. Also, the U.S. sloop *Louisiana* eased down the river and helped force the British column along the river to withdraw. In another attempt to silence Jackson's artillery, Pakenham erected a battery about 700 yards from the U.S. ramparts. On New Year's Day 1815 British guns opened fire, but U.S. fire silenced them. On the dawn of January 8, in the Battle of New Orleans, the desperate Pakenham, fearing that further delay would demoralize his army, made three head-on assaults during a half hour period. His casualties were heavy, but Jackson's were light. Seldom, if ever, had an experienced British force of such valor and numerical superiority met such an overwhelming defeat at the hands of a force of irregulars.

In 1855 the State of Louisiana began erecting a 100-foot monument on a 13-acre tract on the site of the U.S. line. The Federal Government completed the monument after the War Department acquired the grounds in 1907. In 1939 Chalmette was established as a National Historical Park. A visitor center, including a battle museum, is located in the Beauregard House, a restored ante bellum mansion once owned by Judge

René Beauregard, son of the famed Confederate general. The park includes an inactive military cemetery. It totals more than 135 acres, almost 83 acres of which are in Federal ownership.

Fort McHenry National Monument and Historic Shrine, Maryland

Location: About 3 miles from the center of Baltimore, off U.S. 301 and Md. 2, on East Fort Avenue; address: Baltimore, Md. 21230.

This national shrine, where the flag flies day and night by Presidential proclamation, commemorates that surge of inspiration, amid "bombs bursting in air," that impelled Francis Scott Key to create the classic expression of U.S. ideals and patriotism contained in our national anthem, "The Star-Spangled Banner." The morning after a day- and night-British bombardment of Fort McHenry in 1814, during the War of 1812, the inspired Key, glimpsing the U.S. flag above the embattled ramparts of the fort, penned his immortal lines.

As early as the War for Independence, military authorities recognized the strategic importance of the Baltimore peninsula, located on the Patapsco River. In 1776, to protect Baltimore Harbor, they constructed Fort Whetstone, a temporary fort. In the 1790's, when war with France seemed imminent, both the Federal Government and the citizens of Baltimore contributed funds for the construction at the same site of a permanent harbor defense, consisting of outer batteries and a star fort. It was named Fort McHenry, in honor of James McHenry, Secretary of War between 1796 and 1800.

Late in the War of 1812, following Napoleon's defeat in 1814 and the temporary restoration of peace in Europe, the British sent large numbers of troops, including "Wellington's Invincibles," to the United States. Most of them moved into the Great Lakes area. Some, before participating in an attack on New Orleans, were sent to the Chesapeake Bay area. After the easy capture of Washington, the British army moved toward Baltimore, larger and of more commercial significance, where they planned to join naval forces in a joint attack.

On September 12, 5,000 troops disembarked at North Point, downriver from Fort McHenry, and moved rapidly to Baltimore. On North Point Road they clashed with U.S. troops. The next morning the British moved to within 2 miles of Baltimore, and at the same time 16 warships dropped anchor in the Patapsco River and commenced a 25-hour bombardment of the fort. Because most of the U.S. garrison was stationed on outerworks, casualties at the fort itself were only 4 killed and 24 wounded. The critical hour came shortly after midnight on the 14th, when a sizable force of British sailors tried to penetrate the Ferry Branch, a channel on the Patapsco River on the vulnerable south side of the city. But half of them mistakenly entered the North West Branch, the channel opposite the fort. U.S. forces detected them and drove them off, as well as the rest of the group at the Ferry Branch. Because the U.S. troops had sunk the hulks entering the North West Branch, the British commander, prevented from entering the channel, withdrew his land troops to their transports. The Battle of Baltimore was over and the British repulsed. They moved to the island of Jamaica for rendezvous with other troops before attacking New Orleans, where Andrew Jackson defeated them.

"The Star-Spangled Banner" reflects the emotions of Francis Scott Key as he watched the 25-hour attack on Fort McHenry from the decks of a U.S. truce ship, detained by the British fleet. During the day, able to see the flag waving defiantly over the ramparts, he was reassured. As long as the British continued to fire, he knew the fort was continuing to resist. Then shortly after midnight the firing ceased, and he feared that the fort had surrendered. He was unaware that the bombardment had been halted to enable a landing force to storm the fort. Anxiously he waited for daylight, and at dawn saw the flag again. On the back of a letter, he penned the first version of the poem that became the national

View of the parade ground from the sally port, Fort McHenry, Maryland. In 1814 the British bombardment of the fort inspired Francis Scott Key to write our national anthem, "The Star-Spangled Banner."

anthem. When released, he had a revised copy printed in handbill form. Soon people were singing the poem to the music of a popular English song, "To Anacreon in Heaven." As time passed, the song increased in popularity. In 1931 Congress made "The Star-Spangled Banner" the official national anthem.

Although the strategic importance of Fort McHenry decreased after 1814, it continued to play a part in the Nation's emergencies. During the Mexican War the Maryland Volunteer Artillery mobilized at the fort, and during the Civil War Confederate prisoners, as well as Baltimore residents suspected of Southern sympathies, were detained there.

Fort McHenry was first established in 1925 as a National Park and redesignated by Congress in 1939 as a National Monument and Historic Shrine. It includes the pentagonal brick fort and surrounding area of slightly more than 43 acres. The visitor center interprets the history of the site. Buildings within the fort serve as museums; of special interest are exhibits of the flag and its evolution. A numbered self-guiding tour of the fort includes all principal features.

Fort Washington, Maryland

Location: Prince Georges County, along the Potomac River, 5½ miles below the District of Columbia line, on the southern boundary of a 341-acre reservation, just off Md. 210; address: Regional Director, National Park Service, 1100 Ohio Drive NW., Washington, D.C. 20242.

This fort, constructed during the period 1814–24, is an outstanding example of a 19th-century coastal defense. The first erected to defend the Nation's Capital City, it was designed to withstand attack by wooden naval vessels, armed with smooth-bore artillery. Its high masonry walls, gun positions, dry moat, and drawbridge illustrate some of the then prevailing principles of military science and architecture.

Despite the construction of the Capitol at Washington and the relocation there late in 1800 of the Government from Philadelphia, almost a decade passed before Congress took any steps to provide for the defense of the city. Congressional reluctance to do so was not dispelled until Europe's Napoleonic Wars came dangerously near U.S. shores. In 1808, after the repeated seizures of U.S. seamen and the detention and search of the U.S. Frigate *Chesapeake* by a British warship, Congress appropriated funds for harbor and port defense.

Just after the War of 1812, the U.S. Government constructed Fort Washington, Maryland, to guard the Capital City from attack. Although never attacked, the fort remained active through World War II.

George Washington originally selected the site of Fort Washington, where Fort Warburton, completed in 1809, had at first been situated. In 1814, however, during the War of 1812, the commander destroyed and abandoned it without resisting a British naval and military force en route to join that which had attacked Washington. Wartime anxiety for the safety of the Capital induced Acting Secretary of War James Monroe to engage the French engineer Maj. Pierre Charles L'Enfant to reconstruct the fort. L'Enfant had more or less free rein. In 1815, by which time the British threat had subsided, Monroe, concerned over expense, replaced L'Enfant with the economy-minded Lt. Col. Walker K. Armistead. Fort Washington was completed in 1824 at a cost of $426,000.

Extensive modifications during the 1840's, still visible today, included construction of 88 permanent gun platforms for barbette carriages, erection of a new drawbridge, the addition of a bastioned outerwork to strengthen the south wall, and improvement of the powder magazines. Early in the Civil War the Secretary of the Navy assigned 40 marines to the fort, the only fortification defending Washington. As a naval attack became less probable, its importance declined, particularly after the completion of Fort Foote, opposite Alexandria, in 1864. In 1872 the Government abandoned Fort Washington and 13 years later removed the obsolete muzzle-loading guns. During the period 1896–1921 it was headquarters for the Defenses of the Potomac. Eight concrete batteries, erected during this period, may still be seen. From 1921 until 1939, when transferred from the War Department to the Department of the Interior, the fort was headquarters of the 12th Infantry Division. Shortly after the Japanese attack on Pearl Harbor, it reverted to the War Department; later it was transferred to the Veterans Administration. Finally, in 1946, it was returned to the Department of the Interior for park purposes. Rehabilitation began in 1957 under the Mission 66 Program.

The fort area is open to the public daily. A small museum interprets its history. The masonry fort has been little altered in basic form since 1824. It is entered by a drawbridge across a dry moat at the main gate. Approximately 60 feet below the fort is an outer V-shaped water battery. Two half-bastions overlook the river above and below the fort. Below the ramparts of these two structures are the casemates, or bombproof gun positions. Guns of the water battery, casemate positions, and ramparts could deliver a devastating fire against an enemy fleet on the Potomac from three different levels. On the parade ground are the officers' quarters and soldiers' barracks, near which are magazines. A guardroom, containing two narrow cells, and a museum are located in the main gateway structure.

Adams National Historic Site, Massachusetts

Location: Norfolk County, bounded by Adams Street, Furnace Brook Parkway, and Newport Avenue, Quincy; address:'135 Adams Street, Quincy, Mass. 02169.

This site, which features the Adams Mansion, is a memorial to four generations of the Adams family, distinguished in American politics and intellectual life. In the mansion resided Presidents John Adams and John Quincy Adams; Charles Francis Adams, U.S. Minister to Great Britain during the Civil War; and the celebrated writers and historians Henry and Brooks Adams.

John Adams (1735–1826) was the first Vice President and second President of the United States. He was graduated from Harvard College in 1755, a decade or so later actively opposed the Stamp Act, and in 1774 represented the colony of Massachusetts as a delegate to the First Continental Congress. After fighting began at Lexington, he took a leading part in the Second Continental Congress, was one of those involved in the movement for independence, and helped choose Washington as commander in chief of the Army. Adams was also one of the Committee of Five, which drafted the Declaration of Independence.

After Burgoyne's surrender at Saratoga, in 1777, Adams was appointed commissioner to France and with his 10-year-old son, John Quincy, sailed for Europe in 1778. Later he served as Minister Plenipotentiary to Holland, from which country he obtained loans. Together with Benjamin Franklin and John Jay, on September 3, 1783, he signed the peace treaty with Great Britain that recognized the independence of the United States. In 1785 he served as Envoy to Britain, where he remained until 1788. Few contributed more to independence and foreign recognition.

Together with Franklin and Jefferson he selected the motto *E Pluribus Unum* (One Out of Many) for use on the Great Seal of the United States. In the Government under the Constitution, he held the office of Vice President. Elected to the Presidency in 1796, he served ably and prevented a war with France. In 1801 he retired to his home in Quincy, but never lost his avid interest in public questions. He lived to see his son elected to the Presidency, and died on July 4, 1826, the same day as Thomas Jefferson. John's wife, Abigail, a remarkable woman in her own right and first mistress of the White House, was the only woman in our history to have been the wife of one President and the mother of another.

"Peacefield," or the "Old House," in Quincy, Massachusetts, was the home of four generations of the Adams family, including Presidents John and John Quincy Adams. The Adams Mansion is now a part of Adams National Historic Site.

John Quincy Adams (1767–1848) as a boy accompanied his father to Europe, in 1778. During his father's ministry to Great Britain, he returned to America and in 1787 was graduated from Harvard College. Seven years later Washington commissioned him Minister to the Netherlands, and during his father's Presidency he was Minister to Prussia. In 1803 he won election to the U.S. Senate, where he demonstrated independence of mind by supporting Jefferson's embargo as an alternative to war. In 1809 President Madison appointed him Minister to Russia, where he witnessed many stirring events in the reign of Tsar Alexander I. Refusing a nomination to the Supreme Court of the United States, he remained in Europe as one of the U.S. peace commissioners for the War of 1812. On December 24, 1814, he signed the Treaty of Ghent, which ended the war. In Paris he witnessed Napoleon's triumphal return from Elba, the prelude to Waterloo.

Adams next went to England as Minister to the Court of St. James. In 1817 he became President Monroe's Secretary of State and negotiated with Spain for the cession of the Floridas, which culminated in the Adams-Onís Treaty of 1819. He took a prominent part in the recognition of the Latin American Republics and was jointly responsible with the President for the promulgation of the Monroe Doctrine. In 1825 he became the sixth President of the United States. Four years later he retired to Quincy, hopefully to write history. But within 2 years he was elected to Congress, where he served continuously for 17 years—the only ex-President to become a Member of the House of Representatives. At the age of 81, stricken on the floor of the House, he literally died at his post.

Charles Francis Adams (1807–86), son of John Quincy, followed his father and grandfather in public life and fathered four distinguished sons. His father took him at the age of 2 to St. Petersburg and later to Paris. In 1825 he was graduated from Harvard University, and 4 years later was admitted to the bar. After serving in the Massachusetts Legislature, in 1848 he was nominated for Vice President on the Free Soil ticket with Van Buren. He was elected to Congress in 1858 and 1860. The following year President Lincoln chose him as Minister to the Court of St. James, a post held by his father and grandfather, in which he served with distinction throughout the Civil War. Resigning in 1868, he declined the presidency of Harvard University and retired to Quincy. He returned to Europe as one of the arbitrators who passed upon the *Alabama* claims at Geneva. An accomplished historian, author, and biographer of his grandfather, he also published the letters and diaries of various members of the family.

The four sons of Charles Francis Adams—John Quincy II (1833–94), Charles Francis, Jr. (1835–1915), Henry (1838–1918), and Brooks (1848–1927)—all had highly successful careers. All of them, like their father, grandfather, and great grandfather before them, graduated from Harvard. And they distinguished themselves in politics, literature, historiography, and public service.

The Adams Mansion, named "Peacefield" by John Adams, but known later to the family as the "Old House," was dear and close to all of them. In 1731 Maj. Leonard Vassall, a wealthy West Indian sugar planter who had come to Massachusetts some 8 years before, built the oldest part of the house. It consisted of only three rooms on the ground floor, two bedrooms on the second floor, and three smaller rooms in the attic. The kitchen and servants' quarters were not attached to the house.

John Adams, while still Minister to Great Britain, bought the house in September 1787 from the major's grandson, Leonard Vassall Borland, and on his return in 1788 took possession of the property. During his Presidency he built the large gabled ell containing the long room, east entry, and upstairs study. In 1836 John Quincy Adams added the passage along the north side of the house connecting the two ells. In 1869 Charles Francis added 30 feet to the kitchen ell for servants' quarters, and the following year built the stone library overlooking his grandmother's garden, and, in 1873, the stone stable. In 1906 Brooks added the present entrance gates.

After his retirement from the Presidency, in 1801, John Adams lived in the house the year round until his death, in 1826. John Quincy Adams and Charles Francis Adams made it their summer home, and both Henry and Brooks spent many summers there. Much of the furniture within the house reflects the diplomatic background of John, John Quincy, and Charles Francis Adams, for they all returned with prized possessions from their European missions.

The continuity of life in the house is best shown by the furnishings, for the various objects are of successive periods—each generation contributing something. The house is not a "period piece" but one that clearly shows the ever-changing style and taste of its occupants, from 1788 to 1927.

In 1946 the Adams Memorial Society donated the property to the

Federal Government. Consisting of almost 5 acres, it includes the house, library, garden, and stables. It is open to the public from April 19 through November 10.

Salem Maritime National Historic Site, Massachusetts

Location: Essex County, Derby Street, Salem; address: Custom House, Derby Street, Salem, Mass. 01970.

The group of buildings and wharves at this site memorializes U.S. maritime greatness and the pioneering enterprise upon the sea that strengthened the young Nation. Surviving from the period of Salem's supremacy as a port are Derby Wharf; Derby House; Hawkes House; and the Old Custom House, in which Nathaniel Hawthorne worked.

Founded in 1626 by Roger Conant as the plantation of Naumkeag and established 2 years later as the first town in the Massachusetts Bay Colony, Salem owed its prosperity to a seaboard location and was a major port long before the Nation was formed. Prior to the settlement of Boston, it was the principal debarkation point for the Puritan migrations from England in the 1630's.

From the beginning, American colonists depended upon the ocean for communication with the homeland and, because of the lack of roads, with the other colonies. Many colonists lived within reach of the sea and naturally turned to it for adventure, livelihood, and even riches. Indeed, the sea was the first frontier as well as the first highway. The colonies in New England, more than most others, grew up on the sea and for more than two centuries aggressively followed its calling. Much of the land was rocky and agricultural possibilities meager, but the coastal waters yielded an abundance of fish and the virgin forests afforded materials for building ships. The Salem colonists soon became actively engaged in maritime pursuits, particularly fishing and shipping.

Salem and other New England ports figured prominently in the colonial and early republican economy. Beginning soon in the 17th century, sailing vessels based at Salem plied the sealanes of the world. As early as 1643 Salem merchants sent fish, lumber, and provisions to the West Indies in exchange for sugar and molasses, which were brought home and made into rum. Gradually the orbit of trade was extended to Europe, for the most part to Portugal and Spain, which offered a ready market for dried fish and supplied salt, wine, fruit, iron, and Spanish dollars in return.

Old Custom House, Salem Maritime National Historic Site, Massachusetts, commemorates the era of Salem's maritime supremacy. Nathaniel Hawthorne, the noted author, at one time worked in this building, erected in 1819.

This trade and that with the West Indies—which after 1700 developed into the "triangular trade" between New England, the West Indies, and Africa—thrived until 1763, when the long struggle between France and England for the mastery of the American continent finally came to an end and the English Government began to enact and enforce new measures that stringently limited the commerce of the American colonies. Under these conditions the economic life of Salem, like that of all Atlantic ports, came to a standstill, and a discontent engendered that grew into resistance and eventually rebellion.

During the War for Independence Salem was a base for privateers, swift and formidable ships that ravaged British shipping. Because it was the one major port in the United States that did not fall into British hands during the war, it was active in privateering. During the years 1776–82 an average of 50 Salem vessels were continually at sea preying on enemy shipping and engaging enemy ships.

For nearly three quarters of a century after that time, until the era of the clipper ships, Salem continued to be a key New England port. At the end of the war the energy that had been shown in privateering found an outlet in a worldwide search for new markets. Between the War for Independence and the War of 1812, especially, Salem emerged as one of the major seaports in the Western Hemisphere. Not a large city, it gained wealth and fame from the work of a small but bold population of shipmasters and sailors, sponsored by a small group of enterprising merchants. The latter included the Derby family, particularly Richard, Elias Hasket, and Elias Hasket, Jr.

Salem shipmasters made pioneering voyages into the Baltic and beyond the Cape of Good Hope to the fabulous East Indies and China—voyages that helped to usher in the first golden age of foreign trade and to achieve for Salem the reputation of a "New World Venice." On some of those voyages, vessels were away as long as 2 years and might take on and dispose of several cargoes before returning to their home port from the Far East.

After the French Revolution brought on the general European war that broke out in 1793, it was not markets of the East alone that lured U.S. merchants. As France and England once again came to grips in a titanic struggle, ships of the neutral United States attempted to transport a large share of the goods of both belligerents. The U.S. vessels were exposed to constant danger of capture by privateers in the quest of plunder or by men-of-war that seized any shipping going in or out of enemy ports.

At first, British aggressions were the more serious, particularly in French West Indies waters. Negotiation of the Jay Treaty in 1794 somewhat reduced the friction between the United States and England, but it created resentment on the part of the French Republic, which accused the United States of repudiating the friendship formed during the War for Independence. The French increased their depredations on U.S. shipping, and Congress took warlike measures for the protection of U.S. trade. In 1798 it organized the Navy Department and abrogated all treaties with the French. The Navy could not provide all the necessary war vessels, so during the summer of 1798 citizens of the seaport towns were requested to build ships by subscription. Salem raised $74,700 in a few weeks for the construction of the *Essex,* a 32-gun frigate, which became famous in naval annals.

The embargo President Jefferson imposed on U.S. shipping in 1807 and the War of 1812 were severe blows to Salem and were the first of several factors that in but a few decades led to the decline of her commerce. During the War of 1812, however, privateering took the place of trade as it had in the War for Independence. At the end of hostilities, Salem displayed the same pioneering instinct that had been in evidence at the close of the War for Independence. Merchants and captains explored new channels of trade to Africa, Australia, and South America. After the discovery of gold in California in 1848, Salem shipowners were among the first to reap profits from the trade around Cape Horn to San Francisco. However, the great increase in the size of vessels that came with the decade of the clipper ships, 1850–60, brought Salem's maritime activities abruptly to a close. Her harbor was too shallow to accommodate the large ships, and the deep water ports of Boston and New York absorbed her commerce.

Salem Maritime was designated a national historic site in 1938. It occupies an area of almost 9 acres bordering on Salem Harbor. Capt. Richard Derby began building Derby Wharf soon after 1762. After the War for Independence it became a mercantile center of the Republic. One of the major survivals from Salem's era of maritime supremacy, it was restored in 1938. It extends nearly 2,000 feet into the harbor. Directly opposite the wharf is the Custom House, constructed in 1819, where Nathaniel Hawthorne once worked and collected materials for his distinguished novel *The Scarlet Letter*. The oldest surviving brick house in Salem is the Derby House, erected in 1761–62 by Capt. Richard Derby for his son, Elias Hasket Derby. Other buildings of interest are the Hawkes House and the Rum Shop.

Jefferson National Expansion Memorial, Missouri

> *Location: St. Louis, downtown; address: 11 North 4th Street, St. Louis, Mo. 63102.*

This memorial celebrates the vision of President Thomas Jefferson, architect of westward expansion, and all aspects of that vital national movement.

St. Louis, "gateway to the West," was founded in 1764 by Frenchmen from New Orleans and became a center of French-Canadian culture and Spanish governmental control until 1803, when the United States acquired it from France as part of the Louisiana Purchase. The continent-spanning Lewis and Clark Expedition, which stimulated the opening of the West, embarked in May 1804 from its base camp, just north of St. Louis on the Illinois side of the Mississippi at the mouth of the Wood River. A couple of months earlier Meriwether Lewis, accompanied by a few soldiers, had witnessed in St. Louis the formal transfer of Upper Louisiana from France to the United States. Prior to that time he had visited there to obtain permission from Spanish officials, in control despite the nominal cession of Louisiana to France in 1803, for his expedition to proceed.

Jefferson National Expansion Memorial, St. Louis, Missouri, commemorates the Nation's trans-Mississippi expansion, which was greatly facilitated by the Louisiana Purchase, in 1803. The late Eero Saarinen designed the gigantic arch, which symbolizes St. Louis' role as "Gateway to the West."

For decades after the Louisiana Purchase, St. Louis was a key town on the Western U.S. frontier. Conveniently located in relation to the mouths of the Ohio, Missouri, and other Mississippi tributaries, it was the hub of midcontinental commerce, transportation, and culture—the place where East met West and point of departure for the wilderness beyond. A base of operations for traders, travelers, scientists, explorers, military leaders, Indian agents, and missionaries, it was also the headquarters of the Western fur trade and focus of advanced scientific and political thought in the West.

Along the St. Louis waterfront, hulking steamboats from the East and South met the smaller river boats that served the frontier communities and outposts on the upper Mississippi and Missouri Rivers. At this major transfer point, a small but teeming city, mercantile establishments, boatyards, saloons, and lodginghouses served and supplied the westbound settlers and other frontiersmen who congregated there before setting out across the Plains to Oregon, California, Santa Fe, and other points.

To dramatize westward expansion and the broad cultural, political, economic, and other benefits that accrued to the Nation from the Louisiana Purchase of 1803, the National Park Service and the Jefferson National Expansion Memorial Association, a nonprofit organization of public-spirited citizens, have undertaken an extensive development program for the memorial. As part of a broad urban renewal program, crowded, obsolescent industrial buildings have been cleared away.

The dominant feature of the memorial—on the west bank of the Mississippi River on the site of the original village of St. Louis—is a 630-foot-high stainless steel arch, designed by the noted architect Eero Saarinen and completed in 1965. It symbolizes the historic position of St. Louis as gateway to the West. A transportation system carries visitors to an observatory at the top. Scaled to the heroic dimensions of such other famous structures as the Washington Monument, the Eiffel Tower, and the Statue of Liberty, the Gateway Arch ranks with them in size and grandeur.

A Museum of Westward Expansion—temporarily located in the Old Courthouse—will soon be constructed underground at the base of the arch. Museum exhibits portraying the experiences and contributions of Western explorers, fur traders, statesmen, overland emigrants, soldiers, miners, Indians, cattlemen, and farmers will present our Western heritage in new dimensions.

In 1935 the Jefferson National Expansion Memorial was designated as a national historic site by Executive order. It occupies an area of slightly more than 85 acres.

Castle Clinton National Monument, New York

Location: New York County, on the Battery, New York City; address: New York City National Park Service Group, 28 East 20th Street, New York City 10003.

Castle Clinton, built as a New York Harbor defense fortification early in the 19th century, successively served as a promenade and entertainment center, a major immigrant receiving depot, and finally as a popular aquarium. Because of such varied usage, it symbolizes a century and a half of U.S. growth and change and is a unique link with the 19th century.

Castle Clinton was the last of a series of forts which, beginning in 1626, guarded the lower end of Manhattan Island and the great commercial city of New York. During the Napoleonic Era, some 2 years after the renewal of the conflict between England and France in 1803, the British began seizing U.S. ships and impressing U.S. sailors into the Royal Navy. The troubled months that followed were climaxed in mid-1807 by a British attack on the U.S. Frigate *Chesapeake*. In mass meetings in New York the citizens, realizing that the city was virtually defenseless, agitated for protection. The U.S. Government subsequently built four new fortifications in New York Harbor, one of which was the circular West Battery, some 200 feet off the southwest point of Manhattan Island. Built in 1808–11 and renamed Castle Clinton in 1815 in honor of Gov. DeWitt Clinton, it was designed for 28 guns in one tier of casemates. Its 8-foot-thick walls of red sandstone stood on a massive foundation of rough stone. Officers' quarters were located on each side of the sally port passageway; no barracks were provided for the enlisted garrison. After the War of 1812, in which Castle Clinton was never attacked, it became headquarters for the Third Military District, and in 1823 the Federal Government transferred it to the city of New York.

Castle Clinton National Monument, at the edge of Battery Park, on Manhattan Island, overlooks New York Harbor. Though constructed early in the 19th century for harbor defense purposes, Castle Clinton later served as an entertainment center, immigration depot, and aquarium.

The following year the fort, which the city leased to private interests, opened as Castle Garden, a place of public entertainment—for concerts, fireworks, balloon ascensions, and scientific demonstrations, among them the Morse telegraph in 1842. The interior of the fort was converted to a garden, which in time included a fountain. The gunrooms, decorated with marble busts and a panoramic mural, served as a promenade from which patrons, in boxes for eight, could watch the entertainment. The top of the fort's wall, where an awning covered a 14-foot-wide walkway, was another, even more popular, promenade. The officers' quarters became a saloon, which served liquors, confections, and ices.

The Marquis de Lafayette began his tour of the United States in 1824–25 from the Castle, where citizens of New York also later listened to orations by Daniel Webster and Henry Clay, viewed John Quincy Adams as he lay in state, and honored Presidents Jackson, Polk, and Tyler. In the 1840's the lessees enlarged and remodeled the fort as a theater, where they began to present operas in concert form. In 1850 it was the setting for the musical event of the century—P. T. Barnum's introduction of Jenny Lind, the "Swedish Nightingale," in her American debut.

Under lease to the New York State Commissioners of Emigration, in 1855 the Castle became an immigrant receiving depot, operated with virtually no Federal controls. Through it passed the floodtide of the mid-century migration from Europe, consisting primarily of Irish and Germans, and after 1882 increased numbers of eastern and southern Europeans. The Castle protected the immigrants from the undesirables who roamed the wharves of New York and tried to take advantage of them; provided medical care; and dispensed information on travel routes and accommodations. Until 1890 more than 7 million immigrants, two out of every three arriving in the United States, passed through the Castle. In that year control shifted to the U.S. Superintendent of Immigration, and the Barge Office became the temporary landing depot, pending the opening in 1892 of a newer, more commodious center at Ellis Island.

In 1896, once again altered, the Castle opened as the New York City Aquarium. Millions visited it until 1941, when it was closed preparatory to being torn down to make room for the Brooklyn-Battery Tunnel approaches. But determined New Yorkers saved the building, and destruction stopped short of the original fort walls. In 1946 Congress authorized Castle Clinton National Monument, and in 1950 the 1-acre monument was established. Restoration began at that time and is still continuing.

Federal Hall National Memorial, New York

Location: New York County, at the corner of Wall and Nassau Streets, just off Broadway, in lower Manhattan; address: New York City National Park Service Group, 28 East 20th Street, New York City 10003.

This memorial commemorates a series of momentous events in our history. On the site of the memorial once stood Federal Hall, the realtered and renamed City Hall. Federal Hall was the first Capitol of the United States under the Constitution and the meeting place of the First Congress. On its balcony General Washington took the oath of office as President. In it Congress created the Departments of State, War, and Treasury, and the Supreme Court; and adopted the Bill of Rights. City Hall was also the scene of many historic events. In that building the trial and acquittal of John Peter Zenger marked the first major victory in the continuing struggle for freedom of the press and speech in the United States; the Stamp Act Congress protested "taxation without representation;" and the Second Continental Congress adopted resolutions calling the Constitutional Convention at Philadelphia, transmitted the completed Constitution to the State legislatures for ratification, and adopted the Northwest Ordinance.

A view of Wall Street, including Federal Hall and Trinity Church, in 1789. The First Congress convened in Federal Hall. Lithographed from a contemporary print (the Cornelius Tiebout view). Courtesy, Library of Congress.

Prior to the building of City Hall, in 1699–1700, the city government had been quartered in the old Dutch *Stadt Huys*. Not until late in 1703 did it transfer its functions to the new building. In 1734 John Peter Zenger, charged with publishing "seditious libels" in his newspaper, the *New-York Weekly Journal*, was imprisoned in the garret of City Hall. The following year his defense attorney, Andrew Hamilton, one of the most brilliant lawyers in the colonies, won acquittal and helped pave the way for a free press and freedom of speech. During October 1765 the Stamp Act Congress convened at City Hall and offered the first united colonial opposition to English colonial policy. Delegates from 9 of the 13 Colonies participated. The Congress sent an address to the King, petitioned Parliament, and drew up a Declaration of Rights and Grievances. The following year Parliament voted to rescind the Stamp Act.

In September 1774 the First Continental Congress convened at Philadelphia in Carpenters' Hall, now a part of Independence National Historical Park. It appealed in vain to the King and the people of Great Britain for the redress of colonial grievances. Before the Second Continental Congress convened in May 1775, the War for Independence was in progress. The next year Congress adopted the Declaration of Independence. After the war the Continental Congress selected New York City as the seat of government and in January 1785 began meeting in City Hall. Here, in February 1787, it adopted the resolution calling for the convening of a Constitutional Convention at Philadelphia. Late in September, after 4 months of labor by the Convention, Congress transmitted the Constitution from City Hall to the States for ratification. While the Constitutional Convention had met, the Continental Congress adopted the famous Northwest Ordinance of 1787, which provided for the government of the Territory Northwest of the Ohio River.

In September 1788 Congress designated New York City as the capital of the United States under the Constitution. The New York City Council promptly offered the use of the City Hall and approved the expenditure of funds for repairing the building. In 1788–89 Maj. Pierre Charles L'Enfant supervised the construction. At the time the First Congress under the Constitution held its initial session, in March 1789, the building, then known as Federal Hall, was said to be the most beautiful in the United States. In an upper chamber the electoral votes were counted, and an announcement was made of the unanimous election of George Washington as first President. On April 30, 1789, Washington took his oath of office on the balcony. Between July and September Congress created the Departments of State, War, and Treasury, and the Supreme

Court; adopted the Bill of Rights; and transmitted the latter to the States for ratification.

In July 1790, during the second session of the First Congress, Congress selected a 10-mile-square site on the banks of the Potomac as the site of the permanent capital, to be called the District of Columbia, land for which was ceded by Virginia and Maryland. On the last day of August, the Federal Government moved from New York to Philadelphia, where it remained for about a decade while the permanent Capital was being constructed. Utilized alternately for State and city offices during the following two decades, in 1812 the crumbling Federal Hall was sold for salvage for $425.

In 1842 the present structure, an outstanding example of Greek Revival architecture, was completed on the site of Federal Hall. It served as the New York City Custom House until 1862, when it became the United States Sub-Treasury. Later it housed the Federal Reserve Bank of New York and a number of minor government offices. Subsequently most of these were relocated. Civic and patriotic organizations in and about New York then conceived the idea of preserving the structure as a memorial to the founding of our Federal form of government. The building was designated a national historic site in 1939 and became a national memorial in 1955.

Federal Hall National Memorial is administered by the National Park Service with the cooperation of the Federal Hall Memorial Associates, Inc. On exhibit are historic objects and documents associated with the site. One room, set aside as a memorial to John Peter Zenger, features exhibits showing the struggle of the colonies for freedom of the press. The stone on which Washington traditionally stood to take his oath of office is preserved in the rotunda.

Hamilton Grange National Monument (Authorized), New York

> *Location (Proposed): New York County, at West 130th Street and St. Nicholas Terrace, overlooking St. Nicholas Park, on the campus of the College of the City of New York, New York City; Hamilton Grange to be moved to above site from its present location, 287 Convent Avenue, adjoining St. Luke's Protestant Episcopal Church, near West 141st Street, New York City (Not Open to the Public).*

In 1962 the President signed the act of Congress that authorized creation of Hamilton Grange National Monument in honor of Alexander

Hamilton, Founding Father, first Secretary of the Treasury, and brilliant financial and political leader. The Hamilton Grange, now in poor condition but one of the few Federal-period houses still standing in New York City, is the only home ever owned by Hamilton and the only extant structure that possesses an intimate association with Hamilton. The other houses that he occupied in New York City have been torn down, and the House of Morgan building occupies the site of his law office, across from Federal Hall National Memorial.

In 1795 Hamilton resigned as Secretary of the Treasury and returned to New York to practice law, although he continued to take an active part in national affairs. In 1800 he purchased a 16-acre tract of land on the pleasant wooded hills overlooking the Hudson River, north of the town of New York; later he purchased the adjacent 16 acres. Workmen constructed the house in 1801–2 at a cost of £1,500. The architect was John McComb, designer of New York City Hall and other distinguished buildings. Taking much pleasure in planning and supervising the construction, Hamilton named the estate "The Grange" after that of his paternal grandfather, Alexander Hamilton, Laird of the Grange, in Ayrshire, Scotland.

Hamilton lived in the house only 2 years, until July 11, 1804, when he died after a duel with Aaron Burr. Hamilton spent the night before the duel in his study writing a farewell letter to his wife. After his death Mrs. Hamilton moved to downtown New York and in 1833 sold the house, which had a series of owners until 1889. In that year St. Luke's Protestant Episcopal Church purchased it, moved it 500 feet from its original location, and used it as a temporary chapel. At that time workmen removed the front and back porches and made other alterations. In 1924, when the threat to the preservation of the house became acute, two financiers, George F. Baker, Sr., and J. P. Morgan, purchased it, conveyed it to the American Scenic and Historic Preservation Society, and set up a $50,000 trust fund to maintain it as a memorial to Hamilton and a museum of his times.

Encroachments on the present location have obscured Hamilton Grange, which is not now open to the public. Despite modifications, the basic structure is intact, though it needs extensive renovation. Its design is simple but dignified. The two-story frame structure has brick-filled walls and partitions. The original siding, hand-hewn attic beams, hand-split lath, and ornamental plaster mouldings are preserved. In 1962, to make possible a National Monument to Hamilton in a suitable location, the American Scenic and Historic Preservation Society donated the house to the Federal Government and the city of New York deeded the land for the proposed relocation. The National Park Service plans to move the Grange to the new site, completely restore it, furnish it with some of the Hamilton furniture and memorabilia now in the house and others promised by family descendants, and open it to the public.

Perry's Victory and International Peace Memorial National Monument, Ohio

> *Location: Ottawa County, on South Bass Island in Lake Erie, about 4 miles from the mainland, accessible during the summer by ferry; address: P.O. Box 78, Put-in-Bay, Ohio 43456.*

This memorial near Put-in-Bay, where Commodore Oliver Hazard Perry won a decisive naval battle in the War of 1812, also commemorates the many decades of peace between the United States and Canada and the principle of international peace by arbitration and disarmament as symbolized by the unfortified boundary between two North American neighbors. Perry's victory over a British fleet in the Battle of Lake Erie, as the engagement near Put-in-Bay is known, had far-reaching results on the War of 1812. It assured control of the lake for the United States and made possible a successful advance by Gen. William Henry Harrison's army into Canada, where it defeated a British-Indian force at the Thames River. The combined land and naval successes enabled the United States to retain the old Northwest under the terms of the Treaty of Ghent, in 1814. Just 3 years later, representatives of Britain and the United States signed the Rush-Bagot Agreement, which limited naval warships and armaments on the Great Lakes and was the first step toward permanent disarmament of the 4,000-mile boundary between the two countries.

In 1812 an unprepared United States declared war on Great Britain because of the violation of her commercial and naval rights during the struggle between Great Britain and Napoleonic France that began in 1793. On land, during the first part of the war, U.S. military operations failed. Despite brilliant individual victories by American ships in duels with British vessels, the British effectively blockaded the ocean coastline and controlled the vital Lake Erie lifeline for troops and supplies.

In mid-1813 a British squadron under Commodore Robert H. Barclay

Perry's Victory and International Peace Memorial National Monument, Ohio, commemorates Perry's triumph over a British fleet in the Battle of Lake Erie (1813). It also symbolizes more than a century and a half of peace between the United States and Canada.

was blockading Erie, Pa. There Commodore Oliver H. Perry was building ships, behind the low sandbar protecting the harbor, to contest British domination of the lake. Early in August Barclay relaxed his watchfulness for a few days, and Perry seized the long-awaited opportunity. Moving his nondescript fleet across the sandbar, he freed it for action. He established headquarters at Put-in-Bay, on South Bass Island, so that he could observe Barclay. He then made contact with General Harrison, commander of the U.S. Army in the Northwest, at the time in northern Ohio.

On September 9 Barclay left his base at Fort Malden, on the Detroit River, and sailed into the lake. The next morning the two fleets, each of which had assigned about 440 men, met about 10 miles west-northwest of South Bass Island. Seeking to take advantage of his edge in firepower, Perry assigned each of his nine vessels one of the six enemy ships to fight. His flagship, the *Lawrence*, bore the brunt of the battle. By mid-afternoon, four-fifths of the crew were casualties, and the ship was a floating wreck. Under heavy fire, Perry transferred in a rowboat to the

Niagara and continued to direct the desperate fight. Only minutes thereafter the wounded Barclay, his flagship destroyed and his other ships badly disabled, surrendered. British casualties were slightly larger than the American, but both sides had losses of more than 100. Perry sent General Harrison a concise and dramatic message that announced his victory to the world: "We have met the enemy and they are ours: Two Ships, two Brigs one Schooner & one Sloop."

The memorial covers more than 22 acres. The monument is constructed of concrete and pink Massachusetts granite. The fluted shaft is one of the most massive Doric columns ever built. It consists of 78 courses of granite, is 352 feet high, and is 45 feet in diameter at the base. Its cap serves as an observation platform, reached by an elevator, above which is a bronze urn 32 feet in height, 18 feet in width, and weighing 11 tons. The rotunda is constructed of Tennessee and Italian marble, Indiana limestone, and granite. Carved on the walls are the names of the U.S. vessels and casualties. In a crypt beneath the floor are the remains of the three American and three British officers killed in the battle. In the west doorway of the rotunda is a bronze tablet, upon which is engraved the provisions of the Rush-Bagot Agreement of 1817.

Fort Necessity National Battlefield, Pennsylvania

Location: Fayette County, on U.S. 40, about 11 miles east of Uniontown; address: Route 1, P.O. Box 311, Farmington, Pa. 15437.

This battlefield primarily commemorates the opening engagement of the French and Indian War (1754–63), in which the English won from the French control of the North American Continent. Within the park area, however, stands the original Mount Washington Tavern, which has some significance in the phases of history treated in this volume. The tavern was a stage station on the National, or Cumberland, Road, which in the 1800's was a principal artery of traffic between the Atlantic seaboard and the Ohio Valley.

French-English rivalry in the trans-Allegheny territory and in North America approached a climax in the 1750's. In 1754 the British sent Lt. Col. George Washington and a small force from Virginia to contest French possession of the Forks of the Ohio, where the French had erected Fort Duquesne. After defeating a French scouting party at Great Meadows, as the Fort Necessity area was then called, Washington built a temporary fort, which he called "Fort Necessity." In an ensuing clash, Washington's first major battle, the French forced the colonials to surrender, allowed them to return to Virginia, destroyed Fort Necessity, and returned to Fort Duquesne. This battle sparked the French and Indian War, which the British eventually won.

In 1769 Washington acquired a 234½-acre tract of land at Great Meadows. He owned it until his death and in his will directed that it be sold along with his other properties. Judge Nathaniel Ewing later purchased it for a farm, and in 1818 erected a large house, which he called Mount Washington, near the newly opened National Road. Constructed of brick molded and burned from kilns on the farm, the house was the only substantial building for miles along the road, and Ewing soon opened it as a tavern and stage station. It subsequently passed through several hands and was a popular stopping place until the stagelines went out of business in the 1850's. After the mid-19th century Godfrey Fazenbaker owned it and used it as a farmhouse. His heirs donated it to the Commonwealth of Pennsylvania. The tavern overlooks the site of Fort Necessity. Now Fort Necessity Museum, it contains relics of the Washington and Braddock campaigns; it also exhibits household furnishings and industrial, agricultural, and military equipment.

Fort Necessity National Battlefield became a part of the National Park System in 1933. In 1962 it absorbed Fort Necessity State Park, including sections of Great Meadows, scene of the 1754 battle and part of which Washington later owned. A stockade, storehouse, and entrenchments have been reconstructed on the exact site of the original structures. The site of Washington's skirmish with the French scouting party and the grave of Gen. Edward Braddock, commander in chief of the British forces in the Battle of Monongahela (1755), also may be seen.

Independence National Historical Park, Pennsylvania

Location: Philadelphia County, in downtown Philadelphia; address: 311 Walnut Street, Philadelphia, Pa. 19106.

In this 22-acre park, in the old part of Philadelphia, is located a group of historic buildings that notably commemorates the founding and initial development of the Nation. Probably no other similar group, except possibly that in Washington, D.C., has such broad and special historical significance and is associated with so many momentous national events.

These include meetings of the First and Second Continental Congresses; adoption of the Declaration of Independence, which marked the creation of the United States; the labors of the Constitutional Convention of 1787, which perpetuated it; and George Washington's second inauguration as President. This area was also the second Capital of the United States under the Constitution, from 1790 to 1800. As the historian Carl Van Doren has said: "On account of the Declaration of Independence, [Independence Hall] is a shrine honored wherever the rights of man are honored. On account of the Constitution, it is a shrine cherished wherever the principles of self-government on a federal scale are cherished."

Independence Hall was originally the State House for the Province of Pennsylvania. In 1729 the Provincial Assembly set aside funds for the building of a statehouse, and during the next four decades acquired all the property that is today Independence Square south to Walnut Street. In 1732 ground had been broken for construction of the statehouse, completed in the 1750's. Designed in the dignified style of the Georgian period and considered to be one of the most beautiful buildings of the colonial period, it was planned by Andrew Hamilton, a lawyer, and its construction supervised by Edmund Wooley, a master carpenter.

In 1750 the assembly authorized erection of a belltower on the south side of the statehouse, and the following year ordered a bell from England. The "Proclaim Liberty" inscription, engraved on the bell to celebrate the 50th anniversary of William Penn's Charter of Privileges (1701), is the source of the Liberty Bell's name. After the bell arrived in 1752, it was cracked during testing and was twice recast. As the official statehouse bell, it was rung on public occasions. In 1777, before the British occupied Philadelphia, the Government moved temporarily to Baltimore and had the Liberty Bell removed to Allentown. When the British threat subsided, it was returned to Independence Hall, in Philadelphia, where it rests today. Traditionally the bell cracked once again, in 1835, while tolling the death of Chief Justice John Marshall. It is a worldwide emblem of liberty.

As opposition increased in America to England's colonial policy, Philadelphia, the principal city of the English colonies, became the center of organized colonial protest. In Carpenters' Hall, near Independence Square, built in 1770 for use as a guild hall by the Carpenters' Company of Philadelphia, the First Continental Congress met in 1774 to decide how the colonies should meet British threats to their freedom. The Congress united the colonies behind a policy of resistance to oppressive meas-

Independence Hall, in Philadelphia, is one of the most historic buildings in the Nation. There the Second Continental Congress signed the Declaration of Independence and adopted the Articles of Confederation; and the Convention of 1787 created the Constitution.

ures. In 1775 the Second Continental Congress met in the Pennsylvania State House (Independence Hall) and decided to move from protest to resistance. Warfare between the colonists and British troops already had begun in Massachusetts. In June the Congress appointed George Washington General and Commander in Chief of the Army, and he announced his acceptance. Congress then organized the Government. On July 4, 1776, it adopted the Declaration of Independence, read 4 days later to the citizens of Philadelphia in Independence Square.

Following the Declaration of Independence came the long hard years of war. During the winter of 1777–78 the British occupied Philadelphia, while Washington's army kept watch at Valley Forge. After the departure of the British, the seat of Government returned from its temporary location in Baltimore to Philadelphia. On November 3, 1781, the Congress proclaimed the news of the surrender of Lord Cornwallis at Yorktown. Independence practically had been won.

The Articles of Confederation and Perpetual Union had been drafted during the war, and in 1781 the Continental Congress adopted them at

Independence Hall. Under the Articles, Congress met in various towns, about half the time in Philadelphia. There, in Independence Hall, for 4 months in 1787, the Constitutional Convention conducted its highly secret sessions to organize a better government. The sessions were held in the same chamber in which the Declaration of Independence had been adopted; no other room in the United States has been the scene of such political courage and wisdom.

Just before Philadelphia became the second Capital (1790–1800) under the Constitution, after the Government moved from New York, Independence Hall acquired two new neighbors: City Hall on the east and the County Court Building on the west. About the same time, the American Philosophical Society, the oldest learned society in the United States, founded in 1743 by Benjamin Franklin, was granted a lot in the square. During the period 1785–89 the society constructed Philosophical Hall, the only privately owned building in the square today; visitors are allowed. Beginning in 1790, Congress sat in the new County Court House (now known as Congress Hall) and the U.S. Supreme Court in the new City Hall. In Congress Hall George Washington was inaugurated for his second term as President, as was John Adams, for his single term.

In 1799 the State government moved from Philadelphia to Lancaster, and later to Harrisburg. In 1800 the Federal Government moved to Washington, D.C., and Congress Hall again was used as the County Court House. During the period 1802–26 Charles Wilson Peale, the eminent artist, operated a museum in Independence Hall. His paintings, purchased by the city of Philadelphia, form the basis for the park's present collection of heroes of the War for Independence. In 1818 the city of Philadelphia had bought Independence Hall from the Commonwealth of Pennsylvania and has preserved it ever since. In recent years, to enhance the setting of the area, the Commonwealth of Pennsylvania began a project to provide a mall in the three blocks directly north of Independence Hall.

The structures and properties in Independence National Historical Park, most of which are open to the public, include those owned by the city of Philadelphia but administered by the National Park Service. These consist of Independence Hall, Congress Hall (old County Court House), Supreme Court Building (old City Hall), and Independence Square. Federally owned buildings include the First and Second Banks of the United States; the Deshler-Morris House, located in Germantown, Pa., and administered by the Germantown Historical Society; the Dilworth-Todd-Moylan House; the Bishop White House; New Hall; Franklin Court; and the Philadelphia Exchange. Those buildings privately owned and whose owners have cooperative agreements with the National Park Service include Carpenters' Hall and Christ Church. The American Philosophical Society has reconstructed and operates Library Hall, on federally owned land, as its library. The original building had been erected in 1789–90 by the Library Company of Philadelphia.

The First Bank of the United States (1791–1811) and the Second Bank of the United States (1816–36) provided a sound financial basis for the young Nation. The First Bank building, erected in 1795, is probably the oldest bank building in the country; in 1797 the First Bank moved into it from Carpenters' Hall, where it had been located since its inception. The Second Bank building, a splendid example of Greek Revival architecture, was built between 1819 and 1824 and occupied by the Second Bank during the period 1824–36. New Hall, another building in the park, has been reconstructed and houses today a Marine Corps museum. The Carpenters' Company of Philadelphia erected the original building as a new meeting hall, and it served in 1791–92 as the office of the War Department. The Bishop White House, constructed in 1786–87, is an excellent example of an early Philadelphia row house. During the summers of 1793 and 1794 President George Washington resided in the Deshler-Morris House, erected in 1772–73. The graveyard in St. Mary's Church contains the tombs of Thomas FitzSimmons, a signer of the Constitution, and Commodore John Barry.

Other buildings and sites in the park that are mainly of interest in other periods of history than that treated in this volume include: The Philadelphia Exchange; the Dilworth-Todd-Moylan House; Franklin Court, the site of Benjamin Franklin's home, where he died in 1790; Christ Church; St. Joseph's Church; St. George's Church; Mikveh Israel Cemetery; and Gloria Dei (Old Swede's) Church National Historic Site.

In 1948, upon the recommendation of the Philadelphia National Shrines Park Commission, Congress passed an act that authorized Independence National Historical Park. The purpose of the act was to provide for the Federal Government's part in the preservation and commemoration of Independence Hall, Carpenters' Hall, Christ Church, and surrounding historic sites and buildings in Philadelphia. This activity includes cooperative agreements with three groups, which own major structures, and the acquisition and interpretation of additional significant sites and buildings east of Independence Square. The entire undertaking is guided by an advisory commission of distinguished citizens.

Fort Sumter National Monument, South Carolina

Location: Charleston County, on a shoal at the entrance to Charleston Harbor, about 3½ miles from the Charleston Battery by boat; address: P.O. Box 428, Sullivans Island, S.C. 29482.

This fort, scene of the bombardment that began the Civil War in 1861 and of a determined Confederate defense during the years 1863–65, is of primary significance in relation to the Civil War. It was, however, one of the forts constructed by the Government after the War of 1812, planned and begun during the period of history treated in this volume, to remedy deficiencies in coastal defenses that the war had revealed.

During the War of 1812 the British did not attack Charleston Harbor, protected by Forts Moultrie, Johnson, and Pinckney, nor many other Atlantic ports. In 1814, however, various officials of States along the coast expressed alarm at the vulnerability of their ports. Soon after the war, military authorities determined to correct the situation. In 1816 President Madison formed a Board of Engineers to devise a system of coastal de-

Initial phases of excavation, in 1956, at Fort Sumter National Monument, South Carolina. Since that time all the ruins of the original fort that are extant have been excavated.

fenses for the entire country. In 1821 it proposed a chain of about 40 coastal fortifications in strategic locations, including Charleston.

In 1826 the board surveyed Charleston Harbor and decided to supplement the older defenses there with a new fort, upon a shoal about equidistant between Forts Moultrie and Johnson, which would command the main ship channel into Charleston Harbor. In 1827 the board adopted plans for the five-sided fort, 1 year later received congressional appropriations, and the following year began construction. The fort was named for a South Carolina patriot of the War for Independence, Thomas Sumter. Construction was not essentially completed until 1860, the year before the Civil War broke out. The fort had 5-foot-thick brick walls that towered 48 feet above low tide. Four sides, 170 to 190 feet long, were designed for three tiers of guns; the gorge, which accommodated officers' quarters, supported guns only on the third tier. Enlisted men's barracks paralleled the parade side of the flank gunrooms. A sally port pierced the gorge and opened onto a quay and a wharf. Full armament was about 135 guns, but by 1861 only 60 cannon had been mounted.

On April 12, 1861, a mortar shell fired by Confederate forces from nearby Fort Johnson, on James Island, burst almost directly over a beleaguered Federal garrison at Fort Sumter, and marked the beginning of the Civil War. It was a signal for a 3,000-shell bombardment that lasted 34 hours. On April 14 Maj. Robert Anderson, the Federal commander, evacuated the fort. The next day President Lincoln issued a call for 75,000 volunteers. The Civil War, so long dreaded, had begun.

In 1948 Congress established Fort Sumter National Monument, which consists of about 24 acres and includes Fort Moultrie, on Sullivans Island. Today both forts reflect numerous changes made between 1865 and 1900, particularly those that occurred during the Spanish-American War. Few changes were made in the 20th century. The battery dominates the central section of Fort Sumter, where a small museum is located. Markers and interpretive exhibits point out features of interest.

Custis-Lee Mansion, Virginia

> *Location: Arlington County, in Arlington National Cemetery; address: Regional Director, National Capital Region, National Park Service, 1100 Ohio Drive SW., Washington, D.C. 20242.*

At this mansion, splendid ante bellum home of the Custis and Lee families, Robert E. Lee in 1861, torn between devotion to his country and to his native State of Virginia, wrote his letter of resignation from the U.S. Army. Designated by Congress in 1955 as a permanent memorial to Lee, it has primary associations with the Civil War period. It also, however, has some associations with the phases of history treated in this volume. Furnished today with historical appointments, it preserves for posterity the atmosphere of gracious living enjoyed by the Custis, Washington, and Lee families. It has been for many years a treasury of Washington heirlooms.

Arlington House, now known as the Custis-Lee Mansion. The house is preserved today as a memorial to Gen. Robert E. Lee. From a lithograph by Pendleton, published in *The Washington Guide,* 1830. Courtesy, Library of Congress.

George Washington Parke Custis, builder of Arlington House, as the Custis-Lee Mansion was originally known, was the grandson of Martha Washington and the foster son of George Washington. When Martha Dandridge Custis became the wife of Col. George Washington, she was a widow who had two children, Martha Parke ("Patsy") Custis and John Parke Custis. Martha Parke Custis died in her teens without having been married, but in 1774 John Parke Custis married Eleanor Calvert of Maryland, and upon his death at the close of the War for Independence left four children. The death of John Parke Custis was a shock, not only to his mother, Mrs. Washington, but to General Washington as well. He is reported to have remarked to the grieving mother at the deathbed, "I adopt the two youngest children as my own." Their names were Eleanor Parke Custis (Nelly) and George Washington Parke Custis. They were reared at Mount Vernon.

In 1802, the year his grandmother, Mrs. Washington, died, George Washington Parke Custis began building Arlington House on the estate of nearly 1,100 acres that his father had purchased in 1778 from the Alexander family. He named the estate "Arlington" and the home "Arlington House" in honor of the ancestral homestead of the Custis family on the eastern shore of Virginia. Two years later, at the age of 23, he married Mary Lee Fitzhugh of Alexandria and "Chatham." George Hadfield, a young English architect, drew the plans for the house. The north wing was built first, and the south wing was completed in 1804. The foundation stone and timber came from the estate. The bricks with which the house was built were burned from native clay. The portico and large center section were not finished until 1817.

In 1824–25 General Lafayette visited the house. Not long thereafter, in 1831, Mary Ann Randolph Custis, only child of the Arlington Custis family and the great-granddaughter of Martha Washington, married Lt. Robert E. Lee, a young West Point graduate, in the family parlor. Much of her married life was spent at the estate, sometimes with her husband, sometimes awaiting his return from the Mexican War or other distant tours of duty. Six of the seven Lee children were born there. George Washington Parke Custis, who died in 1857, bequeathed the estate of Arlington to his daughter for her lifetime, and afterward to his eldest grandson and namesake, George Washington Custis Lee. Because of the rundown condition of the Arlington plantation upon the death of Mr. Custis, Robert E. Lee, as executor, felt that his presence at Arlington was necessary if he were to give proper attention to the estate. He therefore obtained extended leave from the Army and settled down to the life of a farmer. More than 2 years elapsed before he rejoined his regiment.

Following the news of the secession of Virginia, news that he had hoped never to hear, Lee on April 20, 1861, resigned his commission in the U.S. Army. The next day, at the request of the Governor of Virginia, he departed for Richmond. Mrs. Lee remained at Arlington engaged in the work of dismantling her home and sending family possessions to a place of safety. Soon after she left Washington, Federal troops occupied the lands between Washington and Alexandria. The few remaining family possessions were later taken from Arlington to the old Patent Office in Washington, but not before many things, including some of the Mount Vernon heirlooms, had been carried away.

Situated on the line of fortifications guarding Washington, the Arlington estate soon became an armed camp. Headquarters of the general commanding the forts in the vicinity was located in the mansion. Confiscated by the Government when Mrs. Lee was unable to appear personally to pay taxes as required, about 200 acres of the estate were set aside for a national cemetery in June 1864. Upon the death of Mrs. Lee, in 1873— General Lee having died in 1870—Custis Lee took steps to recover the Arlington property willed to him by his grandfather, George Washington Parke Custis. His case was carried to the U.S. Supreme Court, where a decision favorable to him was obtained. He then consented to give the United States clear title to the property for $150,000, and in 1883 Congress appropriated the necessary funds.

For years after the war, the mansion stood an empty shell—an office for the superintendent of the cemetery and a place for his tools. In 1925 Congress empowered the Secretary of War to undertake restoration of Arlington House to its pre-Civil War condition, including as many furnishings as possible. For original furniture that could not be obtained, similar period pieces and a few copies have been substituted. In 1933 the War Department transferred Arlington House to the Department of the Interior.

The front of the two-wing mansion extends 140 feet. The wings are identical, except that in the north wing the space corresponding to the state dining room in the south wing was divided into small rooms for the temporary accommodation of Mr. and Mrs. Custis while the house was being built and was never changed. The central portion is divided by a wide central hall. A large formal drawing room with two fine marble fireplaces lies south of this hall. To the north of it is the family dining room and family parlor, separated by a north and south partition broken by three graceful arches. The second story is also divided by a central hall, on either side of which are two bedrooms and accompanying dressing rooms. A small room used as a linen closet is at the end of this hall. The third floor attic was used only for storage purposes. The grand portico facing the Potomac has eight massive Doric columns. At the rear two buildings used as servants' quarters, smokehouse, workroom, and summer kitchen form a courtyard.

The mansion is open to the public daily and National Park Service personnel conduct tours. Not far away, beyond the formal garden, is a special museum devoted to the career of Robert E. Lee.

George Washington Birthplace National Monument, Virginia

Location: Westmoreland County, on the Potomac River, just off Va. 3, about 38 miles east of Fredericksburg; address: c/o Fredericksburg National Military Park, P.O. Box 679, Fredericksburg, Va. 22401.

The memorial mansion at this site symbolizes "Wakefield," where George Washington was born, on February 22, 1732, and spent the first 3 years of his life. His family then moved farther up the Potomac, to the Hunting Creek plantation that later became known as Mount Vernon. Four years later the family moved again, to the "Strother estate," on the Rappahannock River opposite Fredericksburg.

In 1718 Augustine Washington, George's father, bought 150 acres fronting on Popes Creek, 1 mile southeast of his Bridges Creek home. On this tract he built Wakefield, probably between 1723 and 1726. It was about 6 years old at the time of George Washington's birth. George never owned it. Upon the death of his father, it passed to George's half-brother, Augustine, Jr., who lived there until he died, in 1762. The farm eventually passed to his son, William Augustine, who was living in the home during the War for Independence, when fire accidentally destroyed it. It was never rebuilt.

In 1882 Washington heirs and the Commonwealth of Virginia donated to the United States the old Washington family burial ground and a small plot of land at the house site. A year later the U.S. Government bought an additional 11 acres and in 1896 erected a granite shaft where members of the family had placed a stone marker in 1815. In 1923 the Wakefield National Memorial Association organized to recover the birthplace grounds and restore them as a national shrine. Several years later Congress authorized the erection of a house at Wakefield as nearly as possible like the one built by Augustine Washington. By 1931 the association, aided by John D. Rockefeller, Jr., was able to transfer to the Government enough land to bring the holding to 394 acres.

Wakefield, a replica of a typical Virginia plantation home of the 18th century, has been constructed to represent the boyhood home of George Washington.

Because extensive research on the birthplace house and grounds failed to yield reliable information about the appearance of the original house, the reconstructed memorial mansion is only a general representation of a Virginia plantation house of the 18th century. Its design is based on tradition and surviving houses of the period. Archeological excavations by the National Park Service and others, however, have revealed foundation remnants that might well have been those of the original house.

Reconstruction took place in 1931–32, at which time workers moved the granite shaft to the present location. The Federal Government paid part of the cost of building the house and landscaping the grounds. The house has eight rooms, four downstairs and four in the half story upstairs. A central hallway is located on each floor. The bricks were hand-made from the clay from an adjoining field. A tilt-top table in the dining room is the only surviving piece of furniture reported to have been in the original house. The furnishings are designed to portray life in the early 18th century.

Plantings near the land-front door of the house may be derived from those that grew on the place when Washington lived there as a boy. The boxwood, well over 100 years old, was brought from the home of Sarah Tayloe Washington, a daughter of the last owner of the birthplace home, and probably is descended from boxwood originally at Wakefield. In the garden near the house are found only those flowers, vines, herbs, and berries common to Virginia gardens of the period. About 50 feet from the house is a typical colonial-period frame kitchen, built on the traditional site of the old kitchen. It is furnished to represent a plantation kitchen of the period of Washington's youth, and displays artifacts recovered on the plantation.

About 1 mile northwest of the memorial mansion, on the banks of Bridges Creek, are the family burial plot and the site of the home that John Washington, George's great-grandfather, purchased in 1664. The burial plot includes the graves of George Washington's father, grand-father, and great-grandfather. Washington himself was buried at Mount Vernon.

George Washington Birthplace National Monument was established in 1930. It consists of more than 390 acres, all in Federal ownership.

Harpers Ferry National Historical Park, West Virginia-Maryland

Location: Near the West Virginia-Maryland-Virginia boundary, situated in the States of West Virginia and Maryland, visitor center in Harpers Ferry, W. Va.; address: P.O. Box 117, Harpers Ferry, W. Va. 25425.

Most of the remaining and restored buildings at this scenic and historic park, situated at the strategic confluence of the Shenandoah and Potomac Rivers in the Blue Ridge Mountains, have primary associations with John Brown's Raid and the Civil War. As the site of one of the first Federal armories and an early center of industry and transportation, however, the park is also pertinent to the phases of history treated in this volume. Gateway to a river-carved passage through the mountains, meeting place of two mighty rivers, and convenient source of waterpower, it figured prominently in the industrial evolution and westward expansion of the young Nation. Then, in 1859, John Brown—who conceived himself as an instrument of providence—led a violent raid on the town that helped goad the Nation closer to civil war. When the sectional passions exploded into conflict, the oft-flooded juncture of mountain and valley at Harpers Ferry became an important military objective, changing hands several times. Its capture in 1862 by Gen. Thomas J. "Stonewall" Jackson was a dramatic prelude to the Battle of Antietam, which ended the first Confederate invasion of the North. And when peace finally came again, the town of Harpers Ferry lay prostrate—a burned and battered casualty of war.

Peter Stephens, a trader, was the first settler at the site of Harpers Ferry, in 1733. Fourteen years later a millwright named Robert Harper purchased "Peter's Hole," as the place was called, and began to operate a ferry. Seeing the possibilities of using the readily available waterpower, he also built a mill. Around these enterprises grew a small village that was known as "Shenandoah Falls at Mr. Harper's Ferry" until shortly after the War for Independence, when it was shortened to Shenandoah Falls; in 1851 the town incorporated as Harpers Ferry.

In 1795, during the Presidency of George Washington, Congress authorized the establishment of a second Federal armory, at Harpers Ferry—Springfield Armory having been authorized a year earlier. Washington himself chose the site, which he felt was "the most eligible spot on the river." It offered waterpower, supplies of iron, hardwood forests for making charcoal to fuel the forges, and a watercourse on which to ship finished products to the future national Capital in the District of Columbia. In 1801 the armory completed its first arms and by 1810 was producing 10,000 muskets a year. Nine years later the Government

The U.S. Armory in Harpers Ferry, West Virginia, in the 1850's. Established by the U.S. Government late in the 18th century, by 1801 it had begun production. From a lithograph by Rau and Son, after a sketch by Edward Beyer. Courtesy, Library of Congress.

awarded John Hall, a Maine gunsmith and inventor, a contract to manu-
facture 1,000 unique, breech-loading flintlock rifles of his own invention.
These were made on so exact a scale that all parts were interchangeable.
This was the first completely successful application of the principle that
led to modern mass production. Two buildings on Virginius (Virginious)
Island were assigned for Hall's use. His rifle proved so successful that
the contract was repeatedly renewed, and in the ensuing years Hall's
Rifle Works produced thousands of them. In 1843 a new Federal rifle
factory replaced the works.

As one of the few water-level gateways through the Blue Ridge Mountains, Harpers Ferry gap early attracted the attention of transportation
interests. The first of these was the Patowmack (Potowmack) Co., whose
first president was George Washington, and which operated between
1785 and 1828. Though not a financial success, this canal complex was
the forerunner of the Chesapeake and Ohio Canal, on the Maryland side,
which carried freight on mule-drawn barges from the 1830's until the
1920's. The Patowmack Co. improved navigation to perfect a canal
system in the Potomac and Shenandoah Valleys.

The Potomac River Valley, as a westward route, has figured prominently in the growth of our Nation. Through it have passed the Indian
trail, colonial wagon road, canal, railroad, telegraph and telephone, and
the modern superhighway. These improving means of communication
linked the East and West socially and commercially. Before the War for
Independence, internal transportation was largely confined to the East
along the tidewater reaches of the rivers and bays. Soon after the settled
frontier had extended beyond the Allegheny Mountains, enterprising men
made plans to connect the East and West by a navigable waterway.

As early as 1754 George Washington, then still in his twenties, promoted a system of river and canal navigation along the Potomac Valley.
Largely through his efforts the Patowmack Co. organized in 1785 to
carry out his plan. As the first president of the company, Washington
actively engaged in the project until he became President of the United
States in 1789 and resigned. By 1802 the company had substantially
completed five short skirting canals with locks around falls and rapids between Georgetown and Harpers Ferry to provide for navigation as far
as Cumberland, Md. These canal-locks, in order from Georgetown to
Shenandoah Falls (Harpers Ferry), were located at Little Falls, Houses
Falls, Great Falls, Seneca, and Shenandoah Falls. Of these, Houses Falls,
Great Falls, and Seneca were on the Virginia side of the river.

The largest of the five canals skirted the impassable Great Falls of the Potomac. Some 1,200 yards long, 25 feet wide, and 6 feet deep, it passed boats through a series of lift locks over an elevation of more than 76 feet. Moss-covered remnants of about half a mile of this canal, retaining pools, and buildings may be observed today in Great Falls Park, an 800-acre park that recently became part of the National Park System and is jointly operated with the Fairfax County Park Authority. Also visible are ruins of Matildaville, envisioned by George Washington and Henry ("Lighthorse Harry") Lee as a large city but which never came to fruition. The four other canals, each shorter than the one at Great Falls, had a total length of slightly more than 3 miles. The one at Shenandoah Falls (Harpers Ferry) had three locks.

Such early canal systems were not long towpath canals like the later Chesapeake and Ohio Canal, but rather a series of wing dams and sluices to improve existing river channels. Occasionally, however, short canals as noted above were constructed to bypass river rapids. Small raftlike boats, poled with the aid of the currents, brought furs, lumber, flour, corn, whisky, pig iron, and farm produce from as far as Cumberland to Alexandria, a distance of 180 miles. These boats were either poled back empty or with light cargoes along the shoreline aided by towpaths along swift stretches. One-way log rafts were dismantled at Harpers Ferry or George Town and sold for lumber or firewood. Some of the timbers, which came downriver beneath a load of flour or whisky, can be identified in Harpers Ferry and Georgetown houses today.

Low water often hampered the flow of traffic, and the total tonnage of freight was limited. Toll collections varied from $2,000 to $22,500 per year. After about three decades of operation the Patowmack Canal was superseded by the far more efficient Chesapeake and Ohio Canal. And almost immediately the latter faced serious competition from the railroads. In the 1830's a spirited race occurred between the Chesapeake and Ohio Canal, being built from Washington, D.C., and the Baltimore and Ohio Railroad, which started at Baltimore, Md. Their goal was Cumberland, Md., and after that the Ohio Valley. In November 1833, more than 1 year ahead of its rival, the canal reached Harpers Ferry. But only the railroad pushed on to the Ohio Valley; the canal stopped at Cumberland, which it reached 8 years later than the railroad. In 1836 the Winchester and Potomac Railroad, which crossed Virginius Island and connected with the Baltimore and Ohio, began operations. This line was destroyed and rebuilt during the Civil War. [John Brown's Raid and Union-Confederate military activities at Harpers Ferry will be treated in the volume of this series dealing with the Civil War.]

The city of Virginius, on Virginius Island, now a part of Harpers Ferry, has an interesting history. It originated later than Harpers Ferry, shortly after the year 1803, when George Washington's Patowmack Co. deepened the channel of the Shenandoah River on one side of the island into a canal in order to bypass the Shenandoah rapids, during the course of which the river drops 12 feet. At harvest time a steady stream of river craft used the canal to avoid the Shenandoah's riffle-strewn lower falls. Even more important for the town's development, the rapids were a valuable source of waterpower. Mills of many kinds and residences soon dotted the island, and it became the incorporated town of Virginius, later absorbed by Harpers Ferry.

Virginius is an excellent example of a town that—in the days before steam engines, gasoline, and electricity—naturally grew up around river rapids. Power could be conducted only as far as a shaft or a belt could be run from a water wheel or turbine, operated by water usually forced into tunnels. Ruins of various 19th century mills, including cotton, paper, and flour mills, are visible today on Virginius Island, as well as those of a dam. The line of the Winchester and Potomac Railroad, now owned by the Baltimore and Ohio, is the only active survival today of life on the island. One after the other the industries of Virginius succumbed to the blight of the Civil War and floods.

Harpers Ferry National Historical Park, authorized in 1944 by Congress as a National Monument and redesignated in 1963 as a national historical park, consists of a total of 1,500 acres, about 1,251 of which are in Federal ownership. The National Park Service recently acquired a large tract of park land in Maryland, which is not yet developed for park purposes. The visitor center shows an orientation film and features various exhibits. Visitors may take a marked walking tour of downtown Harpers Ferry or journey by auto to nearby Bolivar Heights and "John Brown's Farm." Many of the buildings in Harpers Ferry contain historical exhibits, and archeological remnants of the armory are visible. The National Park Service has inaugurated a major restoration program. A park trail leads from Jefferson's Rock to Loudoun Heights, where it meets the Appalachian Trail. The 1½-mile self-guiding trail that encircles Virginius Island is not only of historical interest but also leads to a veritable nature wonderland.

B. National Historic Sites in Non-Federal Ownership

A few national historic sites in non-Federal ownership are located throughout the United States. These are not units of the National Park System but, as authorized by the Historic Sites Act of 1935, are administered by the owners under the provisions of cooperative agreements with the Department of the Interior. The owners agree to maintain the property in a manner consistent with good preservation practices, for which purpose they may receive assistance from the National Park Service as provided in the agreements. The Park Service provides bronze plaques for the sites. The following site illustrates the phases of history treated in this volume.

Chicago Portage National Historic Site, Illinois

Location: Cook County, Old Chicago Portage Forest Preserve, junction of Portage Creek with Des Plaines River, just west of Harlem Avenue on the line of 47th Street, River Forest, Ill.

Chicago owes its very existence to its strategic location on the Chicago-Illinois River route, one of the natural arteries leading from the St. Lawrence River system to the Mississippi. In September 1673 Père Jacques Marquette and Louis Jolliet discovered the portage at Chicago as they returned from their voyage of exploration down the Mississippi River. Marquette, in failing health, spent the winter of 1674–75 near the portage, and passed over it on other trips, as did also René Robert Cavelier,

Sieur de la Salle, and his lieutenant Henry de Tonty, plus many other Frenchmen. About 1700 Indian hostility kept Europeans out of the area, but the Indians continued to use the portage extensively.

During the French and Indian War and the War for Independence, the portage acquired renewed importance. In the Treaty of Greenville (1795), the Indians ceded to the United States "a piece of Land Six Miles Square, at the mouth of Chickago River, emptying into the southwest end of Lake Michigan, where a fort formerly stood." In 1803 U.S. soldiers from Detroit erected the first Fort Dearborn at the river's mouth, considered to be a strategic location in Northwest Territory. Opposite the fort on the north bank of the river stood a number of cabins occupied by Frenchmen and their native wives. Trade continued actively until the beginning of the War of 1812, when the 140 or so inhabitants of the fort and settlement evacuated it, after the British and their Indian allies captured Fort Mackinac. They began the trip to Fort Wayne, but before they had gone 2 miles Potawatomi Indians murdered or captured most of them and then set fire to the fort.

In 1816 soldiers reconstructed Fort Dearborn, new settlers arrived, and trade again resumed over the portage. It diminished in importance, however, as the Illinois fur trade declined, though it continued to have commercial value into the 1830's. On the site grew the city of Chicago. Work began in 1836 on the Illinois and Michigan Canal—finished in 1848—which followed the water-and-portage route, as does the present Sanitary and Ship Canal.

The western end of the Chicago portage route, where Marquette and Jolliet landed, is located in the Old Chicago Portage Forest Preserve, which is managed by the Forest Preserve District of Cook County, Illinois. The two Fort Dearborns were located on the lakefront, outside of the commemorated area, at the eastern end of the portage route, on the north end of present Grant Park. In 1952 a cooperative agreement between the Cook County Forest Preserve District and the Department of the Interior authorized the designation of Chicago Portage as a national historic site.

C. Sites Eligible for the Registry of National Historic Landmarks

Most of the historic sites in this group have been judged by the Advisory Board on National Parks, Historic Sites, Buildings, and Monuments to meet the criteria of "exceptional value" for commemorating or illustrating the phases of U.S. history treated in this volume. A few, however, which have primary associations with other phases of history, have been included because of their secondary associations with the period covered in this volume. As historic sites of national significance, all of them have been declared by the Secretary of the Interior to be eligible for inclusion in the Registry of National Historic Landmarks. Some have already been designated Registered National Historic Landmarks, and others will receive the designation upon application of the owners. A few have been proposed for addition to the National Park System.

Fort Morgan (Fort Bowyer Site), Alabama

Location. Baldwin County, at the terminus of Ala. 180, on Mobile Point, at the entrance to Mobile Bay.

Ownership and Administration. State of Alabama; Department of Conservation.

Significance. Fort Morgan, guarding the entrance to Mobile Bay, is a Registered National Historic Landmark relating primarily to the Civil War. However, an earlier fort on the same site, Fort Bowyer, was involved in the War of 1812, a phase of history treated in this volume.

Resenting Spanish collaboration with British forces and the latter's use of the Spanish port of Mobile, long coveted by the United States, in 1813 President Madison ordered Gen. James Wilkinson, U.S. commander at New Orleans, to capture the city. After taking Fort Charlotte, the major inland defense, Wilkinson began to construct the "Seraf" (soon thereafter named Fort Bowyer) on Mobile Point, facing the sea approach, at the mouth of Mobile Bay. The new commander, however, questioned the defensive value of the wooden fort and stopped construction. The next year, 1814, Gen. Andrew Jackson, upon visiting Mobile and noticing the strategic location of the uncompleted fort, ordered it completed, refitted, and garrisoned. The sea approach was guarded by a semicircular battery 400 feet long, flanked by two curtains (sidewalls) 60 feet long that joined a bastion facing the land approach. The interior of the fort was 180 feet long from the summit of the bastion to the parapet of the battery; the parapet was 15 feet thick. Artillery pieces numbered 20, but the fort had no casemates and was open to artillery fire from high mounds of sand a few hundred yards to the rear.

The British, seeking to regain Mobile, twice attacked the fort with numerically superior forces. In September 1814 some 130 British soldiers and 600 Indian allies attacked it from the land approach, but Maj. William Lawrence's forces repulsed them. Two days later four British ships attacked; one was damaged and ran aground not far from the fort, and the other withdrew to Pensacola. This victory, involving the loss of only four soldiers, aided the morale of U.S. Army troops and convinced them that they had a chance of winning the war.

The second British attack on Fort Bowyer was made early in February 1815, just before the ratification of the Treaty of Ghent, by 5,000 British troops, who had been defeated 1 month earlier at the Battle of New Orleans. Landing 3 miles from the fort, they captured it but soon abandoned it when they learned that the war was over. It then fell into ruins.

In 1819 the U.S. Army began constructing Fort Morgan, a brick fort, on the site and completed it in 1834. Two years later Federal troops occupied it and remained until the outbreak of the Civil War, at which time Confederate forces seized and garrisoned it. It remained an unthreatened Confederate stronghold until August of 1864, when Union forces captured it.

Present Appearance. No remains of Fort Bowyer are extant. Fort Morgan, repaired by Union forces after its capture in 1864, is in fine condition and is part of Fort Morgan State Park. A huge concrete gun mount and several concrete batteries constructed during the Spanish-American War may also be seen.

Fort Toulouse (Fort Jackson), Alabama

Location. Elmore County, on a gravel road, at the junction of the Coosa and Tallapoosa Rivers, 4 miles southwest of Wetumpka.

Ownership and Administration. State of Alabama; Department of Conservation.

Significance. In 1814, after defeating the Creek Indians at the Battle of Horseshoe Bend, Andrew Jackson and his Tennessee Militia constructed Fort Jackson on the site of Fort Toulouse, a French fort, whose moat remained. From its construction in 1717 until the end of the French and Indian War, in 1763, Fort Toulouse had been the offensive-defensive eastern outpost of French Louisiana. Situated just below the southern tip of the Appalachian Highland, at the junction of the two main tributaries of the Alabama River, it protected the French settlements from Mobile Bay westward to New Orleans. It was also the spearhead of the French effort to wrest control of the present Southeastern United States from the Spanish and English. By the Treaty of Paris, in 1783, it passed to the United States.

After Jackson had constructed Fort Jackson on the site, in August 1814 it was the scene of the Treaty of Fort Jackson that officially ended the Creek War. The Creek Nation surrendered half its land, and the treaty formed the boundaries of the remaining land so as to pacify the Creeks by separating them from the Spanish, to the south; the Choctaws, to the southwest and west; and the Chickasaws, to the west and northwest.

In September 1814 about 100 of the militiamen at the fort, claiming that their term of enlistment was over, marched back to Tennessee. Because this mutiny seriously weakened the garrison, Jackson captured and tried the men and executed six of them. During his later campaign for the Presidency, Jackson's opponents used this act to attack him. The fort was garrisoned until 1817, when settlers staked out a town nearby and the fort was abandoned.

Fort Toulouse is a Registered National Historic Landmark relating primarily to French exploration and settlement.

Present Appearance. The Coosa and Tallapoosa Rivers follow nearly parallel courses for some distance just above their junction, and form a narrow peninsula a mile long and only a few hundred yards wide. A privately owned tract that extends upstream from the junction includes the site of a prehistoric Indian village, where one large mound is discernible and the ground is liberally sprinkled with sherds. East of the tract is the 6-acre Fort Toulouse tract, owned by the State.

Adjoining the tract on the south and east is private property containing the Isaac Ross Cemetery, which dates from at least the War of 1812. In 1897 about 200 bodies were relocated from this cemetery to the national cemetery in Mobile. Most of them were the remains of men who had been assigned to Andrew Jackson's army, but some may have been Frenchmen. Amateur archeologists have carried on excavations at the Indian village site, but not at the State-owned Fort Toulouse tract. The fort area includes two monuments and the remains of what appears to have been a powder magazine.

Old State House, Connecticut

Location. Hartford County, Main Street at Central Row, Hartford.

Ownership and Administration. City of Hartford.

Significance. Standing among modern office buildings in downtown Hartford, the Old State House is a link with history. The first of numerous public buildings designed by Charles Bulfinch, it is today one of the most carefully restored civic structures of the Federal period. While it served as State Capitol between 1796 and 1879, it was the meeting place of the Hartford Convention, at which some New England States expressed opposition to the War of 1812. From 1879, when a new State Capitol building was completed, until 1915, the Old State House was used as the Hartford City Hall.

Authorized in 1792 by the Connecticut General Assembly, the Old State House was not completed until 1796 because of financial difficulties. Although its excellent proportions and design are typical of the work of Bulfinch, his association with the building was not as intimate as with some of his other structures. It therefore reflects not only his genius, but the skills and talents of local artisans as well. The artist John Trumbull supervised construction. By 1918, when the city of Hartford began a major restoration of the building, the foundations and outer walls were discovered to be in excellent condition, but the wooden beams were replaced with steel ones and steel trusses were added in the roof and cupola.

Between December 15, 1814, and January 5, 1815, the Hartford Convention met in the Old State House. Called by the Massachusetts Legislature, the immediate result of a dispute between the U.S. Secretary of War and New England Governors over control of New England State militia, the convention was an expression of New England Federalist opposition

Designed by Charles Bulfinch and completed in 1796, the Old State House, Connecticut, is an excellent example of Federal-style architecture. It was the meeting place of the Hartford Convention, which opposed U.S. policies during the War of 1812.

to the War of 1812 and to Democratic-Republican control of the National Government. Twenty-six delegates attended, sent by the legislatures of Massachusetts, Connecticut, and Rhode Island and scattered Vermont and New Hampshire counties. In the secret debates of the convention, a minority group favored New England's secession from the United States, but the less extreme majority prevailed. The convention adjourned in January 1815 and forwarded a number of resolutions to the New England legislatures urging them to assert themselves against Federal encroachments on the rights of the States. The convention also sent three representatives to Washington bearing proposed constitutional amendments to limit Southern political influence and restrict Federal Government controls. The proposed amendments came to nothing. New England's protests were forgotten with the news of Jackson's victory at New Orleans and the signing of the Treaty of Ghent.

Present Appearance. The Old State House, open to the public as a historic building, measures 120 by 50 feet. The first story is constructed of Portland (Connecticut) freestone, 3 feet thick; the upper story, 2 feet thick, is built of brick, in Flemish bond. The 40-foot wide porticoes on the east and west sides formerly opened into the central corridor, which has since been walled in and doors and windows added; the white-columned portico on the east is one of the building's major architectural features. The balustrade and cupola, though added in 1815 and 1822 respectively, were both probably specified in Bulfinch's original design. In the interior, the staircase that rises on either side of the central corridor, and which has been restored to its original design, has elaborately turned balusters. The Secretary of State's office is situated on the landing. On the first floor are located the Superior Court Chamber, now considerably altered, and executive offices. On the second floor, which best reveals the original design, are the Senate and House Chambers.

City Hall (District Court House), District of Columbia

Location. 451 Indiana Avenue NW., Washington.

Ownership and Administration. District of Columbia government.

Significance. A fine example of Greek Revival architecture and one of the first public buildings in the District of Columbia, the old City Hall, now known as the District Court House, has been the scene of many legal trials of national interest. Included were those of John Suratt, one of the accused conspirators against the life of Lincoln; Charles Guiteau, the assassin of President Garfield; and the Teapot Dome Case.

In July 1820 the Washington City Council authorized the mayor to advertise in the newspapers for a design for a city hall and appointed a commission to select a site and supervise its construction. The commission selected the site of present Judiciary Square because of its convenient location. George Hadfield, one of the architects of the Capitol, won the architectural award. Laying of the cornerstone took place in August 1820, accompanied by an oration by John Law, music of the Marine Band, and gun volleys from the Navy Yard and Fort Washington.

In 1822 the main, or central, part of the building was half completed and ready for partial occupancy, though the pillared porticoes on the

City Hall, District of Columbia, now known as the District Court House. One of the first public buildings in the District, it has been the scene of many legal trials of national interest. From a lithograph by E. Sachse and Company. Courtesy, Library of Congress.

front and the colonnades of the two wings had not been added, the rough bricks of the walls were exposed, and the bare building stood neglected—for lack of funds. Nevertheless, the mayor and registrar moved in and the city council convened. In 1823 Congress appropriated $10,000 to complete the central portion of the building in return for space to house the U.S. circuit court. In 1826 the city completed the east wing, and in 1849 the west wing. Meanwhile, because of the city's inability to finance construction and upkeep of the building, the Federal Government began to take over additional office space and by 1871 occupied most of the building. Two years later the city transferred jurisdiction of the building to the Federal Government, which immediately undertook its completion and restoration, and in 1881 completed a north extension.

During the period 1916–20 the Federal Government rehabilitated the building. The original architectural lines were preserved, but extensive renovation, rebuilding, and modernizing occurred. In 1920, on the 100th anniversary of the laying of the cornerstone, ceremonies were held rededicating the building as the U.S. courthouse. In the 1950's it became the national headquarters of the Selective Service System, but jurisdiction over the building recently reverted to the District of Columbia government.

Present Appearance. The three-story gray stone building, in the

Greek Revival style, is E-shaped and has two wings facing south. The approaches, steps, sills, and superstructure are faced with Indiana limestone. A large portico of ten Ionic columns, supporting a stone cornice and pediment, highlights the main center entrance. The end wings feature large columned porches and cornices, set between abutting piers. The building is used today by the District of Columbia government and is a place of public business.

Decatur House, District of Columbia

Location. 748 Jackson Place NW., at the corner of H Street, Washington.

Ownership and Administration. National Trust for Historic Preservation.

Significance. This house, the first private dwelling on Lafayette Square, is a fine example of a Federal-period townhouse and is one of the few original houses that have survived on the historic square. Built by the distinguished naval hero, Commodore Stephen Decatur, throughout the years it has housed a number of prominent foreign diplomats and U.S. political and military leaders.

In 1818 Decatur, naval hero of the War of 1812 and of the War with Tripoli, decided to build a permanent residence in Washington with prize money he had won during his naval career. He purchased a small tract of land a few hundred yards away from the White House and retained Benjamin H. Latrobe, architect of nearby St. John's Episcopal Church and parts of the White House and Capitol, to design a house. Latrobe, designing a townhouse as rugged and compact as a ship, restricted external ornamentation. Late in 1818 workmen finished the house, and early the following year the Decaturs moved in. They lived there for little more than 1 year, however, for in 1820 at the age of 41 Decatur died in the house after a duel with Commodore James Barron at the Bladensburg dueling ground. Decatur, member of a board that had courtmartialed Barron, had gained Barron's enduring enmity, and Barron had challenged him to a duel.

After Decatur's death the house became headquarters for the French Legation and home of the French Minister to the United States, Baron Hyde de Neuville. In 1822 De Neuville returned to France, and the Russian Minister, Baron de Tuyll, moved in. Three Secretaries of State were the next occupants: From 1827 to 1829, Henry Clay, Secretary under John Quincy Adams; from 1829 to 1831, Martin Van Buren, Secretary under Andrew Jackson and later Vice President and President;

Decatur House, one of the few surviving original buildings on historic Lafayette Square, is a Federal-style townhouse built in 1818 by naval hero Stephen Decatur. It has been the residence of many national and international dignitaries.

and from 1831 to 1833, Edward Livingston, also Secretary under Jackson. From 1834 to 1835 Charles Vaughan, British Minister to the United States, lived in the house, after which John Gadsby purchased it. After his death, in 1844, his wife leased the house to various tenants, including George M. Dallas, Vice President under Polk, and several Congressmen.

Following the Civil War, during which the Federal Government used Decatur House for emergency offices, Gen. Edward F. Beale, a Californian and hero of the Mexican War, purchased the house. He added heavy sandstone trim around the entrance and first-floor windows on the front facade, and installed gaslights. In the drawing rooms he laid parquet floors of rare California woods and embellished the floor of one room with the California State seal. After 1870 he divided his time between Decatur House and Rancho Tejon, in California. Following his death, in 1893, his son, Truxtun, inherited the house. Truxtun Beale died in 1936, but his widow continued to occupy the house. In 1944 she retained Thomas T. Waterman, a noted architect, to restore it according to 11 original Latrobe drawings in her possession. In 1953 she bequeathed it to the National Trust for Historic Preservation.

Present Appearance. Decatur House, an elegant three-story brick townhouse in Federal style, has spacious rooms with high ceilings and artistic doorways. On the first floor are a dining room and library. Extending back from the dining room is a long wing, once containing servants' quarters, which partially encloses a formal rear garden. A large entrance hall leads through two archways and up a curving staircase to two drawing rooms on the second floor. Preserved in the house are original furnishings and artifacts associated with the various owners. The remodeled stables and carriage house at the rear of the house are now the Truxtun-Decatur Naval Museum, operated by the Naval Historical Foundation. Though preserved as a historic house museum, Decatur House is also used by the U.S. Navy for official entertaining.

Octagon House, District of Columbia

Location. 1741 New York Avenue NW., Washington.

Ownership and Administration. American Institute of Architects.

Significance. Built between 1798 and 1800 by Col. John Tayloe, a rich Virginia planter, this house is a superb example of an 18th-century Georgian townhouse. President and Mrs. Madison temporarily resided in it in 1814–15, while the White House was being rebuilt and renovated following its burning by the British during the War of 1812. While living there, Madison signed the Treaty of Ghent, ending the war, in the room that he used as a study.

Colonel Tayloe had planned to build a townhouse in Philadelphia, but his close friend, President George Washington, persuaded him to build it in the new Capital City. In 1797 Tayloe purchased a lot and obtained the services of Dr. William Thornton, architect of the Capitol. Built between 1798 and 1800, the house was considered to be one of the finest in the Nation, and in it Colonel Tayloe entertained many distinguished guests, including Madison, Jefferson, Monroe, Adams, Jackson, Decatur, Webster, Clay, Lafayette, and Calhoun. In 1814, after the British set fire to the abandoned White House, as well as the Capitol and other public buildings, Colonel Tayloe and other Washington residents offered their homes to President and Mrs. Madison during the rebuilding of the White House. They first chose Octagon House and lived there for nearly 1 year, in 1814–15. Madison, who used the tower room above the entrance as a study, on February 17, 1815, signed there the Treaty of Ghent, which ended the War of 1812. The Madisons resided in a suite on the east side of the second floor, consisting of a large room and two small dressing rooms. In 1815 they moved to "Seven Buildings," on Pennsylvania Avenue, where they lived out the President's term of office.

After Mrs. Tayloe's death, in 1855, the Tayloe family no longer lived in the house and it soon fell into disrepair. In 1865 the St. Rose's Technical Institute, a Catholic school for girls, occupied the house, and from 1866 to 1879 the Government rented it for the use of the Hydrographic Office. Until about 1885, when the Tayloe heirs entrusted it to a caretaker, it was

Octagon House, District of Columbia. After the British burned the White House, during the War of 1812, President and Mrs. Madison lived for a time in this 18th-century Georgian townhouse. In the room he used as a study, Madison signed the Treaty of Ghent, ending the war.

used as an office and as a studio dwelling. As early as 1889 the American Institute of Architects expressed interest in acquiring the building for its national headquarters, and in 1897 agreed to rent it for 5-year periods. The institute rehabilitated the dilapidated house, took formal possession in 1899, and 3 years later purchased it.

Present Appearance. Octagon House is a three-story red brick building, trimmed with Aquia sandstone, and has been well preserved. It is open to the public. Stone steps lead to a circular entrance area that opens into a foyer. The institute uses the two downstairs rooms leading from the foyer as reception rooms for social functions. From the foyer a spiral staircase curves upward to the Madison Room, or Treaty Room, which has been restored, and includes, among other things, the table on which Madison signed the Treaty of Ghent. Other second-floor rooms, including the ones used by the Madisons for living quarters, are now exhibition galleries. In 1940 the institute erected an administration building along the eastern line of the Octagon plot, in 1950 restored the garden, and in 1953 converted the stable into a library.

St. John's Episcopal Church, District of Columbia

Location. Corner of 16th and H Streets NW., Washington.

Ownership and Administration. St. John's Parish.

Significance. This "Church of Presidents," across from Lafayette Square, is an excellent example of the Federal style of architecture and was the first building after the White House to be built opposite the square. It is today among the few surviving Federal-period structures around the square, which also include the White House, Decatur House, Dolley Madison House, and the Benjamin Ogle Tayloe House.

The distinguished architect Benjamin H. Latrobe designed St. John's, constructed in 1815–16, in the form of a Greek cross. A lantern cupola sitting above a flat dome dominated the gabled roofline, which towered above the high sidewalls. The transepts had four massive pillars at their intersection. Surrounding the interior was a graceful circular gallery, which had a railing and was supported by columns. The aisles were of brick and the pews high-backed. Within the chancel was a communion table, above which was a movable wine-glass pulpit, reached by a spiral staircase. Four years after completion of the church, workmen erected a major addition on the west side, fronted by a Doric-columned portico

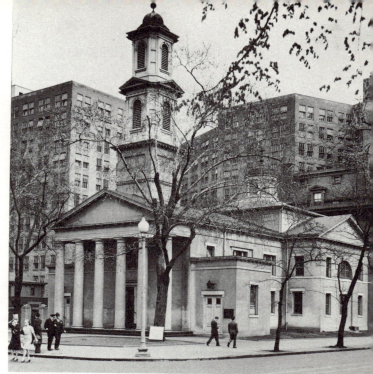

St. John's Episcopal Church, one of the first buildings on Lafayette Square, is known as the "Church of Presidents." Since its construction, in 1815–16, a pew has been reserved for the President.

which became the new main entrance, and above which rose a high steeple. New flat-roofed vestibules, just behind and lower than the portico, created the form of a Latin instead of a Greek cross. In 1842 church officials replaced the old pews and subsequently made other minor modifications, but over the course of the years restored many original features.

From the time of the opening of the church, church officials reserved one pew for the President. Madison chose Number 28, later redesignated Number 54, and the next five successive Presidents—Monroe, Adams, Jackson, Van Buren, and Harrison—occupied the pew. Since then, by tradition, pew 54 has been set aside for the President. Recent Presidents who have attended services in the church include Franklin D. Roosevelt, Harry S. Truman, Dwight D. Eisenhower, John F. Kennedy, and Lyndon B. Johnson.

Present Appearance. St. John's Church, in fine condition today, is still an active parish church and is open to the public. The basic structure is much the same as at the time of the original construction and subsequent major enlargement. Twenty-seven handsome memorial windows adorn the building. Many of the Presidents have autographed an 18th-century prayerbook, placed in the President's pew. A silver chalice donated by

John Tayloe, builder of the Octagon House, and a solid gold communion chalice, encrusted with jewels, are among many notable treasures of the church.

Tudor Place, District of Columbia

Location. 1644 31st Street NW., Washington.

Ownership and Administration. Privately owned.

Significance. This two-story mansion, also known as Tudor Mansion and Tudor Hall, which sits on the crest of a knoll in Georgetown, is of historical, as well as architectural interest, because of its association with the Washington, Custis, Lee, and Peter families.

Between 1794 and about 1805 Francis Loundes, wealthy tobacco merchant who planned an imposing mansion, built two unconnected wings of the house. In the latter year Thomas Peter and his wife, Martha Parke Custis, granddaughter of Mrs. George Washington, purchased the unfinished house and 8-acre tract. They retained Dr. William Thornton, architect of the Capitol and the Octagon House, to design a central building joining the wings. He chose an ellipse, a modified version of which he had used for the Capitol and the Octagon House. Tall Doric columns extending almost to the second story supported the dome roof. Construction of the center portion occurred between 1807 and 1816.

Brittania Peter, one of Thomas' daughters, was a popular belle of Georgetown and one of the bridesmaids at the wedding in Arlington House of her first cousin, Mary Ann Randolph Custis, to Robert E. Lee. In 1842 Brittania married Commodore Beverly Kennon, who subsequently died. After her parents' death, she inherited the estate and lived at Tudor Place with her daughter, Martha Custis Kennon. In 1867 Martha married a distant cousin, Dr. Armistead Peter, and the house has remained in the Peter family ever since. In the 19th century, Tudor Place, a center of Georgetown society, entertained the Marquis de Lafayette, George Mason, various leaders of the Federalist Party, and Gen. Robert E. Lee.

Present Appearance. Tudor Place remains today essentially the same as originally constructed. It is a two-story structure, built of stuccoed brick, painted pale buff. The exterior is unchanged except for a slight modification in the second-story balcony. The only change in the interior is the addition of a large kitchen in the central portion and bathrooms in each wing. The original kitchen with its equipment has been maintained. The formal entrance on the north opens into a central hallway, crossed by a transverse hallway. In the angles of the **T** are spacious living rooms. The delicate plaster friezes, the marble mantelpieces, and the wide plank flooring are original. The east wing contains a conservatory adjoining a drawing room. The west wing consists of a parlor, dining room, and office.

Much of the furniture is original, and the house contains many interesting heirlooms of the Dandridge, Washington, Custis, Randolph, and Lee families. A number of interesting portraits, including some by Gilbert Stuart, hang on the walls. The gardens on the present 6½-acre tract are of much interest. Tudor Place is not open to the public.

United States Capitol, District of Columbia

Location. Capitol Hill, Washington.

Ownership and Administration. U.S. Government; U.S. Congress.

Significance. An architectural masterpiece reminiscent of an ancient Roman temple, the Capitol of the United States sits on the crown of a hill dominating the Capital City. It is not only a national shrine but also a symbol of liberty to the free world and a monument to the hopes and aspirations of all mankind. Since 1800, except for one short period during and shortly after the War of 1812, it has been the seat of the Congress of the United States; the flag flies over it night and day. Within its walls, political forces affecting the destinies of our land have recurrently clashed in dramatic conflict. They have been resolved in the enactment of laws affecting the lives of all Americans. From the east portico most of the Presidents have taken their inaugural oath, and inside many have personally delivered their annual State of the Union messages to joint sessions of the Congress. In the Capitol, too, are preserved scores of priceless artworks and furnishings that commemorate historic events and leading citizens.

The Capitol sits on Jenkins Hill, as specified by Maj. Pierre Charles L'Enfant in his plan for Washington. In 1792 Dr. William Thornton, a physician by profession but an architect by avocation, won the architectural competition for a Capitol design. In 1793 George Washington laid the cornerstone. Soon thereafter construction began, workers using light gray sandstone from quarries in Aquia, Va. Dr. Thornton, appointed as official architect of the Capitol, clashed with a series of professional

The Capitol, symbol of liberty to the free world. George Washington laid the cornerstone, in 1793. Courtesy, Office of the Architect of the Capitol.

architects who wished to alter his design; in 1794 Stephen Hallet, who had been supervising the construction, was dismissed. Thornton then collaborated with James Hoban, the White House architect, and others. In 1800 Congress moved from Philadelphia to Washington and crowded into the newly finished north wing, the first to be completed.

In 1803, during Jefferson's administration, Benjamin H. Latrobe took over supervision of the construction and 4 years later completed the south wing. In August 1814, during the War of 1812, British troops invaded Washington and set fire to many buildings, including the incomplete Capitol, but a heavy rainstorm and a small group of patriots quenched the flames and saved it from complete destruction. In late 1814 Congress met in the Patent Office Building (formerly Blodgett's Hotel), the only

Government office structure to escape burning, and from late 1815 until 1819 they met in a hastily constructed building, known as the Brick Capitol, which stood on the site of the present Supreme Court Building. Latrobe undertook restoration of the Capitol, but in 1817 Charles Bulfinch replaced him and completed the work 2 years later, at which time Congress returned.

In 1818 Bulfinch had begun construction of the central portion of the building, including the east and west fronts and the central rotunda. By 1824 the rotunda, having a wooden copper-covered dome, was essentially completed. Neither the Senate nor the House assumed any responsibility for the rotunda. For a few years a multitude of hucksters invaded it and turned it into a marketplace; they sold everything from fresh vegetables to ribbons and pianos.

In 1851, to provide Congress with better quarters, work began on the present House and Senate Chambers, extensions of the old north and south wings. By 1859 both had been essentially completed—of Massachusetts and Maryland marble. The House occupied its new quarters in 1857; the Senate in 1859. A few years after the House and Senate had moved into their new chambers, the old south wing became Statuary Hall; and the Supreme Court, which had been meeting in the basement, moved into the old north wing and remained there until the Supreme Court Building was completed, in 1935. In 1855 work crews had begun to construct the present cast- and wrought-iron dome to replace the wooden one in the interest of better architectural proportion with the House and Senate Chambers. Late in 1863, in the middle of the Civil War, Thomas Crawford's bronze "Statue of Freedom" was moved into position on the top of the dome as a symbol of liberty and freedom. As this occurred a 35-gun salute from Capitol Hill was echoed by salutes from 12 fortifications surrounding the city. Thus ended many years of hard labor and ingenious engineering skill in erecting the monumental structure that is the seat of the legislative branch of the U.S. Government.

During the period 1959–61 a major renovation occurred. On the east side of the building, between the Senate and House Chambers, workmen constructed a new marble front, following the design of the old sandstone front, extending beyond the old walls. They also repaired and repainted the dome, built a subway terminal under the Senate wing, cleaned the walls of the wings, improved lighting throughout the building, and made other changes.

Present Appearance. The Capitol rises majestically at the east end of the mall. Containing 540 rooms, it houses the Senate and House of Representatives and also contains a President's Room and an office for the Vice President. The present Senate Chamber has changed little over the years, but contains modern lighting and acoustics for the convenience of the Senators. The mahogany desks, arranged in a semicircular pattern, face the rostrum, where the Vice President presides. Of special interest are the desks once used by Daniel Webster and Jefferson Davis. The chamber is surrounded by visitor galleries, on the second-floor level. The House Chamber is similar to the Senate Chamber in that its walnut desks are arranged in a semicircle around the Speaker's rostrum, and the chamber is surrounded by second-floor visitor galleries. It is, however, a larger room and is used for joint sessions of Congress. A prized historical artifact is a silver mace, an 1841 replica of the one used in 1789 by the First Congress.

Statuary Hall, the old House Chamber, contains statues of leading citizens from the various States. In the central rotunda seven Presidents have lain in state—Lincoln, Garfield, McKinley, Harding, Taft, Hoover, and Kennedy—as well as such notables as the Unknown Soldiers of World War II and Korea, Adm. George Dewey, and Gen. John J. Pershing. Paintings adorn the walls of many rooms and corridors in the Capitol, and on the interior dome of the rotunda is the remarkable fresco "The Apotheosis of Washington," painted from scaffolds by Constantino Brumidi. On this canopy, which measures 4,664 square feet, Brumidi, in a prodigious feat of solitary workmanship, employed his remarkable artistic powers to scale heroic figures to appear life size from below. The frieze, circling the rotunda below the dome and picturing significant events in U.S. history, is partially the work of Brumidi, who, after 22 years of work on the rotunda, died in 1880. In 1953 Allyn Cox completed the frieze. Below it are large paintings by John Trumbull, a popular U.S. artist of the War for Independence period. In the ground floor below the rotunda is the empty crypt and tomb intended for George Washington, who chose to be buried at Mount Vernon.

Other sections of the Capitol consist mainly of private offices, committee rooms, and other facilities for the Congressmen. The Capitol is open daily to the public throughout the year. Guided tours begin in the rotunda and cover all public areas of interest.

Fort San Carlos de Barrancas, Florida

Location. Escambia County, U.S. Naval Air Station, Pensacola.

Ownership and Administration. U.S. Government; Department of Defense.

Significance. This fort, constructed by the Spanish during the 18th century, also has associations with the War of 1812 and the Civil War. During the first phase of its history, because of a three-cornered rivalry between Spain, France, and England in which their American possessions were pawns in a worldwide imperial struggle, it was several times destroyed and rebuilt. Originally erected in 1787 during the last Spanish occupation of West Florida on a high bluff called "Barrancas de Santo Tomé," it occupied the same site as Fort San Carlos de Austria, which dated from the time of the first permanent Spanish settlement on Pensacola Bay, in 1698, and had been completely destroyed in 1719 by the French. From 1763 to 1781 the British controlled Pensacola. Its capture by a Spanish expedition in 1781 marked the beginning of the last period of Spanish rule. Fort San Carlos de Barrancas, a semicircular structure of Pensacola brick, was a defense bastion in West Florida and, with St. Augustine, a foothold in the Southeastern United States.

Fort San Carlos de Barrancas, Florida. In the late 18th century the Spanish constructed the fort to guard Pensacola, the capital of Spanish West Florida.

Spanish collaboration with the British forces during the War of 1812 led Andrew Jackson to move into Pensacola in 1814. The occupying British force retreated rapidly to their warships after blowing up the fort. When Jackson withdrew to New Orleans, the Spanish returned and began to rebuild it. Four years later, near the end of the Seminole Indian War, Jackson again attacked Pensacola. In accepting the surrender of the Spanish Governor in Fort San Carlos de Barrancas, he in effect seized control of West Florida for the United States. Three years later, in 1821, he returned as provisional Governor of the territory and took formal possession of it at ceremonies in the Plaza Ferdinand VII, Pensacola.

As part of the general tightening of the Nation's coastal defenses, following the War of 1812, during the years 1833–44 U.S. troops strengthened the defenses in Pensacola Bay. Immediately in the rear of and connected to Fort San Carlos de Barrancas, they constructed a four-sided brick fortification, Fort Barrancas; and, as a part of the defensive complex, built Fort Redoubt about 1,000 yards to the north. During the Civil War the three forts were first in the hands of Confederate and then the Union forces.

Fort San Carlos de Barrancas is a Registered National Historic Landmark relating primarily to Spanish exploration and settlement.

Present Appearance. The forts are now in poor condition.

Plaza Ferdinand VII, Florida

Location. Escambia County, on Palafox Street, between Government and Zaragossa Streets, Pensacola.

Ownership and Administration. City of Pensacola.

Significance. This plaza is the site of the formal transfer in July 1821 of West Florida from Spain to the United States. The basis for the transfer was the Adams-Onís Treaty (July 1819), which Spain did not ratify until February 1821. In the treaty Spain agreed to cede East and West Florida in exchange for U.S. assumption of $5 million in claims of its citizens against the Spanish Government.

On March 12, 1821, Gen. Andrew Jackson was commissioned as provisional Governor of East and West Florida, which the United States planned to combine into one territory. He dispatched Col. Robert Butler, his adjutant, to act as his representative in accepting the transfer of East Florida at St. Augustine, and he proceeded to Pensacola to accept that of West Florida. Both Jackson and Butler encountered delaying tactics on the part of the Spanish Governors, but the transfer of East Florida took place first, on July 10, at Castillo de San Marcos, in St. Augustine.

On July 17 the transfer of West Florida occurred at Pensacola. On the morning of the ceremony, Jackson met the Spanish Governor, Don José Callava, on the steps of the Government House, located on the site now occupied by City Hall, and the two men entered the plaza. After passing between lines of American and Spanish troops, they stood at attention. While the 4th Infantry band played "The Star-Spangled Banner," the Spanish royal standard was lowered to half-staff and the U.S. flag raised to a level with it. Then, as the U.S.S. *Hornet*, in Pensacola Bay, fired a 21-gun salute, soldiers lowered the Spanish flag and raised the Stars and Stripes to full staff. After the ceremony Jackson set up a provisional government for Florida; divided it into Escambia and St. John's Counties; and designated Pensacola and St. Augustine, respectively, as the two seats of government. In 1822 Congress created Florida Territory.

Present Appearance. The present square is only a remnant of the original one, laid out by the British in 1765. In 1802 a large part of the original square was subdivided and sold as building lots. In 1935 the Pensacola Historical Society erected in the square a monument commemorating the transfer of the sovereignty of West Florida.

Grouseland, Indiana

Location. Knox County, Scott and Park Streets, Vincennes.

Ownership and Administration. Francis Vigo Chapter, Daughters of the American Revolution.

Significance. This mansion, now surrounded by the city of Vincennes, preserves the memory of William Henry Harrison—Indian fighter, military leader in the War of 1812, Governor of Indiana Territory, and ninth President of the United States. He built Grouseland and lived in it during his term as Territorial Governor, when he helped bring peace to the old Northwest and opened to white settlement a vast territory between the Ohio River and the Great Lakes.

In 1800 Congress created the Indiana Territory out of a part of the old Northwest Territory, and President Adams appointed Harrison as Governor. Arriving in the small Territorial capital of Vincennes the next year, Harrison purchased a 300-acre tract of land just north of town, which he called Grouseland, and in 1803–4 built a mansion on it. As Territorial Governor, he sought to protect white settlers against Indian tribes blocking the tide of westward expansion. He negotiated a series of treaties with tribal leaders of the Northwest that called for the cession of Indian lands. In 1810 Tecumseh, the Shawnee leader, warned that his people would fight white encroachment.

William Henry Harrison built this mansion on his Grouseland estate in 1803–4 and lived there while serving as Governor of Indiana Territory. He later achieved fame as a military leader in the War of 1812 and served as ninth President of the United States.

Apparently learning from Tecumseh that he was going south to seek allies, in September 1811 Harrison left Grouseland and traveled northward to Terre Haute, where his troops constructed Fort Harrison to serve as an advance base for an attack on the stronghold of the Shawnees and their allies at Tippecanoe Creek, near present Lafayette, Ind. Late in October he resumed his march northward and at the Battle of Tippecanoe—precipitated by a premature attack on the whites led by Tecumseh's half-brother, "The Prophet"—scattered Tecumseh's followers. Harrison had heavy losses and the victory was indecisive, but he was soon to have his day.

Not long after the Battle of Tippecanoe, once the War of 1812 broke out, Harrison obtained a commission in the Army as brigadier general, left Grouseland to command U.S. forces in the old Northwest, and the next year became a major general. Harrison's forces finally drove the British and their Shawnee and other Indian allies into Canada and decisively defeated them at the Battle of the Thames (1813). After years of diplomatic struggle and frontier war, this victory assured U.S. domination of the old Northwest. It made Harrison a national figure and contributed to his popularity and election to the Presidency in 1840. In 1814, after resigning his commission, he returned to a house that he had built at North Bend, Ohio, instead of to Grouseland; in 1813 he had been replaced as Governor of Indiana Territory.

The next occupant of Grouseland after Harrison was Judge Benjamin Parke, who lived there until about 1819. John Harrison, William Henry's son, Receiver of the Land Office in Vincennes, then resided in the mansion for about a decade. It soon fell into ruins and the city encroached upon it. By 1850 ownership had passed out of the Harrison family hands, and during the decade the mansion served as a grain storehouse and a hotel. From 1860 to 1909 it was again a private residence. In 1909 the Vincennes Water Co. purchased it and planned to raze it, but the Francis Vigo Chapter of the Daughters of the American Revolution collected enough money to acquire, furnish, restore, and open it to the public as a historic house museum.

Present Appearance. Grouseland is a two-story Georgian house. To its rear is a one-story annex, joined by a covered passage. The house contains 26 rooms, an attic, and a basement. The architect is unknown. Features incorporated for protection against the Indians include two false windows in front of the house, a lookout in the attic, heavily barred basement windows, powder magazine, and basement well. All the rooms are furnished with period pieces. On display are articles associated with the Harrisons, as well as with Francis Vigo, fur trader and merchant of Vincennes who was friendly to the American cause during the War for Independence. Adjoining Grouseland is the Indiana Territory Capitol State Memorial, where the first Indiana Territorial Legislature met. This building stood elsewhere in Vincennes until 1919, when it was moved opposite Grouseland.

Joseph Bailly Homestead, Indiana

Location. Porter County, just outside the village of Chesterton.

Ownership and Administration. Privately owned.

Significance. Joseph Bailly was probably the first white settler in northwestern Indiana—at the time a wilderness inhabited mainly by Indians. His homestead was an oasis for travelers, a meeting place for Indians and whites, and a religious and social center.

Bailly, born in 1774 in Canada, began fur trading at Mackinac, the bustling fur capital of the old Northwest, at the age of 18. He built up a thriving business in the Mackinac and Lake Michigan areas and extended it south as far as the Kankakee and Wabash Rivers. His fur business was interrupted by the War of 1812, whereupon he enlisted in the British Army, and as a lieutenant of Canadian *Voyageurs* transported munitions for the British and Indians. Late in 1813 he was captured by a party of Indians loyal to the United States, delivered to U.S. authorities at Detroit, and imprisoned for 3 months. After his release he led several raiding parties against the Americans.

Following the war Bailly's fur trading activities declined, as did those of other traders in the area. In 1818 he became a U.S. citizen. He lived in the Mackinac area until 1819, first on Mackinac Island and later on Drummond Island, some miles distant. In 1822 he settled permanently in northwestern Indiana, an area as yet unsettled by whites, although the central and southern parts of the State had already been bypassed by the advancing line of westward settlement that had reached Illinois and, in places, had crossed the Mississippi River. Some of the displaced Indians had moved into the northwest part of the State. Bailly erected several log cabins to carry on his trading activities. Because the post was located in the wilderness near the trails from Detroit and Fort Wayne to Fort Dearborn, it became a stopping place and social oasis for Indian and white travelers.

In 1834 Bailly started work on his home, but died the following year. His hope of founding a town and bringing in Canadian settlers never came to fruition, but he did manage to sell a few lots. He is best remembered for his missionary-like activities among the Indians. His homestead was a religious center, the only one of its kind between Fort Dearborn and Detroit. The Bailly Homestead has been designated as eligible for the Registry of National Historic Landmarks primarily because of its associations with the fur trade.

Present Appearance. The main house, unfinished at the time of Bailly's death, and one of the log storehouses used in his trading activities are the only buildings that remain. Both have been considerably altered. Now a privately owned memorial commemorating Bailly's activities in northwestern Indiana, they are open to the public.

Tippecanoe Battlefield, Indiana

Location. Tippecanoe County, on Ind. 225, about 7 miles northeast of Lafayette.

Ownership and Administration. State of Indiana; Department of Conservation.

Significance. Although the Battle of Tippecanoe (November 7, 1811) did not destroy the power of Tecumseh or quell the Indian threat in the old Northwest, it strengthened American morale and helped make Harrison a national hero. The battle was followed by increased Indian depredations along the frontier and led the Indians to a closer alliance with the British in the War of 1812. During the war, at the Battle of the Thames (1813), Harrison decisively defeated the Indians and British and left Tecumseh dead on the battlefield.

In the first part of the 19th century, as settlement was spreading westward from the Appalachians, the powerful and resourceful Shawnee Tecumseh began uniting the tribes of the old Northwest. Driven into present Indiana by the advance of white settlement, he and his half-brother, "The Prophet," in 1808 founded a stronghold named Prophet's Town near the mouth of Tippecanoe Creek. From this base Tecumseh attempted to ally Indians in the North and South against the white invaders. While he faced the practical realities of resistance, "The Prophet" preached of visions that foretold the doom of all white men who ventured into Indian lands.

In the Treaty of Fort Wayne (1809) the Delaware and Potawatomi Indians ceded about 3 million acres of land to the United States for a pittance. The following year Tecumseh traveled to Vincennes to discuss the matter of Indian lands with William Henry Harrison, Governor of Indiana Territory. Tecumseh promised peace if white men made no further advances into Indian lands, but Harrison told him that such advance was inevitable. Harrison, also rebuffing Tecumseh's assertion that land cessions made by one tribe could not be binding on all tribes, warned that the newly acquired lands would be settled by force if the Indians resisted. By autumn the frontier was ablaze. British agents in Canada, aware of the increasing tension between Great Britain and the United States, stepped up their aid to the Indians, though probably not to the degree that the Americans believed. After the failure of a last-minute conference in July 1811 at Vincennes, Tecumseh departed for the South with a warning to Harrison that he would invite Southwestern tribes to join the Indian confederacy.

Harrison immediately initiated a campaign against Tecumseh's base at Tippecanoe Creek. In September he mobilized 900 men, consisting of the Indiana Militia, reinforcements from the 4th U.S. Infantry Regiment, and a few Kentucky volunteers, and marched northward to Terre Haute. There he spent most of October building Fort Harrison to serve as an advance base. Late in the month the march resumed. On the night of November 6 he camped near the Indian base. Shortly before dawn about 600 or 700 Indians, who during the night had been incited by "The Prophet," attacked—but without the leadership of Tecumseh. Harrison

Tippecanoe Battlefield State Memorial, Indiana. At this site in 1811 Gov. William Henry Harrison defeated a party of Indians led by "The Prophet," half-brother of the Shawnee chief Tecumseh. Harrison's success in quelling the Indian threat in the old Northwest helped win him the Presidency.

beat them off three times and ordered a countercharge. The Indians broke and fled. The next day Harrison marched to the deserted village of Prophet's Town, destroyed it, and then marched back to Fort Harrison and Vincennes.

Although people in the West regarded the Battle of Tippecanoe as a major victory, it was dearly bought and not decisive. One-fourth of Harrison's army was dead or wounded. Harrison disbanded the survivors at Vincennes. The Indians soon rebuilt Prophet's Town and increased their attacks on white settlers. The frontier became as defenseless as before. Nevertheless, Harrison dispatched to the East an exaggerated account of the battle. Its impression on the frontier mind is evidenced by the campaign slogan of about 30 years later, "Tippecanoe and Tyler, too," when Harrison won the Presidency. Because of the Battle of Tippecanoe, Tecumseh and his followers allied themselves with the British the following summer, when the War of 1812 broke out. In the Battle of the Thames (1813), Harrison finally struck a fatal blow to the Indians. With Tecumseh's death in the battle, the Indian threat in the old Northwest subsided.

Present Appearance. Located on the edge of the village of Battleground, the 16-acre site of the Battle of Tippecanoe is enclosed by an iron fence and commemorated in Tippecanoe Battlefield State Memorial. The area is heavily wooded and relatively isolated from modern intrusion. A towering white monument, near the base of which is a statue of Harrison, and several stone markers identifying the locations where U.S. officers were killed or mortally wounded commemorate the battle.

Fort Leavenworth, Kansas

Location. Leavenworth County, on the eastern edge of Leavenworth.

Ownership and Administration. U.S. Government; Department of Defense.

Significance. Founded in 1827 to protect caravans on the Santa Fe Trail and to help maintain a "permanent Indian frontier," this fort was the central one in a chain ranging from Fort Snelling, Minn., to Fort Jesup, La., that the Army established in the 1820's and 1830's. From that time to the present it has been a major U.S. Army installation. A significant post in the trans-Mississippi West, it figured prominently in the

Indian Wars of the Great Plains, the Mexican War, and the Civil War, and later became a major training center.

As early as 1824 citizens of Missouri petitioned Congress for the activation of a military post at the Arkansas Crossing for the protection of the traders on the Santa Fe Trail. Three years later the Secretary of War ordered the erection of a fort near the western boundary of Missouri to meet the petitioners' needs and quell Indian disturbances. Col. Henry Leavenworth selected a site to the north of Arkansas Crossing, and his troops built a post called Cantonment Leavenworth, later Fort Leavenworth. Strategically located on the Missouri River near the eastern terminus of the Oregon and Santa Fe Trails, for many years it was a key frontier post. From 1827 to 1839 it was headquarters of the Upper Missouri Indian Agency, which had jurisdiction over all the tribes in the Upper Missouri and Northern Plains region, and was the scene of many conferences and treaty councils. Exploring expeditions that used it as a base of operations between 1829 and 1845 included Maj. Bennett Riley's expedition along the Santa Fe Trail, Col. Henry Dodge's expedition to the Rocky Mountains, and Col. Stephen W. Kearny's expedition to Cherokee country and to South Pass and the Rockies.

During the Mexican War the fort was the departure point and supply base for General Kearny's "Army of the West," which occupied New Mexico and California. Following the war the fort was the chief supply depot for Army posts in the West, and in 1854 served as temporary capital of the Territory of Kansas. During the Civil War the Confederates twice threatened the fort, which after the war continued to be a major supply depot. From 1860 to 1874 it was an ordnance arsenal; from 1874 to 1878 the quartermaster depot for the Military Division of the Missouri; and after 1881 a school for infantry and cavalry, reorganized in 1901 as the General Service and Staff School. In the 20th century it has served as an officers' school, induction, and training center. It is a Registered National Historic Landmark relating primarily to Indian-military affairs in the trans-Mississippi West.

Present Appearance. Among the noteworthy historic structures at the fort are the post chapel, erected in 1878; the original home of the General School for Officers; the enlisted men's barracks, constructed between 1881 and 1889; the Syracuse House, built in the late 1860's; and a portion of a wall of the original fort. One of the old cavalry stables at the fort now serves as a transportation museum.

Ashland, Kentucky

Location. Fayette County, Main Street (Richmond Road), Lexington.

Ownership and Administration. Henry Clay Memorial Foundation.

Significance. This estate, in the heart of the Bluegrass region, was the home of one of the Nation's outstanding statesmen and pre-Civil War leaders, Henry Clay—the "Great Pacificator," or "Great Compromiser." From 1812, when he gained national recognition as a leader of the "War Hawks" in Congress, until his death, in 1852, Clay returned to Ashland as often as his busy schedule would permit. While there, he entertained many distinguished guests, worked on legislation, and prepared speeches for Congress. For diversion he dabbled in farming and bred race horses, cattle, and sheep. After his last disappointing try for the presidential nomination, in 1848, he left Ashland for the Senate to do what he could to avert the growing danger of civil conflict. In the fall of 1851 he bade goodbye to his home for the last time as he left to devote his failing strength to the political struggle in Washington, where he died the following year.

In 1811 Clay purchased nearly 400 acres of land from the estate that he had been renting and the following year constructed a brick mansion, designed by Benjamin H. Latrobe, architect of the Capitol and other Washington buildings. Clay christened the home Ashland because of its

Henry Clay, the distinguished ante bellum statesman and Senator, lived in this mansion, on his Ashland estate. Although the city of Lexington, Kentucky, now occupies most of the original estate, a portion of it has been preserved.

location in a forest of ash trees. Even during Clay's lifetime the house revealed serious structural weaknesses. After his death his son razed and reconstructed it on its original foundations; he maintained as closely as possible the original Latrobe design. For many years Nannette McDowell Bullock, Clay's great-granddaughter, lived at Ashland and she deeded it to the Henry Clay Memorial Foundation, chartered in 1926. The foundation preserved it and dedicated it in 1950 as a historic shrine honoring Clay.

Present Appearance. Most of Clay's original estate is today covered by residential areas in Lexington. The Henry Clay Memorial Foundation has preserved 20 acres of the estate, once totaling about 600 acres, as a park. The house is a 2½-story brick structure, covered with vines, and has one-story wings on each side. From these wings, ells project forward and form a court in the front of the main section of the house. On both sides of the doorway are full-length windows and above it is a fanlight. The house is furnished with a great variety of Clay's possessions. Several outbuildings survive, including two cottages, two icehouses, and a smokehouse. At the rear of the house the Garden Club of Lexington maintains a garden on the site of Mrs. Clay's garden. The house and grounds, both in excellent condition, are open to the public throughout the year.

Fort Jesup, Louisiana

Location. Sabine Parish, on La. 6, about 7 miles northeast of Many.

Ownership and Administration. State of Louisiana.

Significance. From its founding, in 1822, until its inactivation, in 1845, this fort was the most southwesterly military outpost of the United States. Because of a dispute over the Texas-United States boundary, in 1806 Spain and the United States designated as a neutral strip an area 30 to 40 miles wide extending eastward from the Sabine River and embracing most of the present western tier of parishes in Louisiana. Under the Adams-Onís Treaty of 1819, the United States acquired this strip, which had become a haven for outlaws and marauders who molested settlers emigrating to Texas, and moved swiftly to occupy and police it. Pending ratification of the treaty, which occurred in 1821, the U.S. Government in 1820 built Fort Selden on the Bayou Pierre near its junction with the Red River just outside the strip on its eastern edge and the following year made plans to set up another post nearer the Sabine.

Reconstructed officers' quarters, which now serve as a visitor center, at Fort Jesup State Monument, Louisiana. For nearly 25 years after its founding, in 1822, Fort Jesup was a key military post in the old Southwest. Courtesy, Louisiana State Parks and Recreation Commission.

In 1822 the Army abandoned Fort Selden. Lt. Col. Zachary Taylor occupied the watershed between the Sabine and Red Rivers and moved to a point 25 miles south-southwest of Fort Selden, where his troops built a group of log cabins. Within a few months Cantonment Jesup, as the post was first called, was the largest garrison in Louisiana, consisting of four companies of the 7th Infantry under Lt. Col. James B. Many. In 1827–28 the troops helped construct a military road 262 miles northwest to Cantonment Towson, in Arkansas Territory; it linked the two most southwestern outposts of the U.S. Army. In 1831–33 Gen. Henry Leavenworth assumed command of the cantonment and garrisoned it with six companies of the 3d Infantry. In 1834 Colonel Many again assumed command. In 1833 the Government, recognizing the enlargement and expansion of the cantonment, redesignated it as the Post of Fort Jesup and created the 16,000-acre Fort Jesup Military Reservation.

After the Texas Revolution began, in 1835, reinforcements arrived at Fort Jesup. Maj. Gen. Edmund P. Gaines assembled 13 infantry companies at the fort and marched to the Sabine, where he founded a temporary post, Camp Sabine. From there he occupied Nacogdoches and remained until the independence of Texas was assured. In 1845, just after President Tyler ordered Gen. Zachary Taylor, commander of Fort Jesup, to move an army into Texas in anticipation of a war with Mexico, the

Army inactivated the fort. It is a Registered National Historic Landmark relating primarily to political and military affairs, 1830–60.

Present Appearance. In 1957 the State of Louisiana created Fort Jesup State Monument. It consists of about 22 acres. The only original building is one of the log kitchens, which has been repaired, reroofed, and refurnished with period reproductions and authentic kitchenware. An officers' quarters, reconstructed for use as a visitor center and park administrative office, contains exhibits that tell the story of the fort.

Jackson Square, Louisiana

Location. Orleans Parish, Vieux Carré, New Orleans.

Ownership and Administration. City of New Orleans.

Significance. On December 20, 1803, in this square in the heart of the French capital of Louisiana, the U.S. flag was raised for the first

Jackson Square, located in the heart of the Vieux Carré district of New Orleans, is of architectural as well as historical interest. Surrounded by buildings dating from the days of Spanish Louisiana, the square was in 1803 the scene of the transfer of Louisiana from Spain to France and from France to the United States. St. Louis Cathedral overlooks the square. Courtesy, New Orleans Chamber of Commerce.

time over the newly purchased Louisiana Territory—the largest single accession of territory in the history of the Nation. Twice in 3 weeks during late 1803 the allegiance of the inhabitants of New Orleans was shifted, from Spain to France to the United States. At noon on November 30 a crowd gathered to hear the announcement from the balcony of the Cabildo that Louisiana had passed from Spanish into French possession. On December 20 they heard that their allegiance again had been changed; the flag of France was hauled down and replaced by the Stars and Stripes.

Present Appearance. Jackson Square, a tree-shaded public park once known as Place D'Armes, is still the hub of the French Quarter, as it has been throughout the years. It offers a fine view of the Cabildo, St. Louis Cathedral, and other historic buildings. In the center of the square, dominating the park, are the famous equestrian statue of Andrew Jackson by Clark Mills and the flagpole marking the site of the symbolic transfer of sovereignty of Louisiana Territory to the United States.

The Cabildo, Louisiana

Location. Orleans Parish, 709 Chartres Street, on Jackson Square, New Orleans.

Ownership and Administration. State of Louisiana; Louisiana State Museum.

Significance. This building, also known as the *Casa Capitular,* was erected in 1795, on the site of two former buildings that had been destroyed by fire, to house the *Cabildo* of Spanish Louisiana, the legislative and administrative council for the province. Two ceremonies within a period of 3 weeks—November 30 and December 20, 1803—were particularly notable in the Cabildo's history. In the first, Louisiana Territory passed to French rule after having been under Spanish control for 40 years. During the brief period of French rule, the building was called the *Maison de Ville* (Town Hall). In the second ceremony, the transfer of sovereignty of Louisiana Territory from France to the United States took place. For the next century the Cabildo continued to provide public offices, but in 1911 it became the Louisiana State Museum. It is a Registered National Historic Landmark relating primarily to Spanish exploration and settlement.

Present Appearance. The architectural historian Hugh Morrison

The Cabildo, or *Casa Capitular,* demonstrates Spanish architectural influence in Louisiana. Constructed in 1795, it housed the *Cabildo,* the legislative and administrative council for the province of Spanish Louisiana. Courtesy, New Orleans Chamber of Commerce.

has commented that the Cabildo, composed of "a full panoply of Renaissance architectural forms" shows the "most markedly Spanish influence in Louisiana." It is a massive structure of stuccoed brick. Alterations in the 1850's included the addition of a third floor, which has a steep-sided mansard roof. The museum of the Cabildo is open to the public.

Casselman Bridge, National Road, Maryland

Location. Garrett County, just north of U.S. 40, on the east side of Grantsville.

Ownership and Administration. Garrett County.

Significance. This bridge over the Casselman River is a fine example of the state of the bridgebuilding art at the time of the construction of the National, or Cumberland, Road—in the first half of the 19th century a major east-west artery of emigration and commerce between the

Atlantic States and the northern Mississippi Valley. The bridge, whose stone arch was the largest in the United States at the time of its erection, in 1813, typifies the numerous stately stone bridges whose handsomely turned arches were as characteristic a scene on the road as the iron mileposts, iron gates, and wooden bridges.

The Congressional Enabling Act in 1802 that created the State of Ohio (1803) specified that a national road be built from Cumberland, Md., to Wheeling, W. Va., on the Ohio River; a later act called for funds from the sale of public lands in Ohio to be used for financing the road. Cumberland was chosen as the eastern terminus because the Frederick Pike already linked Baltimore and Cumberland. In the spring of 1811 construction began, under the supervision of the War Department. Gangs of men, wielding picks and shovels and driving oxen and horses, cleared a 66-foot strip for the roadway, leveled hills, and filled or bridged hollows. They covered 20 feet of the 30-foot-wide road with stones, at least a foot deep. Interrupted for only a short period during the War of 1812, by 1818 workmen had angled the road northwestward through Pennsylvania and reached Wheeling. This remained the western terminus for some years, partly because an extension was not so critically needed as the eastern part of the road and because many westward emigrants used Ohio River steamboats.

In 1820 Congress surveyed a route west of Wheeling and 5 years later appropriated money for an extension of the road. In 1825–26 workers, following the old Zane's Trace, extended the road to Zanesville, Ohio.

Casselman Bridge, Maryland, an arched bridge built along the National, or Cumberland, Road. At the time of its construction, in 1813, its large stone arch was a major engineering accomplishment.

By 1833 additional congressional appropriations had made possible an extension to Columbus and by 1837 to the Indiana border. Finally, in 1852 the road reached its final western terminus, at Vandalia, Ill.—a distance of 834 miles from Cumberland. The route of the road is generally followed today by U.S. 40.

The short Maryland section of the road had barely been completed, during the War of 1812, when the flow of traffic began in both directions—cargo carriers of all sizes, some drawn by 12 horses and carrying 10-ton loads, stagecoaches, Conestoga wagons, droves of animals, and emigrants. At night the travelers rested at the numerous inns and taverns. The heavy traffic, landslides, and rainstorms created the need for regular repairs. In the 1820's and 1830's laborers had to practically rebuild the road. Upon the completion of repairs in 1831, the Federal Government turned the Maryland section of the road over to the State—and later did the same for the other States involved. They all inaugurated toll charges for the use of their sections of the road, whose importance and use declined after 1850 because of the growth of canals, railroads, and the telegraph.

Casselman Bridge continued to be used until 1933, when the State replaced it with a nearby modern steel-and-concrete structure. It is a Registered National Historic Landmark relating primarily to travel and communication.

Present Appearance. Casselman Bridge is in sound condition. In 1911 the State repaired it, but it is essentially the same as when built. It is now owned by Garrett County and is located in the center of a small park.

Maryland State House, Maryland

Location. Anne Arundel County, State Circle, Annapolis.

Ownership and Administration. State of Maryland.

Significance. The Maryland State House, the oldest still in daily use, is one of the most historic buildings in the Nation, located in one of the most historic cities. In this building the Continental Congress ended the War for Independence by ratifying the Treaty of Paris, accepted George Washington's resignation as commander in chief of the Army, and ratified the appointment of Thomas Jefferson as Minister Plenipotentiary. The Annapolis Convention, a forerunner of the Constitutional Convention of 1787, also met in the statehouse.

For nearly 9 months in 1783–84 (November 25–August 13), the statehouse was the seat of the Federal Government under the Articles of Confederation. For 6 months the Continental Congress met in the room known today as the Old Senate Chamber, where on January 14, 1784, it ratified the Treaty of Paris, ending the War for Independence. A few weeks earlier George Washington had appeared before Congress to resign his commission as commander in chief of the Army; in doing so he reaffirmed the old English principle of the supremacy of civil over military authority and the democratic ideal of a government in which no man would become too powerful. On May 7, 1784, Congress appointed Thomas Jefferson as Minister Plenipotentiary, and he then departed for Paris to join John Adams and Benjamin Franklin in negotiating treaties

Maryland State House, Annapolis, today the State Capitol. In 1783–84, under the Articles of Confederation, this building served as the Capitol of the United States. Courtesy, Maryland Department of Economic Development.

of commerce with other powers. After the main body of Congress adjourned on June 3, 1784, a "Committee of States," in charge of Government affairs, remained in the Old Senate Chamber until August 13; in November the Congress reconvened in Trenton, N.J.

In September 1786 the Annapolis Convention met in the Old Senate Chamber. This convention, in which only five States participated, discussed the formulation of a commercial code to govern all the States and finally recommended to Congress that it call another convention to begin at Philadelphia in May 1787 to consider means of strengthening the Government under the Articles of Confederation. Congress acted favorably on this recommendation; the Constitutional Convention was the result.

From the time of the Annapolis Convention to this day, the statehouse has been used exclusively by the State of Maryland. The General Assembly session that convened in March 1780 had probably first used the building. Construction had begun on March 28, 1772, when Maryland's last royal governor officiated at the laying of the cornerstone. Neither the exact date of completion nor the architect are known.

Present Appearance. The brick statehouse, a distinguished two-story building, is topped by a tall octagonal dome and cupola. The main entrance is covered by a one-story Corinthian portico that is pedimented. The portal opens into a wide arcaded hall, under the central dome, that has arched and oval windows and delicate plaster interior ornament. The Old Senate Chamber has been restored to its historic appearance, including six original pieces of furniture. Over the entrance is a curved, balustraded spectators' gallery, supported by fluted Ionic columns. Facing the entrance is a circular speaker's platform. Surrounding the room are 24 sash windows, which have deep paneled reveals and window seats. A classically trimmed fireplace adorns the room. Opposite the Old Senate Chamber is the Old Hall of Delegates, next to which is the Historic and Flag Room, which contains relics of Maryland's part in the Nation's wars. The statehouse today includes a State-office annex, constructed in 1902–5, slightly larger than the original building. The historic parts of the statehouse are open to the public.

U.S.S. *Constellation,* Maryland

Location. Pier 4, Pratt Street, Baltimore.

Ownership and Administration. U.S.S. *Constellation* Commission of

The Star-Spangled Banner Flag House Association, Inc., 844 East Pratt Street, Baltimore.

Significance. This venerable ship has gallantly served the Nation from shortly after its founding through its rise to a world power and is a tribute to the courageous men of the U.S. Navy. Launched at Baltimore in 1797, only about 2 months after the frigate *United States* at Philadelphia, she was the first ship to put to sea fully equipped and manned, to engage and defeat the enemy, to capture an enemy warship, and to carry marines. Though extensively altered and rebuilt during her years of globe-girdling service, the *Constellation* is one of the two surviving early U.S. naval vessels; the other is the reconstructed *Constitution*, today located in Boston Navy Yard. When the Navy finally decommissioned the *Constellation*, in 1955, she had been in service longer than any other naval vessel. Her career spanned the period from the age of fighting sail to the modern era—from the Barbary Wars and the undeclared naval war with France through the Civil War and World Wars I and II.

Immediately after the War for Independence, Congress disbanded the nondescript "navy" for reasons of economy. Early in 1794, however, in the face of raids on U.S. shipping in the Mediterranean by pirates of the Barbary States, it authorized the building of six frigates, four having 44 guns and two 36 guns. Opponents of a naval force inserted a provision that, if peace were made with Algiers, work would be suspended. President Washington, aware of potential enemies more dangerous than the pirates and favoring a permanent navy, directed that construction begin immediately and designated Joshua Humphreys, Philadelphia naval architect, to draw the plans. Keels were soon laid at six different ports: Portsmouth, Boston, New York, Philadelphia, Baltimore, and Norfolk. At the end of 1795 work, which was proceeding briskly, was temporarily suspended by the conclusion of a peace treaty with the Bey of Algiers. Because of French depredations on U.S. shipping, however, construction soon resumed on three of the ships.

In 1797, the year before Congress created the Navy Department, three frigates were launched: On July 10, the 44-gun *United States,* at Philadelphia; on September 7, the 38-gun *Constellation,* at Baltimore; and on September 20, the 44-gun *Constitution,* at Boston. Early in 1798, when war with France seemed inevitable, the three ships were not yet ready for sea duty, but in April of that year, under the command of Capt. Thomas Truxtun, the 1,287-ton *Constellation* put to sea, followed in July by the *United States* and the *Constitution*. Truxtun had been designated to oversee construction of his ship when it was designated only as Frigate "E." He and the builder, David Stodder, supported by various Government officials, had made many modifications in Humphreys' plans in the interest of better clipper design. Measuring 164 feet long and 40 feet wide, the ship could accommodate a complement of about 340 officers and men.

On the *Constellation*'s "shakedown" cruise, during the undeclared naval war with France of 1798–1800, she convoyed a group of 60 merchantmen along the Atlantic coast. Sailing on to the West Indies, infested by French privateers that preyed on U.S. shipping, in 1799 she won her first victory by capturing the 44-gun French frigate *L'Insurgente,* the pride of the French Navy; and the following year damaged the 56-gun *La Vengeance* so badly that she later sank. The *Constellation*'s speed won her the nickname "The Yankee Racehorse." Captain Truxtun pioneered in instituting for his seamen and marines a comprehensive shipboard training program, including gunnery practice, and establishing shipboard procedures.

After refitting at Norfolk, in 1800 the *Constellation* put out to sea once again. Under a new commander, Capt. Alexander Murray, she served at Guadeloupe Station until 1801, by which time the United States had made peace with France. In 1802 she headed for Gibraltar and entered the renewed war against the Barbary pirates. From 1805 until 1812, while she was laid up "in ordinary" at the Washington Navy Yard, workmen rebuilt her and added a few inches to her beam. During the War of 1812, though the British blockade confined her to Chesapeake Bay, she had a part in thwarting a British invasion attempt at Craney Island, Hampton Roads. In 1815, helping in the final subjugation of the Barbary pirates in the Mediterranean, during her last ship-to-ship battle she led a group of four ships that captured the 46-gun frigate *Mashuda.*

Between then and 1841 the *Constellation* served at various foreign stations, but in 1828 was laid up in Norfolk, where in 1831 she was again repaired and rebuilt, her stern being rounded. During the period 1841–44 the *Constellation* cruised around South America to the Orient as the flagship of Commodore Lawrence Kearny, in command of the East Indian Squadron, whose mission was the protection of U.S. interests in China against British encroachment. In the course of negotiations with Chinese officials, Kearny obtained for the United States commercial privileges similar to those the officials had granted to England. The negotiations paved the way for the later Open Door Policy in China.

En route home, Kearny stopped at the Sandwich (Hawaiian) Islands to protest English attempts to take them over. He entertained King Kamehameha aboard the *Constellation* and promised U.S. support for Hawaiian independence. Britain finally refused the cession, and Kearny returned home.

From 1845 to 1853 the *Constellation,* outmoded as a fighting ship, was laid up "in ordinary" at Norfolk. During the next 2 years workmen at Norfolk's Gosport Navy Yard lengthened her by 12 feet and rebuilt her as a sloop-of-war, or corvette. After cruising for a few years in Mediterranean and Cuban waters, in 1858 she was decommissioned at Boston. The following year, recommissioned, she sailed to Africa to serve in the slave trade blockade. In 1861, unaware that the Civil War had broken out, she made the first capture of a Confederate vessel on the high seas—the slaver *Triton* out of Charleston. She remained in European waters until 1864, when the Navy returned her to the United States for blockade duty.

During the final, and comparatively uneventful, active years of the *Constellation,* she carried relief supplies to Ireland during the famine of 1880; served as a training and gunnery ship during World War I; and saw duty as a relief flagship of the Atlantic Fleet during World War II—at the behest of President Roosevelt, an avid student of the ship's history and alterations. After the war a citizen's group saved her from scrapping, and Congress authorized her return to Baltimore, her place of origin.

Present Appearance. Though decommissioned and recommissioned, rebuilt, and repaired numerous times during her long career, the *Constellation* today is an excellent example of an early U.S. ship. As much as a ship of her age can be, the *Constellation* is the warship that was launched in 1797. Perhaps 35 percent of the total hull is original, consisting of live-oak timber and pig-iron ballast. The alterations, representing a normal and orderly reworking of the basic structure to maintain the effectiveness of the ship throughout the years, do not impair her historical integrity. The U.S.S. *Constellation* Commission, which has devoted considerable effort to her restoration, has opened the ship to the public.

Boston Naval Shipyard, Massachusetts

Location. Suffolk County, at confluence of Charles and Mystic Rivers, in the Charlestown area, main entrance on Water Street, Boston.

Ownership and Administration. U.S. Government; Department of Defense.

Significance. For more than a century and a half this shipyard, one of the Nation's oldest, has built, repaired, and serviced U.S. Navy vessels. It has also pioneered in shipbuilding techniques and made many innovations that have contributed to the development of the art.

In January 1797 Congress recommended the appropriation of funds for a shipyard in Boston. Three years later the Government purchased 23 acres of land on the waterfront there at a cost of $19,350, and about 1 year later began construction. By 1811 a commandant's quarters, brick storehouse, Marine barracks, and several other structures had been completed.

The yard has been commanded by a number of naval heroes. The first three commandants—Capt. Samuel Nicholson, Capt. William Bainbridge, and Capt. Isaac Hull—also commanded with distinction the U.S.S. *Constitution,* which had been launched at Boston in September 1797, a few years before the yard was founded. Appropriately enough therefore, the reconstructed *Constitution* (a Registered National Historic Landmark, described separately in this volume) is anchored today at the yard.

Throughout the years, workers at the yard have built and outfitted hundreds of ships. In 1813, 10 years after Paul Revere and Son re-coppered the *Constitution* at the yard, they launched their first ship, the 18-gun sloop *Frolic,* and the next year the 74-gun *Independence.* The yard was particularly active during the War of 1812. About 1858 it launched the *Hartford,* which served as Adm. David G. Farragut's flagship during the Battle of Mobile Bay. Workers constructed numerous other vessels and outfitted many others for the Union during the Civil War. After the war, operations declined. During the two World Wars many ships were constructed and repaired, but since 1946 emphasis has been on conversion and repair work only.

The yard has also been responsible for major innovations in ship-building. In 1813 Captain Bainbridge built a shelter over the ways so that work could continue during inclement weather. Other U.S. ship-yards subsequently erected shelters, as did also the British. In 1855 the yard launched the *Merrimac,* the Navy's first steam propeller-driven frigate—later converted into an ironclad by the Confederacy. In 1864 the yard launched the *Monadnock,* the first ironclad monitor to travel from the Atlantic to the Pacific Ocean; and, in 1874, the *Intrepid,* the Navy's first iron-hulled torpedo boat. Another important innovation at the yard, between 1827 and 1833, was the construction of a stone drydock. In this dock, in 1833–34, the *Constitution* was repaired and re-modeled—the second man-of-war to be drydocked in the United States. Subsequently, workers enlarged and lengthened the dock, but the original section is still being used.

Boston Naval Shipyard is eligible for the Registry of National Historic Landmarks relating primarily to the development of commerce and industry.

Present Appearance. Since its inception the yard has expanded over a large area in the historic Charlestown section of Boston. Between 1811 and 1840 the U.S. Navy acquired the major part of the present yard, though parts of the harbor have since been filled in. Today, the yard covers 201 acres and includes 161 buildings, 21 miles of railroad, and numerous docks, piers, and shipways.

The present yard is an interesting mixture of old and new buildings. The oldest, a three-story brick structure that stands at the entrance to the yard, dates from 1803. Originally used as a storehouse and sail loft, it now houses an officers' club and bachelor officers' quarters. The commandant's house, dating from 1808–9 and reputedly designed by Charles Bulfinch, remains unchanged except for the later addition of a sunporch. The interiors of both buildings have been altered extensively. Other early structures of interest include Dry Dock Number 1, dating from 1833; it and the drydock at Norfolk, Va., were the first in the country. The ropewalk, built in 1836, has a headhouse three stories high and contains machinery for rope manufacturing; for more than a century the U.S. Navy made all its rope in this building. The public may visit specified areas of the base.

John Adams Birthplace, Massachusetts

Location. Norfolk County, 133 Franklin Street, Quincy.

Ownership and Administration. City of Quincy; City Historian.

Significance. This house was the original homestead of the Adams family and the birthplace of John Adams—lawyer, statesman, diplomat, and second President of the United States. Although not architecturally significant, it is historically notable as the birthplace of John Adams and the house in which he grew to manhood before embarking upon his public career. It is next door to the John Quincy Adams Birthplace. In 1720 John Adams' father, "Deacon" John Adams, bought it. Growing to manhood in the house, young John lived there until or shortly before his

The birthplace homes of John and John Quincy Adams, Quincy, Massachusetts. From an engraving, probably by Stephen A. Schouff. Courtesy, Library of Congress.

marriage, in 1764, when he and his bride moved into a neighboring house that in 1761 he had inherited from his father and where in 1767 his son John Quincy was born. In 1774 John purchased his birthplace home from his brother. His public duties kept him away most of the time. By 1783, when he and his family were in Europe, tenants had occupied both the John Adams Birthplace and the neighboring house, the John Quincy Adams Birthplace. In 1788, when John Adams returned from Europe, he settled in a third house, the "Old House," now Adams National Historic Site, in another part of Quincy, and in 1803 sold his birthplace to his son John Quincy. The John Adams Birthplace remained in possession of the Adams heirs until 1940, when they deeded it to the city of Quincy.

Present Appearance. The John Adams Birthplace is of typical New England saltbox design and has been considerably altered over the years. Probably built about 1681, it originally consisted of two lower rooms and two upper chambers and had a massive central chimney. The later lean-to, built early but at an unknown date, added two lower rooms and two small upper chambers having a large attic space between. The house is open to the public.

John Quincy Adams Birthplace, Massachusetts

Location. Norfolk County, 141 Franklin Street, Quincy.
Ownership and Administration. City of Quincy; City Historian.

Significance. This house, directly adjacent to the John Adams Birthplace, was John Adams' law office and the birthplace of his son John Quincy Adams, sixth President of the United States. In 1761 John inherited the house, the oldest part of which may date from 1663, from his father. At the time of his marriage, in 1764, he moved from the neighboring house, his birthplace, to this one, in which he could house his growing library and set up a law office. For several years he used the kitchen as a law office. In the house, on July 11, 1767, John Quincy Adams was born. After 1772 John's growing law practice made it convenient for him to live in Boston most of the time, but his wife and son remained in the house until after the War for Independence. By 1783, when the family was in Europe, tenants were occupying it. After returning to the United States in 1788, John Adams moved into the "Old House," now Adams National Historic Site, in another part of Quincy. In 1803 John Quincy purchased both birthplaces from his father, and from 1805 to 1807 occupied his birthplace house. In 1940 the Adams heirs deeded the house, along with the John Adams Birthplace, to the city of Quincy.

Present Appearance. The John Quincy Adams Birthplace is in excellent condition, though it is not architecturally significant. Like the John Adams Birthplace, it is of typical New England saltbox design, originally consisted of two upper and two lower rooms, and has been extensively altered over the years. John Adams added a lean-to at the rear of the house for a new kitchen during the time he occupied the original kitchen as a law office. The house is open to the public.

Massachusetts State House, Massachusetts

Location. Suffolk County, on Beacon Hill, at Beacon Street and the head of Park Street, Boston.

Ownership and Administration. Commonwealth of Massachusetts.

Significance. Probably the most brilliant work of the Boston architect Charles Bulfinch, later one of the architects of the Nation's Capitol, the Massachusetts State House is a superb example of Federal-period civic architecture. Its lines reflect the influence of English architects such as Gibbs, Wren, and Jones, and beyond them to the architects of ancient Rome. From the late 1790's to the present, the statehouse—considered by Oliver Wendell Holmes to be "the hub of the solar system"—has been the seat of the Massachusetts government, and it commemorates the stirring history of the Bay State.

Massachusetts State House, a fine example of Federal-style architecture, was designed by the noted architect Charles Bulfinch. Constructed in the late 18th century, it is still being used today.

In February 1795 Gov. Samuel Adams approved the resolve of the Massachusetts General Court adopting Bulfinch's design for a new statehouse. In July the Governor, assisted by Paul Revere, Grand Master of the Grand Lodge of Masons, laid the cornerstone—hauled to the site on a wagon drawn by 15 white horses representing the States of the Union. Bulfinch closely supervised all phases of construction. In 1798 the general court occupied the uncompleted building, and within the next 2 years the rest of the Massachusetts government relocated from the old statehouse to the new one. When completed, the building, of red brick in Flemish bond and having white marble lintels and keystones, measured 172 by 65 feet. In 1802 Paul Revere and Son covered the dome, 53 feet in diameter and rising 155 feet, with copper; in 1861 it was gilded and in 1874 covered with gold leaf.

Present Appearance. Major modifications to Bulfinch's design over the years include the construction of a basement and the erection of white marble wings extending to the rear on both sides of the building. During the years 1896–98 the building was fireproofed by the addition of steel beams. Despite these changes, made primarily to accommodate the growing functions of the Massachusetts government, the major part of the building reflects Bulfinch's genius. Surviving interior features designed by Bulfinch include the Doric Hall, the old Senate Chamber, the old House Chamber, and the Council Chamber. The present lantern cupola is a reproduction of the original. On display in the building are various memorial paintings and statuary, Massachusetts battle flags from the Civil War through World War II, and other exhibits. The statehouse is still used by the State government and is open to the public. In the Hall of Representatives hangs the Sacred Cod, the State emblem symbolizing a vital industry.

Springfield Armory, Massachusetts

Location. Hampden County, Armory and Federal Squares, Springfield.

Ownership and Administration. U.S. Government; Department of Defense.

Significance. This armory, founded in 1794, is the Government's oldest manufacturing arsenal. The small arms it has produced have been used in every war since that time and are known for their quality throughout the world. Even before the War for Independence, Springfield, settled by many skilled gunsmiths, blacksmiths, and other artisans, had become a firearm manufacturing center. As early as 1777, during the War for Independence, Gen. Henry Knox proposed that an armory be founded there, but the Federal Government did not act on the proposal.

In January 1787 State and Federal troops at the Federal arsenal in Springfield repulsed an attack by Daniel Shays and his followers—debt-ridden farmers suffering from the depression that followed the War for Independence—and the rebellion collapsed. Indirectly, however, it influenced the adoption of the Federal Constitution, in May 1787, by demonstrating the need for a stronger central Government.

In 1789 the newly elected President, George Washington, inspected Springfield and subsequently recommended it as the location of a national armory. Five years later Congress authorized the founding of an armory there, and the following year production began. Forty workmen turned out about 20 muskets per month. In 1795 Congress authorized a second armory, at Harpers Ferry, W. Va., which a few years later went into production. The first arm made at the Springfield Armory was the U.S. Flintlock Musket, Model 1795, an adaptation of the French Charleville Musket, Model 1763—a weapon that had been widely used by U.S. troops in the War for Independence. Since that time many other types of small arms have been developed and produced at the armory.

Present Appearance. Springfield Armory is today the U.S. Army's principal research and development center and pilot manufactory for small arms. The first permanent building at the armory, a brick structure built in 1807 and known as the West Arsenal, is on Armory Square and now houses the Officers' Club and conference halls. The Middle Arsenal, on the State Street side of the square, built in 1830, is occupied by engineering offices. The present Main Arsenal is located on the west side of the square. The Springfield Armory Museum, open to the public, contains exhibits not only telling the history of the armory, but also interpreting the growth of U.S. military power. The museum displays a prize collection of U.S. and foreign small arms. A boulder adjacent to the armory grounds on State Street marks the site of Shays' attack.

U.S.S. *Constitution,* Massachusetts

Location. Suffolk County, in Boston Naval Shipyard, Boston.

Ownership and Administration. U.S. Government; Department of Defense.

Significance. Like the *Constellation,* the reconstructed *Constitution,* or "Old Ironsides," is a stirring symbol of the early years of the U.S. Navy and the great age of fighting sail. The two ships, both extensively modified during their years of service, are the oldest surviving naval ships. The *Constitution* was the last of three frigates, whose construction had begun in 1794, to be launched, at Boston, on September 20, 1797, and the last to put to sea. Launched before her were the *United States* and the *Constellation.* The *Constitution* served with distinction through the War of 1812. She has never been decommissioned.

Constructed in Boston between 1794 and 1797, the ship was 175 feet long, had a 43½-foot beam and a displacement of 1,576 tons, and mounted 44 guns. Her timbers were of live oak, red cedar, and hard pine. Paul Revere and Son sheeted the lower hull with copper. The ship took part in the undeclared naval war with France, 1798–1800. During the years 1801–5, as the flagship of Commodore Edward Preble, she served in the War with the Barbary States. She attacked Tripoli five times, and on her deck the treaty of peace ending the war was signed.

It was in the War of 1812, however, that the *Constitution* won im-

The reconstructed U.S.S. *Constitution,* "Old Ironsides," docked in Boston Naval Shipyard. Constructed in the late 18th century, she achieved immortal fame in the War of 1812. Courtesy, Massachusetts Department of Commerce.

perishable fame. A few weeks after the war broke out in June, while en route to New York, she narrowly escaped a British squadron in a demonstration of brilliant seamanship by her commander, Capt. Isaac Hull. Later that summer, while returning from a successful raiding cruise into Canadian waters, she defeated the British frigate *Guerrière* in a hard-fought, close-range duel. This victory sent a thrill of exultation through the Nation. According to tradition, during the engagement a seaman, on seeing the enemy's shots rebounding from her sides, dubbed the ship "Old Ironsides."

In December 1812, under the command of Commodore William Bainbridge, the *Constitution* met the British frigate *Java* off the coast of Brazil. The two ships momentarily jammed together and the crew of the *Constitution* beat off a British boarding party. As the ships parted, the *Java's* mainmast crashed down and she was forced to surrender. For long periods during the remainder of the war, the increasingly vigilant British blockade kept the *Constitution* confined along the Atlantic coast, but in December 1814 she escaped to sea. In February the following year, 2 months after the Treaty of Ghent had been negotiated, she met two British warships off Spain—the *Cyane* and the *Levant,* whose combined gunpower was superior. The *Constitution,* however, used her concentrated firepower to advantage and in a few hours captured them. This was her last battle, but she had won her glory and earned her place in the Nation's history.

In 1828, when the ship was condemned as unseaworthy and on the brink of destruction, she was saved in part by Oliver Wendell Holmes' poem "Old Ironsides," which aroused public sentiment. Used as a training ship thereafter, she was rebuilt or partially rebuilt in 1833, 1871–77, and 1906.

Present Appearance. The *Constitution,* which floats today in the harbor where she was originally launched, has undergone such extensive restoration as to be in fact a reconstruction. During the course of several rebuildings, her original rotted timbers were removed. During the period 1927–30 final restoration took place. Bearing her original lines and characteristics, she presents a colorful picture of a frigate. The ship is open to the public.

Mackinac Island, Michigan

Location. Mackinac County, in Lake Huron, about 3 miles east of the southeastern tip of the Upper Peninsula of Michigan, accessible by ferry.

Ownership and Administration. State of Michigan; Mackinac Island State Park Commission.

Significance. This island, lying at the eastern edge of the Straits of Mackinac, is of outstanding significance in the history of the old Northwest and the advance of the frontier. Possessed at various times by France, Britain, and the United States, it was the center of the thriving Great Lakes fur trade and the site of key military outposts in the 17th, 18th, and 19th centuries. The Great Lakes and their related waterways were the main routes into the continent for the French, the first Europeans to penetrate them, who quickly recognized the strategic importance of control of the straits—the connecting link between Lakes Huron, Superior, and Michigan. Possession of the straits insured French hegemony of the American heartland. The Mackinac fur trade was the lifeblood of New

Agents of the American Fur Company on Mackinac Island lived in this building, constructed in 1817.

Warehouse of John J. Astor's American Fur Company, on Mackinac Island, Michigan.

France, the main livelihood of British Canada, and for a while of considerable economic importance to the United States. Mackinac Island was a rendezvous point for the French explorers and traders who probed eastward and southward from the Great Lakes and a key trading and military post for the British. In the first part of the 19th century it was a major military outpost on the U.S. frontier and the heart of John Jacob Astor's fur empire.

In 1671 Jesuit Fathers Claude Dablon and Jacques Marquette arrived at the straits and planted a mission settlement on Mackinac Island, the first in the region, replacing one founded some 3 years earlier farther west, on Lake Superior's Chequamegon Bay. The following year they moved the settlement to the site of the city of St. Ignace, on the mainland on the north side of the straits. In 1698 the French abandoned the straits for a few years but soon returned and erected Fort Michilimackinac on the southern mainland at the site of Mackinaw City. The British occupied the post in 1761, after the collapse of New France, and stayed until the end of the War for Independence. In 1781, threatened by George Rogers Clark's U.S. forces, they transferred their post to Mackinac Island, where they began construction of an elaborate fortification. This fort was not complete when, in 1796, the island passed to the United States under the terms of Jay's Treaty (1794). At the outbreak of the War of 1812 the British recaptured the straits, and they did not revert to the United States until the end of the war, by the Treaty of Ghent.

After the war the U.S. fur trade in the old Northwest centered in the straits area. Subsequent to the failure of his Astoria enterprise, in the Pacific Northwest, John Jacob Astor had focused his efforts in the Great Lakes and Mississippi Valley regions. Just before the end of the War of 1812, he organized the American Fur Co. to compete with the British and set up the company headquarters on Mackinac Island. Foreign traders were by then banned from the fur trade on U.S. soil, and the trade flourished until about 1830. By that time the fur trade had moved farther west, and the straits declined in strategic importance. In 1834 Astor sold his interests.

In the latter part of the 19th century, the island became a popular summer resort. In 1857 it became a national park. In 1895, however, the Federal Government turned it over to the State of Michigan for development as a State park. The Straits of Mackinac are eligible for the Registry of National Historic Landmarks under the themes of history treated in this volume; Fort Michilimackinac and St. Ignace Mission are eligible under other themes.

Present Appearance. Mackinac Island and nearby St. Ignace Mission and Fort Michilimackinac are unsurpassed in their preservation of the dramatic history of the old Northwest. Each site has considerable individual significance; in combination they constitute a record of virtually every aspect of white occupation of a key point on the North American Continent. Most of the island, including practically all the historical features, is State owned. The State preserves the remains of Fort Mackinac, the U.S. fort on the island, including barracks, officers' quarters, and related buildings; the reconstructed Beaumont Memorial House, a stone structure, built by the British North West Co. and used by Astor as a retail store; the Biddle House, the oldest on the island; the 1936 reconstruction of Fort Holmes, the British fort at the time of the War of 1812; and other sites. The city of Mackinac preserves surviving American Fur Co. buildings, including the Fur Warehouse (1810) and the restored Agency House (1817), whose first floor reflects the period 1817–50 and second floor the period 1871–1900.

Fort Snelling, Minnesota

Location. Hennepin County, at the junction of Minn. 55 and 100, South Minneapolis.

Ownership and Administration. Various.

Significance. This fort, constructed in the period 1819–23, was once the most northwesterly military post in the United States. Built to protect frontier settlers from Indians and to promote the fur trade, it became the northern outpost of a line of frontier forts—Leavenworth, Gibson, Towson, Smith, Atkinson, and Jesup—guarding the "permanent Indian frontier." Later, from 1861 to 1946, it also served as a training installation.

Just after the end of the War of 1812, the Army—seeking to extend U.S. control over the upper Mississippi Valley—planned a fort at the confluence of the Mississippi and Minnesota Rivers on land that Lt. Zebulon M. Pike had purchased in 1805 from the Sioux Indians. In 1819 Lt. Col. Henry Leavenworth led a detachment up the Mississippi from Prairie du Chien to build the projected fort and camped for the winter near an Indian village. The following year Col. Josiah Snelling assumed command and within 2 years essentially completed the fort. Originally called Fort St. Anthony, in 1825 it became known as Fort Snelling.

Fort Snelling guarded the vast region between the Great Lakes and the

Fort Snelling, Minnesota. Soon after the War of 1812, the U.S. Government erected a series of frontier forts just west of the Mississippi River. Fort Snelling, the northernmost, guarded a large area extending from the Great Lakes to the Missouri River. From a painting by Seth Eastman. Courtesy, Library of Congress.

Missouri River. Few expeditions departed from the fort to attack the Indians, but officials cooperated with Indian Agent Lawrence Taliaferro in preventing clashes between the Sioux and Chippewas. Troops from the fort quelled the Winnebagos in the Prairie du Chien area, and policed the Canadian border to prevent French-Canadian hunters from crossing it to hunt buffalo. In 1849 troops from Fort Snelling joined dragoons from Fort Gaines to investigate Indian disturbances in Iowa, which later resulted in the founding of Fort Dodge.

After the frontier advanced to the Great Plains, Fort Snelling's importance declined, and in 1857 the Army abandoned it. Reactivated in 1861 as a training center for Civil War troops, it aided in quelling the Sioux uprising of 1862 and from then until 1946 served as a training center. At that time the Army abandoned the fort and transferred it to the Veterans Administration, which has released large portions of the military reservation to the State but still owns most of the original fort. Throughout the years other portions of the original reservation have come under private ownership. Fort Snelling is a Registered National Historic Landmark relating primarily to Indian-military affairs in the trans-Mississippi West.

Present Appearance. Still standing are 4 of the original 16 structures; these consist of the quarters of the commanding officer, the officers' quarters, a hexagonal tower, and a round tower. Excavations by the Minnesota Historical Society in 1957–58 uncovered the foundations of several structures, including the powder magazine, schoolhouse, sutler's store, hospital, shops, cistern, and a portion of the original walls. The fort is open to the public.

Fort Osage, Missouri

Location. Jackson County, on the northern edge of the village of Sibley.

Ownership and Administration. Jackson County.

Significance. Fort Osage, founded in 1808 by William Clark as a military post and Government "factory," was one of the most successful of the 28 Indian trading posts, or factories, in operation between 1795 and 1822. The idea of winning the good will of the Indians by supplying them with goods from official trading posts originated in the colonial period; Pennsylvania and Massachusetts experimented with the idea. In 1793 Congress acted on President George Washington's recommendation that the Government establish a series of trading posts where Indians could secure goods at cost by barter. These posts were intended to strengthen military policy, promote peace on the frontier, protect the Indians against exploitation by private traders, and offset the influence of the British and Spanish over the Indians. In 1795 the system was initiated. The Government appointed a superintendent of Indian trade, who shipped goods, obtained in open market or by bids, to factors at the trading posts. The factors sold the goods to the Indians for furs, skins, or other products. These were shipped back east to the superintendent, who sold them at auction or in foreign markets. Complicated and idealistic, the system proved to be a failure. It suffered from poor administration, the extension of too much credit to the Indians, inferior trade goods and Indian products, and high freight charges. Congressional opposition to the system grew throughout the years and led in 1822 to its abolition.

Fort Osage was also of considerable military importance. It was the first U.S. Army post beyond the Mississippi and between 1808 and 1822 was the principal outpost of civilization on the Missouri River and in western Missouri. At the fort, in 1808, the U.S. Government signed a treaty with the Osage Indians in which they ceded most of their lands in present Missouri. In 1811 the Astorians stopped off at the fort on their journey to the Pacific, where they built Fort Astoria. During the War of 1812 the U.S. Army abandoned the fort; and in 1813 the factor at the fort, George Sibley, moved his trading post to the site of Arrow Rock, Mo., where he built a small fort. After the war, in 1815, both the factor and the garrison returned to Fort Osage. The garrison remained until 1819. In 1821 the fort became the terminus of a road that extended through the newly created State of Missouri from St. Charles, Mo. After 1822, when Congress abolished the factory system, the abandoned fort served as a Government storehouse until superseded in 1827 by the newly built Fort Leavenworth, in Kansas, which served both as a military post and supply depot. Fort Osage is a Registered National Historic Landmark relating primarily to the fur trade.

Present Appearance. No remains of the original Fort Osage are extant. Restorations, authorized in 1947 by the County Court of Jackson and accomplished with the technical assistance of the Native Sons of Kansas City, include five blockhouses, the main one containing original cannon and exhibits; officers' quarters; soldiers' barracks; the"factory"; black-smith's shop; well; and the Little Osage Village. A museum on the second-floor room of the factory features exhibits on the factory system and military artifacts. Fort Osage is open to the public.

Fort Atkinson, Nebraska

Location. Washington County, on a secondary road, about 1 mile east of the town of Fort Calhoun.

Ownership and Administration. Various.

Significance. This fort, which was active between 1819 and 1827, was the earliest of a line of frontier forts extending from Fort Snelling, Minn., to Fort Jesup, La., and was a center of the fur trade. In February 1819 Secretary of War John C. Calhoun ordered Col. Henry Atkinson, commanding the 6th Infantry at Plattsburgh, N.Y., to move his unit westward, up the Missouri River, to build a fortification at Council Bluffs, a site visited by Lewis and Clark. Not until fall did Atkinson and his troops, including women and children, complete the 2,628-mile trek. At the river bottom near the bluffs, they constructed Cantonment Missouri, but after a winter of disease and hardship and a disastrous summer flood, they moved to a site high on the top of the bluffs. In the fall of 1820 they finally completed a brick-and-log fort, soon known as Fort Atkinson.

Buildings at the fort included barracks, officers' houses, a sutler's house and store, an Indian council house, a hospital, powder magazine, laundresses' quarters, stables, and stockade. Near the fort were located a dairy, gristmill, limekiln, sawmill, blacksmith shop, and brickyard.

Fort Atkinson operated more as a frontier village and social center than as a fort. The soldiers, forsaking military science and drill, began farming and stockraising under the supervision of a director of agriculture and a superintendent of livestock, and by 1821 had tilled 504 acres of land. Agricultural industries included dairying, cheesemaking, meat curing, soapmaking, and milling. In their spare time the soldiers hunted and fished or played billiards or cards at the sutler's store. Fur traders brought news from St. Louis or the Indian country. Indians came to the fort to hold councils and trade at the Indian agency. In 1823 and 1825 Colonel Leavenworth and Colonel Atkinson, respectively, led expeditions from the fort against the Arikara Indians. Occasionally, exploring expeditions on their way to or returning from the west stopped by the fort. In 1827 the Army abandoned it; and, to afford better protection for the Santa Fe Trail, moved the garrison down the Missouri to build Cantonment Leavenworth.

Fort Atkinson is a Registered National Historic Landmark relating primarily to Indian-military affairs in the trans-Mississippi West.

Present Appearance. The site of Fort Atkinson lies on a plateau crowning timbered bluffs rising above the west edge of the Missouri River Valley. The only visible remains at the site are low earth mounds on the east edge, the rest of the site having been leveled and placed in cultivation. Archeological excavations by the Nebraska State Historical Society have yielded many artifacts and exposed the building foundations. The site of the post, including the cemetery, the fortified section, and outlying buildings, covers 140 acres. Of these, the fortified section and 90 percent of the sites of outlying buildings are privately owned.

City Hall, New York

Location. New York County, City Hall Park, Lower Manhattan, New York City.

Ownership and Administration. City of New York.

Significance. This hall, a living museum of New York and U.S. history and one of the most important civil buildings in the Nation, uniquely blends architectural beauty and historical significance. In front of the hall,

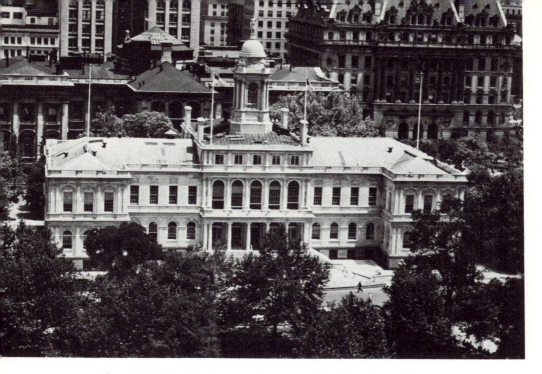

New York City Hall, today the seat of the New York City government, has many associations with New York and United States history. Courtesy, New York Convention and Visitors Bureau.

for more than a century and a half, have passed in review the country's victorious armies—from the War of 1812 to the Korean conflict; the great of this and other nations—Lafayette and Lindbergh, Garibaldi and Eisenhower, MacArthur and Glenn. In front of it have also trudged the humble and the unknown, immigrants, and westward-bound emigrants. The hall reveals much of civic administration and life in the original Capital of our Nation under the Constitution and in one of its first metropolises, trading centers, and seaports. It also memorializes many influential shapers of the U.S. political tradition.

The present hall is actually the third New York city hall; the first was the old Dutch *Stadt Huys,* 73 Pearl Street, and the second was on the site of the present Federal Hall National Memorial. On the third and present site, the old Common, had been located a Liberty Pole, erected in 1765 to celebrate the repeal of the Stamp Act and later razed by the British; the present Liberty Pole, west of the City Hall, was erected on Flag Day 1921. The architect and the city fathers chose the location because they agreed that the city would never extend much farther north and that its life would be centered between the Common and the Battery. In 1803 the cornerstone was laid, and in August 1811 the city government first occupied the building, though it was not fully completed until the following year. The architecture is essentially the work of Joseph F. Mangin, a Frenchman, but his partner and cowinner of a competition for the commission, John McComb, a Scotsman, directly supervised the construction and received most of the contemporary credit.

De Witt Clinton, who fostered the building of the Erie Canal, was the first mayor to serve in the hall. In 1824 General Lafayette and his son arrived in New York City aboard the *Cadmus*. A naval procession escorted him to Castle Garden, where he reviewed the troops, after which a horse-drawn barouche transported him to City Hall. There, officials welcomed him to the city. In 1825 the building was the scene of a celebration marking the opening of the Erie Canal. In 1858, after a fireworks display in honor of the newly laid Atlantic cable, the hall caught fire and was partially destroyed. Architects followed the design of the 1830 alteration of the cupola during the hall's rebuilding. In 1917, however, when the cupola burned again, its reconstruction was identical to the original McComb design. In 1954–56 the city completely restored the hall.

Present Appearance. City Hall, built of marble and brownstone, is a blending of Renaissance and American Colonial architectural styles. It contains the offices of the mayor and other municipal officials. In the Governor's Room, which serves as a museum, is displayed a mahogany table used by George Washington during his Presidency and armchairs used at Federal Hall by members of the first U.S. Senate. Leading figures of U.S. history having associations with New York City are honored in sculpture and paintings throughout the building. It is open to the public.

Erie Canal (Remains), New York

Location. Montgomery County, remains in and around the town of Fort Hunter, 6 miles west of Amsterdam.

Ownership and Administration. Various.

Significance. The Erie Canal, a manmade waterway extending from Buffalo, N.Y., on Lake Erie, to Albany, N.Y., on the Hudson River, and linking the Atlantic Ocean with the Great Lakes, was a significant achievement of 19th-century engineering. Uniting the East and the old Northwest, it also helped break the alliance between the South and the old Northwest that had been strengthened by the latter's use of New

Orleans as a port and helped to create a new alinement of States—an alinement represented in the Federal and Confederate States of the Civil War. Transporting barges loaded with produce eastward from the old Northwest and carrying streams of emigrants and goods westward, the canal stimulated settlement and commerce between the Great Lakes and the Ohio River, and resulted in the founding of numerous towns. Providing a convenient route for European immigrants to move west and a cheap means of sending farm produce directly to the East instead of down the Mississippi River to New Orleans, it made New York the dominant coastal city. The successful completion of the canal introduced an era of canal fever in every section of the country—a fever that abated only with the development of the railroads.

Because of De Witt Clinton's efforts, in 1808 the New York Legislature authorized a survey for a canal between the Hudson River and Lake Erie. The resultant report led the legislature in 1810 to appoint a commission to consider the project further. In 1811 it recommended the waterway as advantageous, but the War of 1812 delayed further progress. After a second commission, which met in 1816–17, reported favorably on the canal, in April 1817 the legislature authorized construction of the ambitious project—only four other short artificial waterways existing in the country at the time. The canal was to be built in three sections: a western section from Lake Erie to the Seneca River, a middle section from the Seneca River to Rome, and an eastern section from Rome to Albany. In July 1817 State officials broke ground at Rome, and by

One of the most impressive remains of the improved Erie Canal of 1841 is Schoharie Aqueduct. This aqueduct eliminated the necessity of towing canalboats across Schoharie Creek.

October 1819 barges were using the eastern section. Although by 1821 both the eastern and central sections were operating successfully, opponents of the canal fought to prevent its completion. Their major antagonist was De Witt Clinton, Governor of New York, who had originally promoted the canal and had served on both canal commissions. Because he crushed the attacks and pushed through legislation authorizing the continuation of the canal, it was dubbed "Clinton's Big Ditch" or "Clinton's Folly." In October 1825 laborers completed the western, and final, section.

The canal—40 feet wide at the top, 28 feet wide at the bottom, and 4 feet deep—stretched across 363 miles and had 88 locks. Except for about 10 miles it formed a completely artificial waterway. It cost $8 million to build, but nominal tolls paid for it within a decade. In 1881 they were finally abolished. Between 1835 and 1862 the State enlarged the canal and in 1897–98 attempted to deepen it. The New York State Barge Canal, constructed during the years 1903–18, replaced the Erie, but follows along some portions of it.

Present Appearance. Each of the Erie Canal's three eras of development—"Clinton's Big Ditch," the Improved Erie, and the New York State Barge Canal—is well illustrated by canal features in and around Fort Hunter. They are bounded on the west by Schoharie Creek and on the north by the Mohawk River. The original canal extends across the town from east to west, and in its dry bed are the only two extant locks of the first canal, both constructed in 1820. In Fort Hunter the bed of the improved canal of 1841 parallels the first channel and then intersects the original bed a short distance east of town. Near the intersection the improved canal passes through the well-preserved Empire Lock of 1841. Still farther east are the Yankee Hill Lock and the Lock Grocery building. West of town, where the improved canal crossed Schoharie Creek, is the Schoharie Aqueduct. Here, before the aqueduct was built in 1841, canal boats were towed across the creek. On the Mohawk River, just north of Fort Hunter, is modern Lock 12 of the New York State Barge Canal, a successor to the two earlier routes.

All of the canal remains are in excellent condition and within walking distance of one another. No special effort is now made to preserve the canal remains or interpret them to visitors, but State authorities and various private groups are considering preservation and restoration of the remains and the creation of a New York State Canal Museum at Fort Hunter.

Fort Stanwix, New York

Location. Oneida County, site bounded approximately by Dominick, Spring, Liberty, and North James Streets, in downtown Rome.

Ownership and Administration. Various.

Significance. Situated at a key location on the route between the Great Lakes and the Mohawk River, the log-and-earth Fort Stanwix was erected by the British in 1758, during the French and Indian War. No action occurred at the fort during that conflict, but in 1768 by the Treaty of Fort Stanwix the Iroquois ceded to the English a vast territory south and east of the Ohio River, and as far west as the mouth of the Tennessee River. By 1774 the British had dismantled and abandoned the fort.

In 1776 American troops occupied the fort. In August the following year they repulsed the western wing of a British invasion of the northern colonies from Canada and checked the possibility of a Loyalist uprising in the Mohawk Valley. Because the retreat to Canada of the western column after the failure to capture Fort Stanwix was a blow to the British strategy of concentration at Albany, it contributed to the defeat of Burgoyne at Saratoga, a few months later. In 1784 the leaders of the Iroquois, who had been seriously weakened during the War for Independence and recognized the futility of further resistance to the white advance, signed the second Treaty of Fort Stanwix. They ceded to the United States a small tract of land in western New York, and all that part of Pennsylvania north and west of the Indian boundary line designated in the first treaty. They also relinquished their claim to land west of the Ohio River—a claim, however, that other tribes disputed.

Fort Stanwix is a Registered National Historic Landmark relating primarily to the War for Independence.

Present Appearance. The cleared site of Fort Stanwix occupies approximately a city block in the heart of Rome, but no physical evidence of the post is visible. Archeological excavations, however, have indicated the exact location of the fort.

Holland Land Office, New York

Location. Genesee County, West Main Street, Batavia.

Ownership and Administration. Genesee County.

Significance. This building housed one of the U.S. offices of the Holland

Holland Land Office, Batavia, New York. In the late 18th and early 19th centuries, foreign land companies helped extend the frontier westward. One of the most successful of these was the Holland Land Company, a Dutch firm.

Land Co., an enlightened and successful land speculation enterprise of the late 18th and early 19th centuries. An example of foreign speculative effort on the early American frontier, the company contributed to the advance of the northern frontier through western New York and northern Pennsylvania toward the Great Lakes.

After the War for Independence thousands of settlers sought economic, social, or political opportunity in the West. Land speculation reached a peak. The fast turnover of lands and the quick and spectacular profits attracted not only fly-by-night speculators but also financially stable investors. European investors, having the capital lacked by many Americans, bought up much land. The Holland Land Co. was one of the largest of these.

After some preliminary reconnaissance in 1789, a group of Dutch banking houses combined to speculate in U.S. lands. In 1796 they formally organized the Holland Land Co., a stock company controlled from Holland by a director and six commissioners. The company purchased for resale to settlers millions of acres of land west of the Genesee River in New

York and in northern Pennsylvania. In 1815 Joseph Ellicott, surveyor and local agent for the company, built at Batavia the third and last land office of the company. From the office he administered the extensive Genesee holdings. After the decline of large land sales on the frontier, the company was forced to dispose of its holdings in small lots and on credit; it liquidated around 1846.

Whatever their faults and abuses, speculators fostered the opening of the West. Responsible land companies assigned land to settlers on an orderly basis, helped them to adjust to life on the frontier, and encouraged the Federal Government to provide roads and protection. Of all the companies, the Holland Land Co. was unsurpassed in its enlightened treatment of settlers.

Present Appearance. During the second half of the 19th century the land office at Batavia fell into ruins, but in 1894 the Holland Purchase Historical Society restored it and it is now in excellent condition. A small gray limestone building, it has a gabled dormered roof, many windows, and four Doric columns at the entrance. A museum commemorating the Holland Land Co. and western New York history, it is open to the public.

Plattsburgh (Cumberland) Bay, New York

Location. In Lake Champlain, between Cumberland Head and the town of Plattsburgh.

Ownership and Administration. State of New York and city of Plattsburgh.

Significance. In this bay occurred the decisive Battle of Plattsburgh (Cumberland) Bay, September 11, 1814, in which Capt. Thomas Macdonough's fleet, supported by a land force, halted a major British thrust into the United States along the invasion route of Lake Champlain and the Hudson River. The victory compelled British troops to withdraw to Canada and leave behind a vast store of supplies. Giving the United States control of Lake Champlain, it thwarted Britain's last hope of conquering the Great Lakes region or of winning a cession of U.S. territory there.

In 1813, after a successful series of raids on towns along Lake Champlain, the British commander constructed a strong war fleet along its northern shores. Meantime, Capt. Thomas Macdonough, USN, constructed additional ships for his flotilla on the lake to allow him to meet the British fleet. The British plan called for a full-scale invasion down the western shore of Lake Champlain to capture Plattsburgh by a force of more than 11,000 regulars, whose left flank would be covered by the British fleet. Defending Plattsburgh was a small force of about 1,500 troops, supported by Macdonough's newly built flotilla.

British forces mobilized late in 1814. Their troops drove advancing U.S. forces back to Plattsburgh and forced them to take a position on the south bank of the Saranac River, just south of town. The British commander intended to triumph by a joint land and sea attack. Macdonough had only 4 ships and 10 gunboats, and the British commander had 4 ships and 12 gunboats. However, Macdonough had chosen his position well—in the confined waters of the bay between the peninsula known as Cumberland Head and the mainland, where lay the town of Plattsburgh. In this area the British *Confiance,* the largest vessel on the lake, would have trouble maneuvering. On the morning of September 11, while U.S. land forces held firm, the British fleet moved in toward Macdonough's fleet, whose flagship was the *Saratoga.* For almost 2½ hours at close quarters,

Thomas Macdonough's fleet clashes with the British at Plattsburgh Bay, in Lake Champlain—a major U.S. triumph in the War of 1812. From an engraving by B. Tanner, after a painting by H. Reinagle. Courtesy, Library of Congress.

the fight continued until Macdonough triumphed. The British commander was killed, and Macdonough was twice knocked unconscious. Demoralized by the naval defeat, his flank unprotected and his supply lines endangered, the commander of the British land forces withdrew his troops to Canada, and left behind a large store of supplies.

Present Appearance. Plattsburgh (Cumberland) Bay is formed by the peninsula of Cumberland Head on the north and east and by the mainland on the west, where the town of Plattsburgh is situated. The bay's open end, facing south, is about 1½ miles wide. The beach area on Cumberland Head provides a fine view of the site of the naval battle in the bay. A good all-weather road encircles the head, at the tip of which is a dock for the ferry that links the New York and Vermont shores of Lake Champlain. The head is a residential area, although much of it is relatively undeveloped. The town of Plattsburgh has grown over and obscured the sites of the land battle. On its bayfront is the Macdonough Memorial, a 135-foot-high obelisk of Indiana limestone decorated with reliefs of symbolic naval scenes and a list of the U.S. ships that won the Battle of Plattsburgh Bay.

United States Military Academy, New York

Location. Orange County, West Point.

Ownership and Administration. U.S. Government; Department of Defense.

Significance. Since 1802 this Academy has trained the nucleus of Regular Army officers who have commanded U.S. troops throughout the world, in peace and war. Its story is woven into the panorama of national growth, from the struggle for independence to the emergence of the Nation as a world power. Its graduates include most of our distinguished military leaders of the 19th and 20th centuries. Because troops have been stationed at the Academy site continuously since January 1778, it is the oldest permanently occupied military post in the country.

Recognizing the strategic importance of West Point as the key to navigation of the Hudson River, a U.S. lifeline during the War for Independence, in January 1778 Gen. George Washington stationed a garrison there. In March, under Washington's direction, Thaddeus Kosciuszko, the Polish engineer, began constructing fortifications at the site. This work continued through the war. For 4 months in 1779 Washington made his headquarters at the Point. The following year Benedict Arnold, the commander, attempted to betray the post to the British, but fled to the enemy when the plot came to light. In 1781 a corps of veterans was assigned to instruct candidates for Army commissions, but the end of hostilities in 1783 and national fear of a standing army led to the near abandonment of the post. During the war the British never directly attacked it.

A parade at West Point. Lithographed by L. Sabatier, figures by V. Adams, from the drawing "Plain of West Point at the Moment of Exercise," by Jacques G. Milbert. Courtesy, Library of Congress.

As early as 1776 Gen. Henry Knox had proposed the founding of a school for the instruction of Army officers. Washington and Alexander Hamilton supported this proposal. When Congress, in 1783, asked Washington for his views on the organization and maintenance of the Nation's peacetime forces, the former commander in chief sought the advice of the officers who had served under him. Among these was the able drillmaster Baron von Steuben, who recommended an academy where cadets would receive a liberal education, supplemented by specialized instruction in engineering and the use of artillery. Taking note of the views of von Steuben and others, Washington recommended a small standing army and one or more military academies. The weak central Government under the Articles of Confederation could do little to carry out these recommendations and rejected the academy proposal as not worth the expense.

In 1790, to save the annual rental charge of $437, the Federal Government purchased the land at West Point from its private owner. In the early part of the administration of Washington, he and his Cabinet again considered the founding of a military academy, but Thomas Jefferson doubted its constitutionality and Congress let the matter die. As the foreign threat became more serious, though, demands increased for adequate seacoast defenses and trained artillerymen and engineers. In 1794 the Government organized an academy at West Point that offered rudimentary training in artillery practice and engineering, but it operated for only a few weeks until fire destroyed the building.

Jefferson, meanwhile, had reversed his views on an academy. When he became President, in 1801, he directed his Secretary of War to re-establish it. The following year Congress formally recognized it, construction began, and the Military Academy opened the following July 4. In the first few years proper equipment and good instructors were scarce. In 1817 Maj. Sylvanus Thayer, who for the previous 2 years had traveled in Europe to observe military schools there and who was an 1808 graduate of West Point, became superintendent. He completely reorganized the Academy and inaugurated many practices that are still followed today.

Present Appearance. The Academy grounds are open to visitors throughout the year, but many of the buildings and training areas are closed to the public. An information center is located at the South (Thayer) Gate. The West Point museum is a point of major interest. At Trophy Point is the West Point Battle Monument, around which are displayed artillery and other relics of U.S. wars. Numerous interesting memorials are located around the grounds. The Cadet Chapel, erected in 1910, is a fine example of Gothic architecture.

Watervliet Arsenal, New York

Location. Albany County, along South Broadway, Watervliet.

Ownership and Administration. U.S. Government; Department of Defense.

Significance. The history of this arsenal and its production of arms illustrates the Nation's growth from a militarily weak and struggling young country to a world power. The arsenal has supplied ammunition, cannon, and other ordnance materiel to our armed forces during all the wars in which they have participated since the War for Independence.

The outbreak of the War of 1812 stimulated the arsenal's founding. In July 1813 the Federal Government, for the sum of $2,585, purchased 12 acres of land, now in the northeast corner of the arsenal, and almost immediately began construction. The main structures were built of brick and arranged in a square. By the end of the war, in January 1815, some 70 or 80 men stationed at the arsenal had not only completed the initial construction but had also manufactured ordnance items and ammunition for use in the northern and western campaigns. In 1821 the Federal Government allowed the State of New York to channel the Erie Canal through the arsenal grounds in return for use of the canal's water to run some machines.

By 1846 the arsenal included 75 additional acres of land and many new buildings. One of the most impressive, a stone structure erected in 1826, could store more than 200,000 muskets. By 1835 the arsenal employed 90 civilian workers, in addition to 45 enlisted men. During the war with Mexico (1846–48), activity expanded; 23 forge fires burned constantly, and about 200 boys were employed to help roll paper cartridges for rifles. After the war the arsenal served as an arms storage and repair center. During the Civil War the arsenal employed about 2,000 people, about a fourth of them children, and consumed up to 10,000 pounds of lead a day. Following the war it resumed its peacetime function of storing arms.

In 1887 a Board of Ordnance Officers recommended the arsenal as the site of a cannon factory, and in 1888–89 a Gun Factory Board prepared a report on the manufacture of cannon. In the latter year construction began on a factory for their production at Watervliet, which was completed in 1891. The north wing, 400 feet long, was finished in 1890, as was also the 166-foot-long central section. The south wing was completed the following year. The production of seacoast cannon had begun in July 1889. By 1896 production began to decline, but 2 years later the Spanish-American War stimulated activities, and the annual output of cannon in 1899 was 134.

Between 1898 and 1902 the factory produced America's first 16-inch gun; it was 49 feet long, weighed 385,400 pounds, and fired a 2,370-

pound projectile about 21 miles. Prior to World War I the factory produced a number of 14-inch seacoast cannon to defend the Panama Canal and Manila Bay. In World War I production burgeoned, and in 1918 the arsenal manufactured 465 cannon. During World War II output reached an all-time peak. Since that time the arsenal has continued to develop and produce weapons and other ordnance, including the Nation's first atomic cannon.

Watervliet Arsenal is eligible for the Registry of National Historic Landmarks relating primarily to the development of commerce and industry.

Present Appearance. The arsenal is still an active U.S. Army installation. The cannon factory, whose total length is 1,300 feet, is the most impressive building. Except for a World War I addition, its exterior remains nearly unchanged from the original appearance. None of the original buildings have survived. The earliest extant buildings include the commanding officer's quarters, a large stone structure completed in 1842; a similar building erected in 1848 for additional officers' quarters; and a stone barracks, completed in 1843. Of special interest at the arsenal is the first all-metal building in the United States, built in 1859 of prefabricated plates that had been cast in New York City. It is now used as a warehouse. Certain areas of the arsenal are open to the public.

Reed Gold Mine, North Carolina

Location. Cabarrus County, on a county road, about 13 miles southeast of Concord.

Ownership and Administration. Privately owned.

Significance. A gold nugget found at this site in 1799 led to the first significant gold rush in the United States—a half century before the major Western rushes began. Miners gained valuable experience in the rush to North Carolina, Georgia, and the southern Appalachians that prepared them for the later and far more lucrative rushes in the West and supplied the national need for gold at a time of limited metal resources.

The Spaniards had vainly sought large gold deposits in the southern Appalachians, and the English colonists searched to no avail for reported Spanish and Indian mines. But not until 1799 were commercially significant deposits discovered. In 1799 Conrad Reed, 12-year-old son of John Reed, found a gold nugget while playing along the creek that ran through his father's farm. Reed at first ignored the discovery, but after finding a 28-pound nugget in 1803 he opened the Reed Mine. The first commercially successful gold mine in the United States, before 1853 the Reed Mine yielded an estimated $10 million worth of gold.

Interest in other gold discoveries spread throughout the State, and by the 1820's newspapers were publishing accounts of new ones in Cabarrus, Anson, Mecklenburg, and Montgomery Counties and in several counties of western North Carolina. Miners poured into the State, founded boom-towns, and then deserted them for richer placer fields. After a new discovery near Dahlonega, Ga., in 1829, prospectors invaded the entire Southeast.

Before 1829 all the gold mined in the United States and coined at the Philadelphia Mint came from the North Carolina mines, and until 1849 from the southern Appalachian States. In the 1830's the Federal Government created branch mints at Charlotte, N.C., and at Dahlonega, Ga., and sanctioned the private Bechtler mint, located near Rutherfordton, N.C., which minted about a third as much as the Federal mints. In the 1830's gold ranked second only to agriculture in North Carolina as a source of income, and mining continued on a broad scale until the Civil War. Total production in the State from 1799 to 1860 is estimated at about $60 million. At the height of operations in North Carolina, at least 56 mines were operating and employing 30,000 men.

The Reed Gold Mine is eligible for the Registry of National Historic Landmarks relating primarily to the development of commerce and industry.

Present Appearance. Numerous diggings of the Reed Mine are extant on the crest of a hill overlooking Meadow Creek, where the first discovery was made. Pits—which seem to have resulted from later vein mining rather than early placer mining—pockmark the hill and reveal an underlying stone strata. On the top of the hill, near a large stone chimney that may have been part of a smelting furnace, appears a deep open pit that may have a horizontal tunnel leading from it. Remnants of what seems to be a crushing machine lie near the narrow road winding up the hill. The creek today runs through a heavily overgrown bottom. The site is not open to the public.

Beginning of the U.S. Public Land Survey, Ohio-Pa.

Location. Columbiana County, Ohio, and Beaver County, Pennsylvania, on the Ohio-Pennsylvania boundary, just east of East Liverpool, Ohio.

Ownership and Administration. Privately owned.

Significance. This site commemorates the inauguration in 1785 of the rectangular land survey system, which was utilized in surveying the millions of acres of land in the States created from the public domain and is still in use. The system facilitated the opening of vast expanses of public land to settlement and thereby contributed to the advance of the frontier. Its indelible imprint on the U.S. landscape is noticeable in the rectangular fields and right-angled section-line roads in many States. As the first mathematically designed and nationally conducted cadastral survey of lands in any modern country, it has often been studied by foreign officials interested in land reform.

The use of the rectangular survey system was specified in the Ordinance of May 1785 "for ascertaining the mode of disposing of lands in the western territory." The ordinance required that all public lands be divided into townships 6 miles square, laid out east and west and north and south of right-angled base lines. Furthermore, each township was to be divided into 36 square-mile sections, which local surveyors could divide into smaller rectangles of any size.

Between June and August of 1785 boundary commissioners representing Virginia and Pennsylvania surveyed a line due north from the southwestern corner of Pennsylvania to the Ohio River, where on the north side of the river they planted a stake marking the beginning point of the survey. The ordinance specified that Thomas Hutchins, the first Geographer to the United States, supervise the running of the first east-west base line. Beginning the survey on September 30, by October 8 he had proceeded westward for almost 4 miles from the beginning point, when an Indian threat forced him to suspend operations. The following August, in 1786, he resumed the survey and extended the base line 2 additional miles. At that point, to create the boundaries of the first township, he surveyed a line south to the Ohio River. He then extended the base line. At the 6 mile markers he directed subordinates to extend lines southward to the Ohio River to create ranges. The surveyors divided these by east-west lines at 6-mile intervals from the base line to create townships. When Hutchins discontinued his direct participation in the survey in September 1786, he had surveyed 45 miles of the base line and his men had completed 4 ranges. In April 1787 Hutchins' subordinates resumed the survey. After they had completed a total of 7 ranges, in July 1788, Hutchins made his final report to the Board of Treasury. Thus ended the first phase of a survey system that is still being used today.

Present Appearance. A stone marker commemorating the survey stands along Ohio 39, about 1,112 feet north of the point where the survey began.

Fallen Timbers Battlefield, Ohio

Location. Lucas County, on U.S. 24, about 2 miles southwest of Maumee.

Ownership and Administration. State of Ohio; Ohio Historical Society.

Significance. Gen. "Mad Anthony" Wayne's victory over the Indians at this site in August 1794 and the ensuing Treaty of Greenville, or Greene Ville, the following year opened the Ohio country to settlement and brought temporary peace in the old Northwest. This victory, coupled with Jay's Treaty (November 1794), in which the British agreed to evacuate their posts in the region by 1796, won for the new Nation a secure foothold there. The refusal of the British to give sanctuary to the Indians defeated in the Battle of Fallen Timbers convinced the Indians that they could expect no decisive help in their resistance to U.S. expansion.

After the Ordinance of 1787 opened the Northwest Territory to settlement, white settlers flowed into the lands of the Shawnees, Miamis, and other tribes in the Ohio country. Conflict inevitably resulted, but the first efforts of the Federal Government to enforce earlier land cessions by the Indians ended in disaster. In 1790 the Indians defeated Gen. Josiah Harmar's expedition at the site of Fort Wayne, and the following year crushed Gov. Arthur St. Clair's force at the site of Fort Recovery. Determined to subdue the Indians and open the region north of the Ohio to settlement, in 1792 President Washington appointed Gen. "Mad Anthony" Wayne to command in the West.

Wayne, a popular hero of the War for Independence, prepared his campaign carefully. After recruiting men at Pittsburgh, in the summer of 1792 he moved to Cincinnati, where he trained them. In the fall of 1793 he moved northward about 70 miles and erected Fort Greenville as his headquarters, where he spent the winter. During that time he erected Fort Recovery, a few miles farther north, on the site of St. Clair's defeat. After an unsuccessful Indian attack on Fort Recovery in the summer of 1794, Wayne led 3,500 men northward into Indian country toward Fort Miami, at present Maumee, built by the British to protect their major base at Detroit from attack by Wayne. On August 20, 1794, after Wayne's advance guard stumbled into an Indian ambush, Wayne ordered a charge against several hundred warriors and a party of Canadian militiamen, who had taken cover in a swath of tangled woods felled by a tornado years earlier. Wayne's adversaries broke from cover and fled to Fort Miami. The British commander at the fort shut out the disillusioned warriors, who dispersed to their villages—villages doomed for destruction by Wayne's men.

Wayne's next step was to build Fort Wayne, in present Indiana, after which, in November 1794, he returned to Fort Greenville. The following June he summoned the demoralized leaders of the defeated tribes to the fort. Cowed by their defeat at the hands of Wayne and rejected by the British, in the Treaty of Greenville they ceded to the United States lands consisting mainly of about three-quarters of the present State of Ohio and the southeastern corner of Indiana.

Present Appearance. Fallen Timbers State Memorial is a 9-acre tract of high ground overlooking the valley of the Maumee River. Within the memorial area, situated on a portion of the battleground, is a monument to Wayne and his victorious army. The surrounding land is farmland. The memorial was a project of the Anthony Wayne Parkway Board, created by the State of Ohio to develop parkways and mark historic sites along the routes of Wayne, Harmar, and St. Clair.

S-Bridge, National Road, Ohio

Location. Guernsey County, just off U.S. 40, about 5 miles west of Old Washington.

Ownership and Administration. Guernsey County.

Significance. This unique bridge, erected in 1828, is a tangible reminder of the National, or Cumberland, Road. The road facilitated the settlement and economic growth of the old Northwest, particularly Ohio. As settlers moved into the interior of Ohio, the road became crowded with traffic. The construction of the road and its background are described under Casselman Bridge, National Road, Md., in this volume.

Work over the low rolling hills of Ohio, between 1825 and 1837, met fewer difficulties than in mountainous West Virginia, Pennsylvania, and Maryland; 1 mile of road in Ohio cost $3,400, in contrast to $9,745 per mile between Cumberland, Md., and Uniontown, Pa. In the 1830's the Federal Government turned the Ohio section of the road over to the State. It immediately set up tollhouses, which between 1831 and 1877 collected

S-Bridge, Ohio, one of four such bridges in the State, represents a unique type of bridge construction used along the National Road.

more than $1 million. S-Bridge, Ohio, is a Registered National Historic Landmark relating primarily to travel and communication.

Present Appearance. The bridge, one of only four of its kind surviving in Ohio, is in excellent condition. The abutments and arch are apparently original. Not used today for vehicular traffic, the bridge is maintained by Guernsey County and is situated in the center of a small roadside park. A marker explains the bridge's construction.

Fort Gibson, Oklahoma

Location. Muskogee County, on the northern edge of the town of Fort Gibson.

Ownership and Administration. State of Oklahoma; Planning and Resources Board through the Division of State Parks.

Significance. One of a line of frontier forts founded early in the 19th century to control the Indians and maintain peace in the Mississippi Valley, this fort was a highly important one. Unlike the other frontier forts—such as Snelling, Leavenworth, Towson, Atkinson, and Jesup—it was located in the Indian Territory and was more directly involved in Indian affairs, particularly the relocation of the Southeast tribes to Indian Territory. It was also a trade and social center and served as a base for several Plains expeditions.

Stockade, sally port, officers' quarters, and southeast bastion, at Fort Gibson, Oklahoma. Erected in 1824, this fort in the heart of Indian Territory protected the relocated Southeastern tribes from the Plains Indians and tried to maintain peace. Until 1889 it remained a major frontier post.

Col. Matthew Arbuckle established the fort in 1824 on the Grand (Verdigris) River near its confluence with the Arkansas River. Its original mission was to prevent Osage attacks on the Cherokees, who were already filtering into Indian Territory. During the period of Indian Removal (1825–40), troops from the fort helped receive and care for the immigrant Cherokees, Creeks, and Seminoles; tried to enforce peace among them; and attempted to protect them from the Plains Indians. For a time the fort housed the Cherokee Agency.

Troops from Fort Gibson provided escorts for surveyors marking the boundaries of Indian lands; founded subposts such as Forts Coffee, Wayne, Holmes, Arbuckle, and Washita to police other parts of Indian Territory; laid out a network of roads; served on patrols to prevent the flow of liquor into Indian Territory; and on occasion furnished escorts for the Santa Fe Trail. Peace commissions met at the fort to conclude treaties with both native and immigrant tribes. Scores of West Point graduates gained their first military experience there, where newly activated units such as the Rangers and the Dragoon Regiment were also tested.

The fort was also the base of operations for three important Plains expeditions that sought to persuade the untamed tribes to conclude peace treaties with the United States. Two of these, in 1832 and 1833, failed; the third, the Dragoon Expedition of 1834, met with the Kiowas, Comanches, and Wichitas. The latter resulted in a treaty, in 1835, in which the Plains tribes promised not to molest travelers on the Santa Fe Trail and to quit warring on the immigrant tribes.

Because of its location near the confluence of the Arkansas and the Grand Rivers, Fort Gibson became a center of trade for keelboats and later river steamers, which sailed up the Arkansas and unloaded at the fort, the traders obtaining return cargoes from Indians. It was also a way station for emigrants, freighters, and traders traveling along the Texas Road.

Originally a four-company post, in 1831 Fort Gibson was expanded to accommodate a regiment, and it became the headquarters of the 7th Infantry. The post consisted of a group of closely packed log buildings surrounded by a log palisade. Blockhouses guarded two of the four corners and commanded all four sides. Log quarters and barracks, the sutler's store, two hospitals, and other structures stood outside the stockade. In 1846 construction began on a stone fort near the log one, but by 1857, when only one building had been completed, the Army moved out of the fort. During the Civil War, Union forces reoccupied it, and Regular troops garrisoned it from 1866 to 1889, when it was finally abandoned. During the latter period, troops completed the new post, which consisted of 7 stone buildings and 10 frame ones.

Fort Gibson is a Registered National Historic Landmark relating primarily to Indian-military affairs in the trans-Mississippi West.

Present Appearance. The original fort fell into ruins, but in 1936 the State of Oklahoma reconstructed the log stockade and a number of outlying buildings almost on the original site. Except for the use of more durable material, the reconstruction is faithful to the original. Interpretive markers on the 55-acre site tell much of the history of the fort. On the ridge overlooking the reconstructed stockade is the site of the second fort of which several stone buildings and ruins are still standing. Much of that site is privately owned. A two-story stone barracks, owned by the State Historical Society, is the most imposing survival. The reconstructed original fort is open to the public.

Forks of the Ohio, Pennsylvania

Location. Allegheny County, "The Golden Triangle," Point State Park, Pittsburgh.

Ownership and Administration. Commonwealth of Pennsylvania; Department of Forests and Waters.

Significance. From about 1750 until 1815 the Forks of the Ohio, where the Monongahela and Allegheny Rivers join to form the Ohio River at Pittsburgh, was a strategic key to the Ohio Valley and the vast territory drained by the upper Mississippi River. Men of three nations fought and died struggling for control of this strategic location, where the bustling city of Pittsburgh—one of the first permanent settlements by the English west of the Allegheny Mountains—arose in the shelter of a series of fortifications. Later the forks became a major gateway to the West for waves of settlers pushing into the Ohio and Mississippi Valleys.

The growing French influence in the Ohio Valley region during the 1750's was incompatible with the westward thrust of Britain's seaboard colonies. In 1753 Maj. George Washington visited the forks, while en route to the French-held Fort Le Boeuf to warn the French away from the Ohio country. Washington endorsed the forks as a strategic position, and in 1754 the English began to construct a fort there. The French seized it that same year, however, completed it, and named it Fort Duquesne. The new fort was the keystone of a defensive line of forts the French founded in western Pennsylvania to block the spread of Anglo-American settlement into the Ohio Valley. The resulting tensions between the two nations led to a 9-year conflict known as the French and Indian War (1754–63) in America and abroad as the Seven Years' War (1756–63). In 1754 the French defeated Washington, who failed in his attempt to recapture the Duquesne area, at Fort Necessity. The following year Fort Duquesne was the objective of the ill-fated force under British Gen. Edward Braddock that suffered a disastrous defeat a few miles east of the forks. Thus for 3 years Fort Duquesne continued to serve as a French base for raids against the English frontier.

In 1758 Gen. John Forbes made a remarkable march with a force of British regulars and colonials through the rugged Pennsylvania wilderness, only to find that the French, weakened by the desertion of their Indian allies, had abandoned and destroyed Fort Duquesne. Its loss, a decisive blow to the French, gave American colonists a convenient entry into the great basin beyond the Alleghenies. The next year the English began to construct a major permanent fortification on higher ground a few hundred yards away from the site of Fort Duquesne; they named it Fort Pitt in honor of the Prime Minister of England. The exterior walls of the pentagonal fort were earthen ramparts faced with brick. Frame and brick buildings were constructed inside, parallel to the interior walls. A town that subsequently became Pittsburgh began to take shape alongside the fort as settlers, mostly Virginians, followed Braddock's trail to take advantage of whatever opportunities might be available at the forks.

Fort Pitt, though besieged, was one of the few English forts to withstand attack during Pontiac's uprising, in 1763–64. A relief column under Col. Henry Bouquet lifted the siege 4 days after decisively defeating the Indians in the Battle of Bushy Run. As an outer work to Fort Pitt, Bouquet built a small brick blockhouse. Fort Pitt served as a base for operations against the British Northwest during the War for Independence. The post then deteriorated, although traces could be seen for many years.

After the war the forks became the center of a rapidly growing frontier settlement, which in 1800 had a population of more than 1,500. By flatboat and wagon thousands of emigrants passed through Pittsburgh en route to the old Northwest, and the town became a commercial and industrial center. With the coming of the steamboat, Pittsburgh became a major port for the traffic that plied the Ohio, the Mississippi, and the Missouri; in this way it served the Western frontier from the Great Lakes to the gulf, from the Alleghenies to the Mississippi, and the Plains beyond.

In the winter of 1791–92, when war with the Indians in the old Northwest flamed anew, the United States built a fifth and last fort, Lafayette or Fayette, at the forks. Located a quarter of a mile above the site of Fort Pitt, which had fallen into ruin, the fort supplied troops in the Whisky Rebellion of 1794 and served as a supply and training depot in the War of 1812.

The Forks of the Ohio is a Registered National Historic Landmark relating primarily to the development of the English colonies.

Present Appearance. A few years ago the point of land at the forks lay beneath a clutter of commercial structures and railroad tracks. However, development of the 36-acre Point State Park, in the shadow of modern Pittsburgh's skyscrapers on the city's "Golden Triangle," has removed the most objectionable modern intrusions and will provide an eloquent historical interpretation. Archeological investigation has provided much useful information about Fort Pitt, whose flag bastion has been restored. Careful plans have been laid for rebuilding the Monongahela Bastion, including a museum under the administration of the Pennsylvania Historical and Museum Commission. The original Bouquet Blockhouse, preserved for years by the Allegheny County Chapter of the Daughters of the American Revolution, will remain at its original site. Attractive promenades have been laid out along the shores of both rivers, and stone bleachers seating 3,000 persons have been placed along the Allegheny River. In summer the city of Pittsburgh anchors a barge in the park, and free concerts and other programs are presented.

Friendship Hill, Pennsylvania

Location. Fayette County, on Pa. 166, about 1 mile south of New Geneva.

Ownership and Administration. Privately owned.

Significance. This mansion was the home of Albert Gallatin—distinguished Secretary of the Treasury, statesman, and diplomat—whose statue today stands in front of the Treasury Department building in Washington, D.C. Born and raised in Geneva, Switzerland, and member of a very prominent family, Gallatin, at the age of 18, emigrated to the

Friendship Hill, Pennsylvania. Albert Gallatin, statesman and Secretary of the Treasury, purchased this mansion in 1788 and lived in it for many years. Courtesy, U.S. Bureau of Outdoor Recreation.

United States, where he sought to fulfill his idealistic dream of a democratic society unblighted by monarchy. After landing in Massachusetts, in 1780, he engaged in trading in Maine; taught French at Harvard; and in 1784 opened a store on the Pennsylvania frontier, where he lost most of his money in highly speculative and unprofitable land purchases.

In 1788 Gallatin purchased Friendship Hill, entered politics, and served at the Harrisburg convention called to consider sending a resolution to Congress requesting revisions in the U.S. Constitution, which Pennsylvania had already ratified. At a subsequent convention, held in 1789–90 to revise the Pennsylvania constitution, Gallatin supported measures to enhance the power of the people and limit that of the executive. While serving in the Pennsylvania Legislature, in 1790–92, he fought for better public education, prison reform, abolition of slavery, and improved fiscal management. Elected to the U.S. Senate in 1793, he was ousted by the Federalists, who claimed he had not been a citizen long enough to serve. Returning to Pennsylvania, in the throes of the Whisky Rebellion (1794), he played a big part in subduing it and preventing civil war. During the years 1794–1800, as a Member of the U.S. House of Representatives, he initiated various fiscal reforms, many of which are still in effect today. His interest in the control of national finances resulted in the creation of the House Ways and Means Committee.

From 1801 until 1814 Gallatin served with distinction as Secretary of the Treasury under Jefferson and Madison, during which time he vigorously applied his fiscal theories to advance his social ideas. He hoped to abolish the national debt, and an amazing increase in trade during the years 1802–7 enabled him to decrease it by millions of dollars, even after various internal taxes had been abolished. In 1808 he initiated a $20 million Federal road and canal building program, which never came to fruition.

When the War of 1812 cut heavily into the budget, Gallatin realized the impracticability of eliminating the national debt and in 1813 began a new career as diplomat. In that year President Madison appointed him to a commission treating Anglo-American conflict. The commission was to have met in St. Petersburg, but Britain refused to attend. Subsequently, as Minister to France and to Great Britain, Gallatin showed exceptional ability as a diplomat, especially in helping to negotiate the Treaty of Ghent. After returning to the United States in 1823 and selling Friendship Hill, he retired from public service, except for occasional diplomatic missions. Settling in New York City, he attempted to create a city university, founded the American Ethnological Society, and from 1844 until his death served as president of the New-York Historical Society. He died in 1849, at the age of 88, still actively interested in national affairs.

Present Appearance. Friendship Hill consists of three sections: The original brick structure of unknown date that stood when Gallatin purchased the estate in 1788; a stone section that he added in 1823–24; and another section added at an unknown date after Gallatin sold the house. Friendship Hill is open to the public.

Fort Hill, South Carolina

Location. Pickens County, on the campus of Clemson University, Clemson.

Ownership and Administration. State of South Carolina; John C. Calhoun Chapter, United Daughters of the Confederacy.

Significance. This estate was the home of the South Carolina statesman John C. Calhoun, prominent advocate of States rights, during the last 25 years of his life. When he acquired it, in 1825, he was at the height of his career, as Vice President. He had gained national recognition as a "War Hawk" Representative in the 12th Congress and as Secretary of War (1817–25) under James Monroe. Though his political career kept him away much of the time, Calhoun always returned to Fort Hill whenever he could.

Fort Hill, South Carolina, on the grounds of Clemson University, was once the home of John C. Calhoun, distinguished statesman.

During the congressional recess of 1828, after Congress had passed what seemed an excessively high tariff, Vice President Calhoun returned home to write his "South Carolina Exposition and Protest," which expounded the previously formulated doctrine of nullification—according to which a State could suspend, within its jurisdiction, a Federal law—as the answer to tariff reform. Declines in the price of cotton and in exports had created an economic depression in South Carolina, which would be worsened by the new tariff. Four years later, when nullifiers in South Carolina—dissatisfied with Congress' revision of the 1828 tariff—won control of the State legislature and called a State convention, Calhoun returned home to guide the proceedings. The convention enacted the Ordinance of Nullification and declared the Tariff of 1828 and its subsequent revision null and void. Calhoun then resigned the Vice-Presidency, under Jackson, to enter the Senate and support his doctrine. He served there between 1832 and 1843. After 1833, when Congress passed a new compromise tariff, Calhoun turned to a defense of slavery and Southern rights; he was an antagonist of the abolitionists. In 1844–45 Calhoun served as Secretary of State under President Tyler and in the latter year was reelected to the Senate, where he took part in the Oregon and Texas controversies and served until 1850, when he died in Washington.

Fort Hill, built in 1803 and originally called Clergy Hall, passed from Calhoun to Thomas G. Clemson, his son-in-law. Calhoun had enlarged and furnished the small house, and Clemson added some furnishings but did not alter the structure. Upon his death, in 1888, Clemson deeded the house and grounds to the State of South Carolina, which founded there the school that became Clemson Agricultural College and then Clemson University.

Present Appearance. The 2½-story, 14-room framehouse, which is open to the public, is completely furnished with items belonging to the Calhoun and Clemson families. Most of the outbuildings have disappeared except for Calhoun's private office and the reconstructed kitchen. Included in one room of the house is a small museum, which contains Calhoun and Clemson articles. The house and gardens are well maintained.

Blount Mansion, Tennessee

Location. Knox County, 200 West Hill Avenue, Knoxville.
Ownership and Administration. Blount Mansion Association.

Significance. This mansion, built in 1792, was the residence of William Blount, Governor of the Southwest Territory and outstanding political figure in North Carolina, Tennessee, and the U.S. Congress. Born in 1749 and raised in North Carolina, he served his native State as a soldier in the War for Independence and later in the State legislature. In 1782–83 and again in 1786–87 he represented North Carolina in the U.S. Congress, and in 1787 took part in the Constitutional Convention. After signing the Constitution, he returned to North Carolina and in 1789 voted for its ratification.

In 1789 North Carolina ceded the Western lands that now comprise the State of Tennessee to the Federal Government, from which in 1790 Congress organized the Territory of the United States South of the River Ohio, commonly known as the Southwest Territory. President Washington appointed Blount Governor of the newly created Territory and Superintendent of Indian Affairs for the Southern Department. When Blount assumed his duties, which he carried out with tact and firmness, he acted as conciliator between the settler, who advocated preventive war against the Indians, and the Federal Government, which opposed such action. On July 2, 1791, he signed the Treaty of the Holston with 41 Cherokee chiefs, by which they ceded a large portion of their lands in present Tennessee. He then chose White's Fort, which he rechristened Knoxville in honor of Maj. Gen. Henry Knox, Secretary of War in Washington's Cabinet, as the capital of the Territory.

There Blount built a two-story framehouse, the first of its kind west of the Allegheny Mountains, which became known as "Governor's Mansion," in which he resided until he died. Building such a house in a remote wilderness was an amazing feat because materials could not be transported across the mountains. The bricks used in the foundations and chimneys were made at a nearby creek and fired on the site, and heavy timbers were probably sawed at a small mill on the creek.

Blount was the foremost figure in winning statehood for Tennessee. He also supported the founding of Blount College, now the University of Tennessee. In 1796 the first legislature of the State elected Blount to the U.S. Senate, but, after he became involved in an intrigue to deliver Spanish Florida and Louisiana to the British, Congress impeached him. The charges were later dismissed. Blount returned to Tennessee, where in 1798 he was elected to the State senate, in which he served as speaker until his death, in 1800.

Present Appearance. The two-story frame mansion is basically Early American. It has no central chimney, stoop, or vestibule, but has large

In 1792, at the time of the construction of this small framehouse on the Tennessee frontier, it was virtually a mansion. William Blount, Governor of the Southwest Territory, erected it and resided there until he died, in 1800. Courtesy, Blount Mansion Association.

Drawing room, Blount Mansion, Tennessee. The rooms in the house have been restored in the late 18th-century style. Courtesy, Blount Mansion Association.

chimneys at the gable ends of the house. Its straight lines are relieved by one-story side wings. The kitchen ell, now rebuilt on its original foundations, is in back of the house, as is the restored office of the Governor. The house and office have been restored as they were in the late 1700's and include furniture of the period and portraits of prominent leaders of the time. The mansion is open to the public.

The Hermitage, Tennessee

Location. Davidson County, on U.S. 70N, about 12 miles east of Nashville.

Ownership and Administration. Ladies' Hermitage Association.

Significance. For more than 40 years, during which Andrew Jackson rose from a frontier militia commander to the Presidency, he made this estate his home. Leading militia forces against the Creek Indians, he defeated them at the Battle of Horseshoe Bend; commanded the army that overwhelmed the British forces at the Battle of New Orleans, the final action in the War of 1812; and, campaigning as a military hero, won the Presidency of the United States.

In 1804 Jackson purchased 1,200 acres of land in central Tennessee, and planted groves of peach and apple trees. He and his wife, Rachel, moved into a two-story log cabin already on the property, which he called The Hermitage. Jackson added a lean-to back of the cabin and to the rear erected a group of log structures, including slave cabins, storerooms, and a smokehouse. The following year he entertained Aaron Burr and undertook and carried out a contract to build flatboats for him. Jackson then settled down to the life of a plantation farmer.

During the Creek uprising of 1813 Jackson commanded the Tennessee Militia and attained the rank of major general. His success at the Battle of Horseshoe Bend (1814) earned him a major general's commission in the U.S. Army, and his victory over the British in 1815 at the Battle of New Orleans, the final action in the War of 1812, made him a national hero. He returned to The Hermitage, where he remained until 1817, when he again left to conduct a 2-year campaign against the Seminole Indians and Spanish forces in Florida. This resulted in the Spanish cession of Florida to the United States and in 1821 to Jackson's appointment as provisional Governor of Florida Territory. After a short tour of duty, however, Jackson resigned and returned to The Hermitage.

In 1818–19, prior to his appointment as provisional Governor of

In 1818–19 Gen. Andrew Jackson, later seventh President, built this brick mansion on his estate, The Hermitage. The mansion and grounds, including the gravesite of Jackson and his wife, are now a historical shrine.

Florida Territory, Jackson had erected at The Hermitage a brick house to replace the log structure he had lived in for 15 years. The new structure had four rooms on the ground floor, each having a fireplace and chimney, and large central hallways opened in warm weather from front to back to form a breezeway. In this house Jackson entertained President Monroe, Lafayette, and other prominent guests.

Elected President in 1828, Jackson left behind at The Hermitage the grave of his beloved wife, who had died a few days earlier. Jackson's two terms were marked by his aggressiveness and strong force of character.

During his first term he enlarged his home at The Hermitage and added wings on both sides. In 1834 fire destroyed much of the interior of the house, but Jackson rebuilt and refurnished it, and it was ready for re-occupancy in May 1835. At the end of his second term, in 1837, Jackson retired to The Hermitage, where he lived out his days as an elder states-man, entertaining the great and near-great. In 1845 he died and was laid to rest beside his wife.

Present Appearance. The Hermitage is open to the public. The house and grounds are in excellent condition, and the mansion is fur-nished with a wealth of Jackson's possessions. Most of the original out-buildings remain, and on the grounds are a small museum and log lodge, used by the Ladies' Hermitage Association, as well as the tomb of President and Mrs. Jackson.

Fort Monroe, Virginia

Location. On U.S. 258, east of 60 and 64, at Old Point Comfort, on the eastern outskirts of Hampton.

Ownership and Administration. U.S. Government; Department of Defense.

Significance. This fort, typical of those that the Government con-structed after the War of 1812 to remedy deficiencies in coastal defenses that the war had revealed, is located on the site of some of the earliest fortifications built by the English in North America and has been almost continuously occupied for more than 350 years.

At the site, in 1609, the Jamestown settlers built Algernourne Fort, a wooden structure, against possible attack by the Spanish. During the period 1630–32 Col. Samuel Mathews reconstructed it and renamed it Point Comfort. It was again reconstructed, this time of brick, during the years 1728–30 and called Fort George, but in 1749 heavy winds destroyed it. During the Siege of Yorktown Count de Grasse strengthened his defenses by placing batteries on the point. The present fort, constructed between 1819 and 1836, was completely surrounded by a water-filled moat and a 40-gun water battery, which stood between the outer banks of the moat and the shore of Chesapeake Bay. It figured prominently in the Civil War, relating primarily to which it is a Registered National Historic Landmark.

Present Appearance. The original brick fort of 40 acres is located in the center of the present, more elaborate post, which occupies about

640 acres and is today headquarters of the Continental Army Command. The old fort is little changed from its 19th century appearance. Three of its casemates have been converted into a museum commemorating Civil War events. The fort is open to the public.

Gunston Hall, Virginia

Location. Fairfax County, on Va. 242, near Woodbridge, about 15 miles south of Alexandria.

Ownership and Administration. Commonwealth of Virginia; National Society of Colonial Dames of America.

Significance. This house, overlooking the Potomac River a few miles south of Mount Vernon, memorializes the life of George Mason (1725–92), patriot and political theorist. He is noted for the various political and constitutional papers that he wrote during and just after the War for Independence. These include the "Fairfax Resolves" of 1774, which asserted the rights of the colonists in their relations with England; the "Virginia Declaration of Rights," in 1776, which influenced the Declaration of Independence and the Federal Bill of Rights; and the "Objections to the Proposed Constitution," in 1788, which expounded the bases of

Gunston Hall, an unpretentious red brick house overlooking the Potomac River, was the home of George Mason, brilliant Virginia statesman and political theorist. The five dormers and the elaborate porches are of particular interest. Courtesy, Charles Baptie, Photographer.

The interior of Gunston Hall, Virginia, is richly ornamented. Of special interest is the intricate woodcarving. Courtesy, Charles Baptie, Photographer.

his opposition to the adoption of the Federal Constitution. Almost as important as his writings was his influence upon younger colleagues, many of whom became leaders in Virginia and national politics.

Mason built Gunston Hall, based on his own design, during the years 1755–58. He employed William Buckland, a skilled craftsman from Oxfordshire, England, to do the interior woodcarving. Buckland also designed and constructed the two porches. The Mason family owned the house until 1867. From then until 1932, when the Commonwealth of Virginia acquired it, it was in the hands of various private owners, one of whom restored it, in 1912.

Present Appearance. The house itself is unpretentious, but it has elaborate porches projecting from both the land and river sides. It is constructed of red brick, laid in Flemish bond. Stone quoins square the corners, and five dormers penetrate the steep roof. The interior of the house is surprisingly spacious and notably well ornamented. The central hall is broken at the stairway by an unusual pair of parabolic arches. In the Palladian drawing room and the Chinese Chippendale room are a variety of intricately carved wood and brocade-covered walls. The house is furnished with period pieces, though few of them belonged to Mason. The grounds feature a boxwood allée, 12 feet high and 250 feet long, surrounded by the restored formal gardens. The house and grounds are open to the public.

John Marshall House, Virginia

Location. Ninth and Marshall Streets, Richmond.

Ownership and Administration. City of Richmond; Association for the Preservation of Virginia Antiquities.

Significance. John Marshall—statesman, diplomat, and probably the most influential Chief Justice of the Supreme Court in history—built this house in 1790, when he was emerging as a leader of the Federalist Party in Virginia, and lived in it intermittently for the next 45 years.

Born in a log cabin and raised on the Virginia frontier, Marshall received an informal education from his father, a member of the Virginia House of Burgesses. When the War for Independence broke out, young

John Marshall built this home in Richmond in 1790, at the beginning of his distinguished career—a career climaxed by 34 years of service as Chief Justice of the Supreme Court. He lived in it until his death, in 1835.

Marshall became a lieutenant in the Virginia Militia. Except for one summer while he attended law lectures at the College of William and Mary, for 6 years he lived the life of a soldier. After the war he set up a law practice in Richmond and soon entered State politics; he was a member of the legislature and participated in the convention that ratified the Constitution. He gained national attention as a result of his diplomatic mission to France in 1797 during the XYZ affair. After returning from France, he ran for Congress and won a seat in the House of Representatives. During his term he became a close friend of John Adams, who, in 1800, appointed him Secretary of State.

Marshall was Chief Justice of the Supreme Court between 1801 and 1835. During that time he greatly strengthened the judiciary branch of the Federal Government and handed down many decisions of long-lasting national significance—based on a broad interpretation of the Constitution and a belief in the supremacy of National over State power. Because the new Jefferson administration viewed the Supreme Court as a stronghold of the defeated Federalists, primarily because Marshall molded the court in his own image, Jefferson frequently clashed with Marshall—especially when the latter acquitted Aaron Burr of treason. Marshall undoubtedly drafted many of his decisions at his home in Richmond, where he also played host to leaders in all branches of U.S. life.

Present Appearance. The house is a square brick building that originally consisted of six rooms and a basement. In 1810 Marshall added a downstairs bedroom at the rear of the house. Exterior ornamentation is simple: A pedimented gable, modillioned cornice, and two small porches. The house is furnished with period items, and a small museum upstairs contains Marshall items, including one of his judicial robes. No original outbuildings have survived. The house, which in 1909 the city of Richmond purchased from the Marshall family, is open to the public.

Monticello, Virginia

Location. Albemarle County, just off Va. 53, about 2 miles southeast of Charlottesville.

Ownership and Administration. Thomas Jefferson Memorial Foundation.

Significance. "Monticello," Italian for "Little Mountain," is an enduring tribute to the genius and versatility of Thomas Jefferson. He spent many years of his long life and is buried there, and his spirit lives on in the architectural perfection of the house and the multitude of ingenious devices with which he equipped it. A splendid specimen of a colonial mansion, classically designed by Jefferson himself, it sits amid pleasant gardens and lawns on a hilltop overlooking Charlottesville; the University of Virginia, which he founded and some of whose buildings he designed; and the green rolling hills of the surrounding countryside, through which he traveled so often on trips of state. Especially after his retirement from public life until his death, at the age of 83, on July 4, 1826, the great men of his age made pilgrimages to Monticello. To this day it is visited by the humble, as well as the great—all who admire Jefferson's character and accomplishments.

In 1757 Jefferson acquired title to the property from his father. Eleven years later he began leveling the hilltop. To make all parts of the hill accessible, he constructed paths, or roundabouts, as he called them, on its slopes at four different levels; the remains of these are visible today. Because of numerous changes and alterations in the plans, all construction was not completed until 1809.

Before Jefferson built Monticello, every plantation had a series of small outbuildings such as the laundry, smokehouse, dairy, stable, weaving-house, schoolhouse, and kitchen. Jefferson sought to render these as inconspicuous as possible by locating them beneath the long terraces terminating in the two balanced out chambers. Connecting these terraces is the all-weather passageway in which are strategically placed the wine room, wareroom, beer cellar, cider room, and rum cellar. Beneath the south terrace are the kitchen, the cook's room, servants' rooms, room for smoking meat, and the dairy. The small pavilion on the end of this terrace is on the site of the first dwelling to be erected—"Honeymoon Cottage," where Jefferson brought his bride, the former Martha Wayles Skelton, in January 1772. The north terrace houses the stables, the carriage house, icehouse, and laundry. Jefferson used the building terminating the north terrace, adjacent to which is the paddock, as an office.

Present Appearance. In 1923 the Thomas Jefferson Memorial Foundation purchased the estate, now consisting of 700 acres, from the Levy family, which had owned it for more than 75 years. The foundation has restored and preserved the house and grounds, which are open to the public. The 3-story mansion consists of 35 rooms, including 12 in the basement, or fourth level. The dominating feature is the central dome, which covers an octagonal room. The spacious 2-wing mansion is fur-

Thomas Jefferson's colonial mansion, Monticello, which he himself designed, reveals the essence of his genius and versatility. The mansion and grounds, in a setting of serene beauty, overlook Charlottesville, Virginia.

nished largely with Jefferson belongings, including such ingenious devices as a 7-day calendar-clock, a folding desk, a dumbwaiter, and a folding quartet music stand. One room contains the first parquet floor in the United States. The second and third stories, accessible only by narrow staircases, are not shown to the public. A small museum in the basement contains a number of personal effects of the Jefferson family. Both house and grounds are well maintained. Jefferson is buried not far from the house in the family graveyard, which he laid out on the hilltop adjacent to the road leading from the house.

Montpelier, Virginia

Location. Orange County, on Va. 20, about 4 miles west of Orange.

Ownership and Administration. Privately owned.

Significance. James Madison, President and statesman, owned Montpelier (Montpellier) for 76 years. He was born in King George County in 1751. In 1760 his father moved to Orange County to settle on a tract of land that had been in the family since 1723. There his father built the central portion of the present house. Madison lived at Montpelier all his life except for periods of public service—notably as a Member of the Continental Congress, 1780–83; as a delegate to the Constitutional Convention, 1787, in which he helped draft the Constitution; as a Member of Congress, 1789–97; as Jefferson's Secretary of State, 1801–9; and as fourth President, 1809–17.

During Madison's first term as President, he retained William Thornton and Benjamin H. Latrobe to remodel the house. They added single one-story wings to both sides and changed the exterior walls from brick to Virginia limestone; apparently Madison later added the huge Doric portico. After serving his second term, he and his wife, Dolley, retired to Montpelier, where they held court for an unending succession of visitors, including Lafayette and Daniel Webster. After Madison's death, in 1836, at the age of 85, Dolley returned to Washington, where she lived until her death, 13 years later. She and her husband are buried at Montpelier.

Present Appearance. In 1907 the owners of the house enlarged the

Montpelier, Virginia, home of President James Madison for 76 years, features a huge Doric portico. It is today a private residence.

wings and raised them to a level with the central portion of the house. Montpelier retains its historic appearance. Except for the Madison family cemetery, it is not open to the public. The grounds are beautifully landscaped and have been carefully maintained, as has the house.

Mount Vernon, Virginia

Location. Fairfax County, on Mount Vernon Memorial Highway, about 7 miles south of Alexandria.

Ownership and Administration. Mount Vernon Ladies' Association of the Union.

Significance. Overlooking the Potomac River, in a setting of serene elegance and beauty, is George Washington's plantation estate, Mount Vernon. Its sweeping lawns, beautiful gardens, magnificent mansion, and carefully planned outbuildings are a superb representation of a Virginia plantation home. Many shrines commemorate George Washington as President, military leader, and statesman, but only Mount Vernon reveals the plantation farmer and country gentleman.

The history of the estate dates back to the late 17th century. In 1674 John Washington and Nicholas Spencer obtained a 5,000-acre grant of land along the Potomac. In 1690 they divided it. Mildred Washington inherited the Washington half, and in 1726 sold it to her brother Augustine, George's father. He deeded it to his eldest son, Lawrence, George's half-brother, who settled on the estate and probably began to construct the present mansion. In 1754, 2 years after Lawrence's death, George Washington inherited the property. Military service in the French and Indian War kept him away until 1759, when he married and brought his new bride there. For 15 years he lived on the estate, whose mansion had by that time been partially built, as a prosperous planter; and planned the mansion and grounds as they appear today. He had hardly begun to enlarge the mansion and carry out his plans, when, in 1775, he went to Philadelphia to serve in the Second Continental Congress. Congress appointed him commander in chief of the Continental Army, and it was 6 years before he again saw Mount Vernon.

While Washington was away, during the War for Independence, a kinsman, Lund Washington, carried out his plans for the estate; he enlarged the main house, built the outbuildings, landscaped the grounds, and extended the gardens. Washington found the mansion completed in 1781, when he stopped off on his way to and from Yorktown. After re-

Mount Vernon, the plantation home of George Washington, is a historic shrine to Americans. Courtesy, Mount Vernon Ladies' Association.

signing his commission, 2 years later, he returned to Mount Vernon. In 1789, elected President, he departed once again and was able to return only about twice a year for the following 8 years. In 1797 he returned for a final time, retired, and died 2 years later. He and his wife are buried on the estate.

Present Appearance. In 1858 the Mount Vernon Ladies' Association of the Union acquired title to Mount Vernon from Washington's great-grandnephew. By that time only the mansion remained; all the furnishings had disappeared. The association has refurnished the house with period pieces, including many of the originals. At its peak, during Washington's lifetime, the estate contained about 8,000 acres and was divided into five farms. After Washington's death four of them were divided and subdivided and only the present 500-acre tract remains.

The mansion is an outstanding example of colonial architecture. Most striking is the high-columned piazza, extending the full length of the structure and overlooking the Potomac. The exterior wood siding is beveled, and its paint contains sand to give the appearance of stone. The first floor of the house is divided by a central hall. From the piazza side, to the right are the musicroom, west parlor, and banquet hall; to the left, the bedchamber, dining room, and library. On the second floor are the blue bedroom, Lafayette's bedroom, the yellow bedroom, Nelly Custis' bedroom, and George Washington's bedroom. The third floor includes three bedrooms and two storerooms. The kitchen and pantries are located outside but adjacent to the house. Various outbuildings have been restored in detail, as have the gardens and lawn. The mansion is open to the public.

Oak Hill, Virginia

Location. Loudoun County, on U.S. 15, about 1 mile north of Gilberts Corner.

Ownership and Administration. Privately owned.

Significance. James Monroe built this palatial mansion at the height of his career, during his first term as President of the United States, drafted the Monroe Doctrine in it, and retired there at the end of his public career. In 1805 he had inherited the property from his uncle, but lack of funds prevented him from beginning construction of a home for

While serving as President, James Monroe built this mansion on his Oak Hill estate. The estate derived its name from the oaks that he planted to represent the States in the Union.

at least a decade. He obtained architectural assistance from James Hoban, architect of the Capitol, and by 1823 had completed the mansion, constructed of brick kilned nearby. Monroe furnished it with pieces from his Ash Lawn estate, which he later sold. Spending much time at Oak Hill, he made horseback trips to and from the Capital. On the grounds, among numerous locust and poplar trees, he planted an oak for each State in the Union, and thereby gave the estate its name. In 1825 he left the White House and retired to Oak Hill, where he entertained such notables as President John Quincy Adams and the Marquis de Lafayette. Financial problems forced him to sell all of his property, and in 1830 he moved to New York to live with his daughter. He died the following year.

Present Appearance. The brick mansion originally consisted of a two-story central portion with small, one-room wings, but in 1923 the owner enlarged the wings. The south portico, two stories high and supported by seven Doric pillars, is the most striking feature of the mansion. A number of outbuildings remain, including a smokehouse, springhouse, and law office. The house and grounds are privately owned and are not open to the public.

Prairie du Chien, Wisconsin

Location. Crawford County.

Ownership and Administration. Villa Louis is owned and administered by the State Historical Society of Wisconsin; the Astor Warehouse, Diamond Jo Warehouse, Dousman Hotel, and Brisbois House are privately owned; the Second Fort Crawford Military Hospital, on the grounds of St. Mary's Academy, is owned and administered by the Charitable, Educational, and Scientific Foundation of the Wisconsin State Medical Society.

Significance. Located on a broad terrace overlooking the Mississippi, 3 miles north of the confluence of the Mississippi and Wisconsin Rivers, Prairie du Chien was a crossroads of the fur trade in the old Northwest. It was a rendezvous point for the hunters, trappers, and traders—white and Indian—who plied the route between Canada and the fur country west of the Great Lakes. Successively occupied by the French, British, and Americans—all of whom contributed to the settlement and development of the old Northwest—it has retained its historical character to a degree unsurpassed in the region. The concentration of historic sites and buildings on St. Feriole Island, center of earliest settlement, constitutes an

Villa Louis, Prairie du Chien, Wisconsin. When built, in 1843, by American Fur Company agent Hercules L. Dousman, this mansion was Georgian in style. Dousman's widow later converted it to Victorian.

Brisbois House, erected in 1808, was one of the earliest homes in Prairie du Chien. A fur-storage area is located in the basement.

outstanding interpretation of the fur trade, the West during the period of the military frontier, and steamboat commerce on the upper Mississippi.

Prairie du Chien, as the western terminus of the Fox-Wisconsin portage, was a vital station on the route between Canada and the vast French-claimed heartland of North America. For more than a century the settlement was a base for French commercial exploitation of the entire region west of the Great Lakes. Soon after Louis Jolliet and Père Jacques Marquette passed nearby in 1673 while journeying down the Wisconsin and Mississippi Rivers, the site became a gathering place for French and Indian trappers, traders, and hunters. For a few years in the mid-1680's the French maintained Fort St. Nicolas at the site. In the mid-1700's French stragglers may have settled there and named it for a Fox Indian chief whom they called *Le Chien* ("the dog"). A land claim made by three French-Canadians in 1781, however, is usually considered the date of permanent occupation.

After 1763, when France ceded her American territory to Britain, British fur traders moved into the Prairie du Chien region. During the War for Independence the British built a fort in the town, from which they and Indian allies launched unsuccessful attacks against Cahokia and St. Louis. Although the British ceded the old Northwest to the United States at the end of the war, until 1796 British troops remained at Prairie du Chien and protected the British traders, who kept a firm grip on the fur trade. Even after that date the British, aided by the Indians, managed to retain their supremacy over the fur trade against the few Americans who attempted to penetrate the Great Lakes region.

In 1814, during the War of 1812, U.S. troops moved up the Mississippi and built Fort Shelby at Prairie du Chien, but the British forces from Mackinac captured the weakly held post, which they renamed Fort McKay. After the Treaty of Ghent, ratified early in 1815, the British abandoned the site and the Americans occupied it. In 1816 U.S. troops erected Fort Crawford on St. Feriole Island, and the town became a major outpost of the American fur trade, which continued through the 1830's. John Jacob Astor established a subheadquarters for his American Fur Co. there, and it thrived as the western terminus of the water route from Mackinac, the central depot, via Lake Michigan's Green Bay and the Fox and Wisconsin Rivers. Fort Crawford was of considerable importance on the Northwest military frontier during the period of pioneer American settlement of the country west of the Great Lakes. At the fort, in 1825 the United States signed the treaties of Prairie du

Chien with the tribes in the region. The treaties involved no cession of land but created Indian boundaries in the region. In another treaty, in 1829, the Winnebagos relinquished their title to lands south of the Wisconsin River. In that same year the Army moved Fort Crawford about 1 mile from St. Feriole Island to the higher ground on the mainland, where modern Prairie du Chien grew up. In 1835 troops from the fort constructed a military road to Fort Winnebago. It subsequently extended to Fort Howard, at Green Bay, and became a major emigrant route. In 1856 the Army abandoned Fort Crawford, but temporarily reoccupied it during the Civil War.

In the meantime the advent of steamboat traffic on the Mississippi, in the 1830's, had made Prairie du Chien a thriving river port and market center for grain and lumber. Further economic stimulation occurred in 1857, when the town became the river terminus of the Milwaukee and Mississippi Railroad, which ran westward from Milwaukee. A few years later the railroad, bridging the river, moved westward.

Present Appearance. The entire city of Prairie du Chien, both the old section on St. Feriole Island and the newer portion that grew up around the second Fort Crawford, on the mainland, appears much today as it did in the 19th century. The most notable historic structure is the palatial Villa Louis, built in 1843 as a Georgian mansion by Hercules Louis Dousman, wealthy and cultured American Fur Co. agent, on the sites of Forts Shelby, McKay, and the first Fort Crawford. In 1872 his widow remodeled the exterior in Victorian style. In the 1930's Dousman's granddaughters and the city of Prairie du Chien restored the mansion to its 1872 appearance. It is a three-story brick structure, furnished with period pieces and family heirlooms. Outbuildings on the 10-acre site include Dousman's office, coachhouse, icehouse, and preserve room; these have not been essentially altered since their construction, in 1843. The mansion is open to the public from May to November.

In 1808 Michael Brisbois, a French-Canadian and one of the earliest settlers in the town, erected the two-story Brisbois House. The basement contains fur-storage space, and the house is furnished with original pieces. It is privately owned but is open to the public. The Astor Warehouse, constructed of stone by the American Fur Co. about 1835, is in fair condition but is now a place of business. In 1864 the Milwaukee and Mississippi Railroad erected the Dousman Hotel, a three-story stone building, to accommodate its passengers. The hotel, somewhat altered, is privately owned and is not open to the public. The Diamond Jo Warehouse, a long one-story structure erected during the Civil War, recalls steamboat days. In private ownership, it is in poor condition and is not open to the public. Only the restored post hospital remains of the second Fort Crawford, the major portion of whose site is occupied by St. Mary's Academy, for girls. Containing a museum of Wisconsin medical history, it is open to the public.

D. Historic Districts Eligible for the Registry of National Historic Landmarks

In some instances, groups of historic buildings located in proximity, when considered collectively, provide outstanding illustrations of a past era. These groups are designated Historic Districts and declared eligible for the Registry of National Historic Landmarks. Such districts sometimes include individual structures that are eligible on their own merits for Landmark designation. The following Historic Districts illustrate the phases of history treated in this volume.

Vieux Carré Historic District, Louisiana

Location. Orleans Parish, the section of the city of New Orleans bounded by the Mississippi River, Rampart Street, Canal Street, and Esplanade Avenue.

Ownership and Administration. Various.

Significance. Covering some 85 blocks, the Vieux Carré is the nucleus of the original city of New Orleans and the scene of many historic events—from the initial French settlement through the French, Spanish, and early American eras. Many of its buildings represent a unique fusion of architectural styles, which reveal the growth of New Orleans in the late 18th and early 19th centuries and the blending of diverse national influences into a cosmopolitan metropolis.

The Frenchman Jean Baptiste le Moyne, Sieur de Bienville, founded New Orleans in 1718, and 3 years later military engineers platted it into 80 rectilinear blocks. In 1722 it became the capital of French Louisiana and, because of its location 100 miles above the mouth of the Mississippi,

St. Louis Cathedral and the Presbytère are situated on Jackson Square, in the Vieux Carré. Most of the buildings in this section date from the late 18th and early 19th centuries. Courtesy, New Orleans Chamber of Commerce.

thrived as a trade center. By the mid-18th century it had gained a reputation for glamorous living and was the cultural center of Louisiana. In 1762, when western Louisiana passed from France to Spain, it became the capital of Spanish Louisiana and grew rapidly. Although fires in 1788 and 1794 nearly destroyed it, its residents erected substantial buildings to replace the old ones.

In 1803 New Orleans officially passed from Spain back to France, and 20 days later from France to the United States. At the very end of the War of 1812, British forces attempted to capture the city, but U.S. forces defeated them in the Battle of New Orleans. After the war the city continued to prosper, particularly because it became the major port for the newly developing steamboat traffic on the Mississippi and its tributaries. The influx of U.S. settlers and traders, Latin American political refugees, and European immigrants made ante bellum New Orleans one of the most cosmopolitan cities in the United States. By mid-century it had become the commercial and financial emporium of the entire Mississippi Valley, the fourth largest city in the United States, and the second most active port. Today, it is a thriving port city and center of culture.

The Vieux Carré Historic District is eligible for the Registry of National Historic Landmarks relating primarily to French exploration and settlement.

Present Appearance. Most of the buildings in the Vieux Carré date from between 1794, when the second of two disastrous fires swept the town, and 1850. They are a mixture of various European styles of architecture, primarily French and Spanish. To some extent, however, they also reflect the Greek Revival style, which swept the country in the 19th century. Sites and buildings in the Historic District that are eligible in their own right for the Registry of National Historic Landmarks and are described separately elsewhere in this volume are The Cabildo and Jackson Square. Some of the other buildings in the district that date back to and are typical of the period of history encompassed in this volume include the following: St. Louis Cathedral, 711 Chartres Street; the Presbytère, 713 Chartres Street; the French Market, extending from Jackson Square to Barracks Street; Montegut House, 731 Royal Street; Nicholas House, 723 Toulouse Street; Bosque House, 617 Chartres Street; Le Petit Theatre, 616 St. Peter Street; Thierry House, 721 Gov. Nicholls Street; Banque de la Louisiane, 417 Royal Street; Bank of the United States, 339 Royal Street; Bank of Louisiana, 344 Royal Street; and the Absinthe House, 238 Bourbon Street.

Colonial Annapolis Historic District, Maryland

Location. Anne Arundel County; the area bounded by Spa Creek, Duke of Gloucester Street, Church Circle, College Avenue, and King George, Hanover, Randall, and Prince George Streets; Annapolis.

Ownership and Administration. Various.

Significance. Although visited by Capt. John Smith in 1608, the Annapolis area was not settled for a few decades. In 1649, the same year that Lord Baltimore's Religious Toleration Act made Maryland a haven for nonconformists, about 300 dissatisfied Puritans emigrated from Virginia to the mouth of the Severn River, near the site of Annapolis. Soon afterward some of them settled at the site—which until 1695 they gave various names, including Proctor's Landing, Arundelton, Severn, and Anne Arundel Town. In that year they renamed it Annapolis in honor of Princess Anne, Protestant daughter of James II.

The year before, the town had been designated the capital of Maryland in place of St. Marys City. A political and mercantile center, the town also had an active social and cultural life. Merchants and planters built elegant homes and entertained legislators. Theaters, horseraces, and taverns provided entertainment. After the turn of the 18th century the affluence of Annapolis increased and during the War for Independence reached its pinnacle. Near the end of the war the Continental Congress met in the Maryland State House, where in 1783 George Washington resigned his commission. Soon after that period, Baltimore began to gain the ascendency as the commercial center of Maryland.

Colonial Annapolis Historic District is a Registered National Historic Landmark relating primarily to architecture and to the development of commerce and industry.

Present Appearance. More brick buildings predating the War for Independence are preserved in Annapolis than in any other U.S. city, thanks in part to the efforts of Historic Annapolis, Inc., which has long been active in protecting the historic residential and harbor areas. The Historic District incorporates much of the original town, one of the first planned cities in the United States. The dominant State Circle and ancillary circle on the west, Church Circle, lie at the heart of the modified radial plan. The streets radiate roughly north and east from the two circles.

Most of the historic buildings date from the 18th century. Some of the more important are as follows: Maryland State House (in its own right a Registered National Historic Landmark and described separately elsewhere in this volume) ; Hammond-Harwood House (eligible for the Registry of National Historic Landmarks relating primarily to the development of the English colonies) ; Chase-Lloyd House; Old Treasury Building; William Reynolds Tavern; William Paca House; Peggy Stewart House; Christopher Hohne-Holland House; and the Brice House. Several buildings, including the Werntz House and the Maryland Inn, are associated from an architectural standpoint with the period of history treated in this volume.

E. Other Sites Considered

In the process of selecting the comparatively few historic sites of such outstanding character as to merit recognition as Registered National Historic Landmarks for the phases of history treated in this volume, a great many throughout the Nation were carefully studied, compared, and evaluated. The sites described below were among those deemed by the Advisory Board to possess noteworthy historical value but not "exceptional value" (national significance) within the special Landmark criteria. Some of them, however, may satisfy the criteria for other volumes in this series. In addition to Landmark sites and those described below, many others—too numerous to list—were judged to be of lesser importance.

Fort Confederation (Fort Tombigbee) Site, Alabama

Location: Sumter County, just off U.S. 11, on the Tombigbee River, near Epes.

Originally the French Fort Tombigbee, whose spelling varies widely in historical records, stood on this site. Constructed in 1735 above the confluence of the Tombigbee and Black Warrior Rivers, in Choctaw and Chickasaw Indian country, it served as an advance base during the Chickasaw War, as a base for trade with the Choctaws, and as a check against British influence in the area. After the French and Indian War the British occupied it, renamed it Fort York, and abandoned it 5 years later. It then fell into ruins.

In 1794 the Spanish rebuilt the fort and renamed it Fort Confederation. They remained until 1797, the year before Congress designated the Mississippi Territory, at which time the fort became a possession of the United States. In 1802–3 Government officials negotiated there one of a series of treaties by which the United States absorbed the Choctaw lands and by which the area along the Tombigbee-Mobile Rivers was opened to settlement. Soon afterwards the fort fell into ruins and was abandoned. The National Society of Colonial Dames of America has placed a marker on the site.

Fort Mims Site, Alabama

> *Location: Baldwin County, on an unimproved road, 4 miles west of Tensaw.*

In July 1813 Samuel Mims, a settler in Alabama, built a stockade around his farm, on the eastern bank of Lake Tensaw. The next month some 500 white and halfbreed settlers, fearing a Creek uprising, took shelter in the stockade, which came to be known as Fort Mims. Maj. Daniel Beasley, the leader of a group of militiamen stationed there, regarded the settlers' fears as unfounded and refused to take adequate precautions. Before the month was out a group of Creeks, led by halfbreeds, attacked the fort and massacred the soldiers and settlers. This massacre spurred military action against the Creeks and marked the beginning of the Creek War (1813–14), during which Andrew Jackson achieved national fame. A monument erected by the United Daughters of the Confederacy marks the approximate site of the fort.

McGillivray Plantation Site, Alabama

> *Location: Elmore County, on County Route 47, about 4 miles north of Wetumpka.*

Alexander McGillivray, halfbreed Creek leader, lived at a plantation on this site during the period of his greatest influence. Son of a Scottish trader and his French-Creek wife, McGillivray acquired a well-rounded education in Charleston and Savannah, but returned to Creek country after the outbreak of the War for Independence. During the war he served as a British agent and sent Indian war parties against the U.S. frontier. Befriending William Panton, the influential trader, he became a leader of the Creeks, whose cause he always held foremost. In 1784 he negotiated on behalf of the Creeks and Seminoles a treaty of alliance and trade with

Spain. In return for his services, McGillivray received a commission as colonel and an annual salary from the Spanish Government. In the following years, from his plantation, he directed Indian attacks on the Georgia frontier and the Cumberland River settlements in Kentucky and Tennessee.

The U.S. Government, recognizing McGillivray's influence, in 1790 persuaded him to negotiate peace in New York. In the Treaty of New York the Creeks and Seminoles agreed not to make alliances with other nations and approved a boundary settlement in Georgia. McGillivray, commissioned a brigadier general in the U.S. Army and awarded an annual salary from the U.S. Government, returned to Alabama, where he secretly abrogated the treaty. Financially stable, having commissions and salaries from both the United States and Spanish Governments, he began to promote a powerful Southern Indian confederation, but he died in 1793. No traces of the plantation buildings remain, though the site, on privately owned farmland, is marked by a boulder placed by the Alabama Anthropological Society.

Boundary Stones, District of Columbia

Location: Various points in Washington, D.C., and Virginia.

These sandstone markers, erected in 1791–92, indicate the original boundary lines of the District of Columbia. The first stone, the cornerstone, was laid in April 1791 just south of Alexandria, Va., at Jones Point, the southern tip of the 10-mile-square District. Forty stones were erected at 1-mile intervals along the four sides of the square—northwest from Jones Point to present West Falls Church, Va.; then due northeast to a point near Woodside; southeast to Chesapeake Junction, now Capitol Heights; and southwest to Jones Point. Each stone was about 1 foot square, having a beveled top, and protruded from 2 to 3 feet above the ground. Carved on the District side was "Jurisdiction of the United States" and the number of the stone; on the opposite side of the stone was carved "Maryland" or "Virginia." For those facing Virginia, "1791," the year of erection, was carved; for those facing Maryland, "1792."

In 1915 the Daughters of the American Revolution recovered, restored, and placed iron fences around 39 of the 40 stones, many of which had been lost in debris. Because the Federal Government in 1846 ceded 36 square miles of the District to Virginia, some of the stones are located outside the present boundaries of the District. Many of the stones can be seen today.

Commandant's House, U.S. Marine Barracks, District of Columbia

Location: 8th and I Streets SE., Washington.

This is the oldest extant building at the Marine Barracks. In 1801 Thomas Jefferson selected the site of the barracks, and by January 1806 they were occupied. In 1814 British troops made their headquarters there when they occupied Washington. At that time the buildings were damaged or partially destroyed, but they were repaired upon the cessation of hostilities. Today, most of them are two-story modern structures, built in 1902. The Commandant's House, erected in 1805, is the only original building. A good example of early 19th-century architecture, it is 2½ stories high and contains 23 rooms. It is not open to the public.

Dolley Madison House, District of Columbia

Location: Southeast corner of Madison Place and H Street NW., Lafayette Square, Washington.

Dolley Madison resided in this house on Lafayette Square for most of the 13 years following her husband's death, in 1836. Richard Cutts, Congressman from the District of Maine, which was then a part of the Commonwealth of Massachusetts, had built it between 1818 and 1820. He was Dolley Madison's brother-in-law and had borrowed from her husband to build the house. In 1829, after he had lost most of his money in unsuccessful business ventures, the house reverted to James Madison. Upon Madison's death, in 1836, his wife acquired it. The following year, after an absence of 20 years from Washington, she returned and took up residence in the house. Her absence had not dimmed her popularity, and until her death, in 1849, she advised the various First Ladies and was prominent in Washington society.

At the time of Mrs. Madison's residence, the house had two stories plus an attic. The gable roof sloped east and west, and upon the west slope were two dormer windows. During subsequent years, owners of the house removed the gable roof and added a story having a flat one; converted the original entrance on Lafayette Square into a window; added a new entrance on the H Street side, in an addition built at the rear of the house; and made other extensive alterations. The interior has been extensively altered. The building is now the property of the Federal Government and is not open to the public.

Dumbarton House, District of Columbia

Location: 2715 Q Street NW., Washington.

George Beall constructed this mansion sometime in the 18th century. A century earlier Ninian Beall, the original owner of the property, had come to the United States as an indentured servant. He acquired large tracts of real estate, and in 1703, as a reward for his services as an Indian fighter, was granted a large tract of land on Rock Creek. The Bealls owned the property until 1796, when Thomas Beall sold it, including the mansion. It subsequently changed hands many times, and in 1813 Charles Carroll bought it. Dolley Madison stayed at the mansion briefly during the British raid on Washington in 1814, after Carroll had assisted her in fleeing from the White House.

Various families owned the house until 1931, when the National Society of Colonial Dames of America purchased it. In 1915 the owners of the mansion had moved it to its present site. The brick mansion is trimmed in white. The central portion, accented by a pillared porch, delicate iron balconies, corbeled cornice, and crowning pediment, is flanked by low service wings. The interior contains furniture of the period 1790–1810. In the exhibition room are displayed personal belongings and costumes of such people as President and Mrs. Washington, Mrs. Madison, George Mason, and Lord Fairfax. Portraits by Peale and Stuart hang in the dining room and parlor. All the books in the library are pre-1810 editions. The mansion, now headquarters of the National Society of Colonial Dames, is open to the public.

Dumbarton Oaks, District of Columbia

Location: 3101 R Street NW., Washington.

In 1801 William H. Dorsey, a judge, erected this mansion in a grove of trees on his estate, Acropolus ("Grove on the Hill"). Subsequently, Robert Beverly bought it, and his son sold it to James E. Calhoun, who lent it to his brother John C. Calhoun. Calhoun lived in it while he served as Secretary of War, Vice President, and Senator. During World War II, in 1944, the Dumbarton Oaks Conference convened there. Attended by representatives of the United States, Great Britain, the Soviet Union, and China, the conference created the Dumbarton Oaks Plan, which served as a basis for the charter of the United Nations.

The mansion has been extensively altered from its original late Georgian style by addition of a mansard roof and other modifications. Its exterior is adorned with carved stone ornaments, classic cornices, and crowning pediments. On the grounds, which are open to the public, is an original greenhouse, containing an orangery, a brook having miniature waterfalls, an orchard, a yew walk, a waterwheel and millstone, stables, and a caretaker's house. The mansion is now owned by Harvard University. The Treaty Room may be viewed.

Navy Yard, District of Columbia

Location: 8th and M Streets SE., Washington.

During the administration of President John Adams, because of French and British aggression on the seas, the Federal Government decided to build six navy yards. By 1801 it had acquired 40 acres of land for the Washington yard, and that same year construction began. Benjamin H. Latrobe, one of the architects of the Capitol, drew up the plans, and Capt. Thomas Tingey supervised construction. In 1805 the yard was completed. Navy ships from the yard figured prominently in the War of 1812. In 1814 officials burned the buildings to prevent their falling into British hands. Soon afterwards, however, the Government rebuilt the yard. Between 1819 and 1840 the U.S. Navy launched there several first-class frigates and sloops-of-war.

During the Civil War the yard served as a base for naval stores and armament and as a military prison. World War I brought about the yard's peak of productivity. At that time employment reached more than 10,000 workers, who produced ordnance and other equipment. The yard was also active during World War II, and it still is today.

Two structures have historical and architectural interest: The entrance gate and the commandant's residence, both designed by Latrobe and built between 1801 and 1805. The Latrobe gate has been remodeled somewhat to allow for construction of a barracks room over it. The commandant's residence stands inside to the left of the entrance. Some parts of the Navy Yard may be visited by the public.

Panton, Leslie and Company Warehouse Site, Florida

Location: Escambia County, Main and Baylen Streets, Pensacola.

This warehouse was the center of the lucrative trade of the influential British firm Panton, Leslie & Co., which dominated Indian trade during the years of the Spanish regime in Florida. William Panton, a Scot, had emigrated to Charleston, S.C. In 1775 he moved to East Florida, where he formed the trading company. He built up trade with the Creek Indians, but his Loyalist sentiments brought him into conflict with South Carolina and Georgia authorities, who during the War for Independence confiscated his property and branded him an outlaw. From 1784, when the British evacuated Florida, until 1801 he lived mostly in West Florida. Spain sought the friendship of the Florida Indians to counter the penetration of Anglo-American backwoodsmen to the north. The Spanish allowed Panton, without loss of British citizenship or freedom of worship, to continue his activities.

At its peak Panton's company monopolized trade with the Creek, Chickasaw, and Cherokee Indians. It maintained a chain of agencies, branches, and trading posts extending from Havana and Nassau to New Orleans and from Mobile to the Chickasaw Bluffs. Despite competition from U.S. traders after Spain withdrew to the 31st parallel in 1795, Panton remained prosperous and left an estate of £10,000. The ruins of the warehouse were removed in the 1940's. On the site the city erected a replica of the original building, on approximately one-third scale. A marker near the replica marks the approximate burial place of Alexander McGillivray, the influential Creek leader, who died in 1793 and was buried in Panton's garden.

San Marcos de Apalache (Fort St. Marks), Florida

Location: Wakulla County, on Fla. 363, about 2 miles south of U.S. 98, at the junction of the Wakulla and St. Marks Rivers, just south of the village of St. Marks.

The Spanish constructed three wooden forts at this site during their first occupation of Florida, from 1565 to 1763. They had begun a stone fort when England acquired Florida in 1763. During the British regime (1763–83), Panton, Leslie & Co. founded a trading center at the site, then known as Fort St. Marks, and remained after the Spanish reoccupation of the San Marcos area, in 1787. San Marcos, as a result, became a thriving center of Indian trade. During his Seminole campaign, in 1818, Gen. Andrew Jackson captured the fort and settlement. He executed two British traders near the fort, one of the episodes that brought United States-Spanish relations to a crisis and influenced the Spanish to sign the Adams-Onís Treaty (1819), by which the United States acquired Florida. During the Civil War the Confederates superimposed entrenchments and fortifications upon the ruins of the earlier Spanish forts.

The State-owned tract, known as San Marcos de Apalache Historic Memorial, is heavily wooded, and only a portion of the stonework from the last Spanish fort stands above ground. The fort site is open to the public. A museum houses artifacts found in the area and exhibits prepared by the Florida State Museum.

[When this volume was in an advanced stage of publication, the Advisory Board declared Fort San Marcos de Apalache to be eligible for the Registry of National Historic Landmarks, relating primarily to Spanish exploration and settlement.]

Fort Hawkins Site, Georgia

> *Location: Bibb County, corner of Emery Highway and Maynard Street, Macon.*

Fort Hawkins was a combined military post (1807–19) and "factory" (1806–17). In 1795 the Federal Government inaugurated the factory system as a means of controlling the Indian trade and negating the influence of Spanish, French, and British traders. The factory at Fort Hawkins was the third, and westernmost, of those on the Georgia frontier. Col. Benjamin Hawkins, "principal temporary agent" for the Southern Indian tribes from 1796 to 1802 and "agent of the United States among the Creek" from 1802 to 1815, selected a hilltop commanding several miles of the Ocmulgee River as the site of the combined military and trading post—authorized by the Treaty of Washington (1805), negotiated with the Creeks. In 1806 the 100-acre tract set aside for the use of the post was cleared; the fort constructed; and the factory, which had been located at Fort Wilkinson (on the Oconee River near present Milledgeville, Ga.), moved to the site. The following year troops who had been stationed at Fort Wilkinson garrisoned the new fort.

Although never attacked, Fort Hawkins was of considerable importance as a supply depot and as a mustering point and base for troops engaged in battles to the west and south during the Creek War, 1813–14; the War of 1812; and the first Seminole War, 1817–18. After 1819 the fort was not garrisoned. Because of the decline of the fur trade in the South, the factory at Fort Hawkins was never very successful. However, it continued in operation until 1817, when it was moved to Fort Mitchell (on the Chattahoochee River near present Fort Mitchell, Ala.).

About 1930 the Nathaniel Macon Chapter of the Daughters of the American Revolution acquired the site of the fort's southeast blockhouse. In 1937–38, through the cooperation of the National Park Service, the Civilian Conservation Corps, and the Works Progress Administration, the blockhouse was reconstructed on its original location. Now owned by the city of Macon, it is open to groups by special appointment.

William H. Crawford Home Site, Georgia

Location: Oglethorpe County, on U.S. 78, on the edge of Crawford.

William H. Crawford lived in a house on this site during the latter half of his life. In 1799 he began his career as a lawyer in Lexington. He was a State Representative during the years 1803–7, after which he acquired a vacant seat in the U.S. Senate. In 1811 he was elected to the Senate. From 1813 to 1815 he served as Minister to France and in 1815 as Secretary of War. Madison appointed him Secretary of the Treasury in 1816, and he remained in that office from 1817 to 1824 under Monroe. He was a Democratic-Republican candidate for the Presidency in 1824. When the victor, John Quincy Adams, asked him to remain as Secretary of the Treasury, he declined and returned to Georgia. In 1827 Governor George M. Troup of Georgia appointed Crawford as Judge of the Northern Circuit, a position he held until he died 4 years later.

Crawford's home, Woodlawn, built in 1804, was a two-story structure, each story having a separate kitchen and porch, and contained 13 rooms. A servants' house, with a high chimney, stood in the side yard. In 1936 fire destroyed the main house. Before that time, the Daughters of the American Revolution had placed a granite marker along the highway. A cemetery, near the house, contains Crawford's grave.

Fort Harrison, Indiana, in 1812. Gov. William Henry Harrison used this fort as a base during his campaign against the Indians in 1811 that culminated in the Battle of Tippecanoe. From a lithograph by Modesitt and Hager. Courtesy, Library of Congress.

Fort Harrison Site, Indiana

> *Location: Vigo County, on Fort Harrison Road, about 3 miles north of Terre Haute.*

Gen. William Henry Harrison erected Fort Harrison in 1811 as a base for his campaign against Tecumseh's Indian confederacy at Prophet's Town, near present Lafayette. Built on a bend in the Wabash River, the fort commanded an unobstructed view of more than 1 mile in both directions. After construction, its complement consisted of more than 1,000 men. It was about 150 feet square; at each corner were 2-story, 20-foot blockhouses, built of logs. Barracks stood between the blockhouses. A large gate, protected by bastions and palisades and a trench about 4 feet deep, gave access to the fort. In the fall of 1811 the troops at the fort marched to northern Indiana, fought the Battle of Tippecanoe, and returned to the fort. Harrison then assigned a small permanent garrison under the command of Capt. Zachary Taylor, later President. Although popularly considered a victory, the Battle of Tippecanoe had been indecisive, and the Indians retaliated by increased depredations in southern

Indiana. In September 1812 a small party of Indians attacked the fort, set fire to it, and then retreated. The garrison held out. The Elks' Fort Harrison Country Club is now located on the site of the fort, of which no remains are extant.

Fort Knox Site, Indiana

Location: Knox County, on a secondary road, overlooking the Wabash River, about 3 miles north of Vincennes.

About 3 miles up the Wabash River from Vincennes is the site of Fort Knox, a frontier fort during the period 1804–14. At this fort several negotiations and conferences took place between Gov. William Henry Harrison of the Indiana Territory and Tecumseh, the Shawnee leader. Harrison trained there the troops that he led into Indian country in the fall of 1811. The climax of that campaign occurred at Tippecanoe, the battleground near Lafayette, where Harrison defeated "The Prophet," Tecumseh's half-brother. This victory, however, only temporarily curtailed Indian depredations. Two future Presidents served at Fort Knox: Harrison, elected in 1840, and Zachary Taylor, elected 8 years later. It was a lost site for some years, but in 1963 the William Henry Harrison Trail Commission located and outlined its boundaries.

Fort Wayne, Indiana

Location: Allen County.

Before the coming of the white man, Fort Wayne was the most important village of the Miami Indians. The date of construction of the first fort at the site, a French fort called Miami, is unknown but may have been as early as the late 17th century. During the French and Indian War, in 1760, the British occupied the fort, but in 1763 surrendered it to Pontiac's followers. In 1790 President Washington sent a force, under Gen. Josiah Harmar, to build a post at Miami Town, as the site was then called. Little Turtle, a Miami chief, attacked and defeated Harmar's force, and the following year defeated a followup expedition, under Gen. Arthur St. Clair, in present Ohio. A third expedition, however, under Gen. Anthony Wayne, defeated Little Turtle at the Battle of Fallen Timbers, in 1794. After the battle Wayne proceeded to Miami

Town and built Fort Wayne. Soon a settlement grew up around the fort. For 20 years Fort Wayne was a crude military and commercial outpost, inhabited by squatters, vagabonds, and traders. The Federal Government maintained there a garrison, an Indian agent, and a factor.

The most renowned Indian agent at Fort Wayne was William Wells, white son-in-law of Little Turtle. Serving from 1799 to 1809, he helped maintain peace between the Miamis and the white settlers. Prior to that time he had fought against the white men, but a few years after Little Turtle's defeat, in 1794, he helped Governor Harrison quell Tecumseh's followers and prevent the formation of an Indian confederacy.

About 1811 the Potawatomi Indians besieged Fort Wayne. Governor Harrison, however, arrived with an army, and the siege was lifted. The last Indian attack on the town was the massacre of Maj. Joseph Jenkinson's men late in 1813. In 1819 U.S. troops evacuated the fort. The town then prospered in the fur trade.

The old Fort Wayne site, at Clay and Berry Streets, is designated by a marker. Another marker indicates the site of Fort Miami, the French fort, on the east bank of the St. Joseph River at Delaware Avenue and St. Joseph Boulevard. The Anthony Wayne Monument, a large equestrian statue of the general, stands at the corner of Hayden Park, on Harmar Street and Maumee Avenue.

Territorial Capitol Building, Indiana

> *Location: Knox County, adjoining Grouseland, the William Henry Harrison estate, Vincennes.*

For the first 13 years following the creation of Indiana Territory, in 1800, Vincennes was the capital. The Territorial Capitol Building housed sessions of the Indiana Territorial Assembly, which governed an area that now comprises Indiana, Wisconsin, Illinois, most of Michigan, and a part of Minnesota. About 1919 the Women's Fortnightly Club of Vincennes, which had purchased the building, donated it to the city, which moved it to Harrison Park. In 1933 the city restored it and in 1949 deeded it to the State, which relocated it adjacent to Grouseland and the following year opened it to the public as a State memorial.

The small frame building, held together by wooden pegs, has two stories. On the ground floor are the offices of the Territorial officials. Furniture includes a desk allegedly used by Governor Harrison and worn

Territorial Capitol Building, Indiana, a State memorial. Between 1800 and 1813, when Indiana Territory consisted of nearly five present States, this small frame building housed sessions of the Indiana Territorial Assembly.

hickory chairs. Heavy hewn timbers, a large fireplace, and whitewashed walls are typical of the period. A narrow stairway along the left wall leads to the legislative hall, which can also be reached by outside stairs. The hall is furnished with plain, hard benches and candle lanterns. Adjacent to the memorial is a replica of the first newspaper office in Indiana, Elihu Stout's *Western Sun*, first printed in 1804 as the *Indiana Gazette.*

William Whitley House (Sportsman's Hill), Kentucky

Location: Lincoln County, on U.S. 150, about 9 miles east of Stanford.

William Whitley, one of the most renowned Indian fighters along the Wilderness Road, built this house between 1787 and 1794. A native Virginian, he had come to Kentucky in 1775 and taken part in the War for Independence. As settlers surged westward after Clark's Kaskaskia campaign of 1778–79, Whitley, a colonel in the Lincoln County Militia, helped protect from Indian attack emigrant parties traveling along the

Wilderness Road. In 1794 he led a militia expedition into Tennessee in pursuit of some renegade Indians. These and his other activities helped bring peace to the wilderness of eastern Kentucky. Although at an advanced age during the War of 1812, he enlisted as a private in the U.S. Army and in 1813 died in the Battle of the Thames.

Sportsman's Hill, Kentucky, was the home of William Whitley, frontiersman and Indian fighter. The initials of Whitley and his wife are inlaid in the front and rear exterior walls.

Sportsman's Hill, perhaps the oldest brick residence west of the Alleghenies, is a 2½-story structure of brick, laid in Flemish bond. The initials of Whitley and his wife are inlaid in large size in the front and rear exterior walls. Some of the interior walls are handsomely paneled in wood. The inner iron supports on the doors served for protection against the Indians. The house is maintained by the State and is open to the public.

Los Adaes, Louisiana

Location: Natchitoches Parish, just north of La. 6, about 2 miles northeast of Robeline.

Los Adaes was the site of an 18-century Spanish mission and presidio and in 1806 the site of a United States-Spanish boundary agreement. Founded in 1721–22 on the site of an earlier mission, the Presidio of Nuestra Señora del Pilar de los Adaes (Adais) was a Spanish outpost and the capital of the frontier province of Texas, seat of 13 Spanish Governors, until 1773. Long after the presidio had been abandoned, in 1806 at the site Ens. Joseph Maria Gonzales of the Spanish Army and Capt. Edward Turner of the U.S. Army signed a boundary treaty by which Gonzales agreed to retreat to Spanish-owned Texas and to cease sending Spanish patrols across the border into the United States. This treaty led to the formal establishment, a few weeks later, of "neutral ground" between Texas and the United States by Gen. James Wilkinson and Spanish Lt. Comdr. Simon de Herrera. The two nations honored the boundary for 14 years.

Only a few unidentified mounds of earth are visible today on the attractive ridge where the presidio stood. Of the 40 acres or so encompassing the presidio, mission, and village sites, more than 9 acres are owned by Natchitoches Parish and are maintained as a historical park. The National Society of the Daughters of American Colonists and the State of Louisiana have erected markers.

Fort Cumberland Site (lost site), Maryland

Location: Allegany County, Cumberland.

In 1750 the Ohio Co., formed by a group of English merchants and Virginia planters, built a trading post and small storehouse in Shawnee Indian country at the site of the city of Cumberland. In 1754 George Washington, on returning from his defeat at Fort Necessity, built Fort Mount Pleasant near the trading post. The following year Col. James Inness expanded the fort and renamed it Fort Cumberland. That same year Braddock, in preparation for his campaign against the French, assembled 2,000 men at the fort and marched through the wilderness toward the Forks of the Ohio, near which his forces went down to defeat.

No attacks were made on the fort during the French and Indian War. Washington commanded the fort there, and in 1756 he became convinced that the major route from Virginia to the West should be through the Cumberland Valley. Later he was president of the Patowmack Co., which opened the Potomac to navigation from George Town to Cumberland. Abandoned in 1765, Fort Cumberland was not occupied again except for a short period in 1794. At that time Washington, making a final visit to the fort, reviewed troops called out to suppress the Whisky Rebellion.

In 1785 Thomas Beall laid out Washington Town adjacent to Fort Cumberland. Two years later the State assembly renamed the town Cumberland, and in 1789 made it the seat of the newly formed Allegany County. At that time large numbers of settlers were emigrating to the regions west of the mountains and making demands on Congress to build a road that would connect the seaboard with the Ohio country. In 1806 Congress authorized construction of the National Road, also known as the Cumberland Road because Cumberland was its eastern terminus. Work began on the road in 1811. Soon a steady stream of wagons rolled in from Baltimore and Pennsylvania, and Cumberland's business increased as the road extended farther westward. The Chesapeake and Ohio Canal gave further hope to Cumberland, but its construction proceeded so slowly that the first train of the Baltimore and Ohio reached the town in 1842, some 8 years before the canal. The probable site of Fort Cumberland is on a hill overlooking Washington and Green Streets.

Gore Place, Massachusetts

Location: Middlesex County, Gore Street, Waltham.

This mansion, a fine example of Federal-period architecture, was the home of Christopher Gore, seventh Governor of Massachusetts and national statesman. Born in 1758 in Boston, Gore graduated from Harvard College, and served in the Army during the War for Independence. He became an outstanding lawyer. In 1796 President Washington appointed him commissioner to England, under the terms of Jay's Treaty. During the next 8 years Gore settled many U.S. merchants' spoliation claims against the British. In 1801 he returned briefly home and planned his mansion, which he built in 1805. While living there he served as Governor of Massachusetts and U.S. Senator. He died in 1827.

The three-story mansion, built of pink brick laid in Flemish bond, consists of a central portion and two flanking wings. A sandstone terrace fronting the two entrance doors was designed to accommodate horsemen and coaches. Inside the mansion on the first floor, marble floors lead to a central State Reception Hall, a semielliptical room having curved doors and thresholds. Immediately beyond the hall is an oval dining room. The left wing contains billiard and music rooms, and the right wing contains servants' quarters. A staircase spirals upward from the central portion and makes a complete circle on the third floor. The second floor includes rooms for entertaining guests, and the third floor consists of bedrooms, Gore's study, and guestrooms. Of the original 400 acres on the estate, 76 are still intact. The estate, maintained and owned by the Gore Place Society, is open to the public from April through November.

Fort Shelby Site, Michigan

Location: Wayne County, 250 West Fort Street, Detroit.

Fort Shelby was the third name of a fort that stood on the site of the city of Detroit. The British had named it Fort Retreat; and the French, Fort Pontchartrain du Detroit. In 1796 the British, carrying out the terms of Jay's Treaty, yielded the fort to Capt. Moses Porter, in command of Gen. Anthony Wayne's advance guard. In 1812 Gen. William Hull invaded Canada from Detroit, but soon retreated and surrendered the Michigan Territory to the British. The next year Gen. William Henry Harrison recaptured Detroit and went on to defeat the retreating British Army in Canada at the Battle of the Thames. He then restored the British fort and renamed it Fort Shelby. A settlement that had grown up around the fort continued to grow slowly until after the completion of the Erie Canal, in 1825. Soon afterward Detroit became an industrial city. At the Fort Street entrance to the Federal Building, a bronze plaque marks the site of Fort Shelby.

Ellicott's Hill, Mississippi

Location: Jefferson County, bounded by Canal, Jefferson, Wall, and Franklin Streets, Natchez.

In 1797 Andrew Ellicott raised the U.S. flag on this hill and asserted

"Connelly's Tavern," a fine example of Spanish Provincial architecture, sits on Ellicott's Hill, Natchez, overlooking the Mississippi River.

U.S. authority over Spanish lands, now portions of the States of Mississippi and Alabama, that had been in dispute between Spain and the United States since 1783. Ellicott had been sent by President Washington to locate the boundary between United States and Spanish lands, specified as the 31st parallel in Pinckney's Treaty of 1795. Realizing that the Spanish had no intention of evacuating lands north of the parallel, especially the area known as the Natchez District—extending along the Mississippi River from Vicksburg through Natchez to Woodville—Ellicott instigated a series of intrigues that resulted in a bloodless revolution. The Spanish Governor ceded his power to a committee of delegates elected by the residents of the district, abandoned attempts to obstruct the execution of the treaty, and withdrew his garrisons from Fort Nogales (Vicksburg) and Natchez. Ellicott then proceeded to the 31st parallel and began surveying the Spanish-American boundary line, which ran from the Mississippi to the Chattahoochee River. In 1800 he completed the survey.

Located on top of the hill is an old two-story frame building, now known as Connelly's Tavern. Restored by the Natchez Garden Club, it is a notable example of Spanish Provincial architecture. Long, narrow, double galleries, having slender columns, overlook the Mississippi. The tavern is open to the public.

Fort Nogales Site, Mississippi

Location: Warren County, in Vicksburg National Military Park, Vicksburg.

In 1790 the Spanish built an outpost on this site, the highest hill in the area, and the following year erected Fort Nogales. At the fort, in 1793, they negotiated the Treaty of Nogales with the Creeks, the Choctaws, the Chickasaws, and the Cherokees. It reaffirmed the Spanish-Indian alliance and commerce treaties of 1784. In the treaty the Indians agreed to defend Louisiana and Florida against attack and the Spanish promised them assistance in obtaining boundary settlements with the United States. Spain agreed to deliver annual supplies and gifts to the tribes and promised to protect them. By further inciting the Indians to burn and ravage American settlements from Georgia to the Mississippi, the Spanish authorities hoped to compel the United States to stay out of the Indian lands and thus create a barrier that would protect Louisiana. In 1797, after Pinckney's Treaty created a new Southern boundary of the United States, the Spanish evacuated the fort. Soon afterward the United States occupied the area, and by 1819 settlers had formed the town of Vicksburg.

Nathan Boone's Home, Missouri

Location: St. Charles County, on a secondary road, about 6 miles northwest of Defiance.

Nathan Boone, Daniel Boone's son, constructed this house, in which the elder Boone spent many of his later years. Daniel Boone led several expeditions into Kentucky from North Carolina and helped to initiate settlement there. After learning that his title to all his Kentucky land holdings was invalid, in 1788 he moved to West Virginia, and in 1799 to Missouri. Boone, his two sons, Daniel and Nathan, his brother, son-in-law, and their families settled in and near the Femme Osage Valley, near the Missouri River. The Spanish Lieutenant Governor appointed Boone civil and military administrator for the area, a position he retained until the Spanish Governor formally transferred Upper Louisiana to the United States in 1804. Nathan Boone built his permanent home between

1803 and 1811, and Daniel lived there sporadically until he died, in 1820. The home, a two-story stone structure, contains three rooms downstairs and four rooms upstairs and has wide halls. Many of the furnishings belonged to Daniel Boone and his descendants. A museum located near the home exhibits items of pioneer days. Although privately owned, the home is administered by the Daniel Boone Shrine Association and is open to the public.

Daniel Webster Birthplace, New Hampshire

Location: Merrimack County, just off N.H. 127, about 2 miles southwest of Franklin.

This small framehouse, built by Daniel Webster's parents and dating from 1780, was 2 years later the birthplace of the renowned statesman and orator. In 1801 he graduated from Dartmouth and 4 years later was admitted to the bar. After practicing law at Boston and Portsmouth, during the years 1813–17 and again in 1823–27 he served in the U.S. House of Representatives. During the period 1827–41, as a U.S. Senator, he gained national fame for his speeches opposing the States rights doctrines of Robert Hayne and John C. Calhoun, both from South Carolina. In 1842, while serving as Secretary of State, he negotiated with Great Britain the Webster-Ashburton Treaty, which settled the long-standing Maine-New Brunswick boundary dispute. He served again as Senator from 1845 to 1850 and as Secretary of State from 1850 to 1852. After failing to win the Presidency in 1852, he retired and died the same year.

Webster's restored birthplace is owned by the State of New Hampshire and is administered by the State Division of Parks. It is open to the public. Furnishings include relics and utensils of the colonial period and a few items that belonged to the Webster family.

Castle Williams, New York

Location: New York County, on Governors Island, in New York Bay, New York City.

This circular stone fortification, designed and built during the years 1807–11 by Lt. Col. Jonathan Williams on the northwestern tip of Governors Island, served as a twin fort with Castle Clinton in guarding the channel between Governors Island and New York City. Known as the "Tower" during construction, in 1810 Castle Williams received its present name. Though never threatened, it has served throughout the years in the defense of New York. Repaired in 1833 and 1836, it served as a prison during the Civil War. Its foundation sits on a rock surface. Its red sandstone walls are 40 feet high and have an 8-foot-thick base and a 7-foot top. The stones in the outer walls are dovetailed. A double row of bombproof arches in the walls once contained two tiers of heavy cannon. The interior of the fort contained two brick buildings and a well; these were removed in 1912 when the fortification was converted into a military prison. In good condition today, Castle Williams may be visited each spring on Armed Forces Day. At other times, visiting arrangements may be made with the Information Officer at Fort Jay.

Fort Hamilton, New York

Location: Kings County, at the entrance to the Narrows, Brooklyn.

This fort—located on the Narrows, the strait separating Staten Island and Brooklyn—for more than a century has been part of the New York Harbor defenses. Although the Dutch and the English, during their occupations of New York, recognized a need for a defense along the Narrows, they erected no permanent fortification. In 1805 Col. Jonathan Williams surveyed New York Harbor and planned a series of fortifications. As a result the city of New York erected Fort Richmond on Staten Island and Fort Diamond (later Fort Lafayette) on Hendrick's Reef, a few hundred yards off the Brooklyn shore. During the War of 1812 the threat of British attack gave renewed impetus to defense projects in New York Harbor. In 1814 New York City donated a tract of land on the Brooklyn shore along the Narrows to the Federal Government. The Army and Navy jointly surveyed the tract, and in 1825 the Army laid the cornerstone for a new fort, Fort Hamilton. Lt. J. K. F. Mansfield supervised construction, completed in 1831.

The fort consisted of a granite, casemated quadrangular inner fort, protected on the land sides by a high earthwork. A ravelin—capable of mounting 70 guns—within the earthwork covered the sally port. Other structures, including officers' quarters and a parade ground, completed the 160-acre reservation. During the Civil War the Army added a shore battery, a south battery, and an east battery. Late in the 19th century it added additional armament facilities. Though never under attack, Fort

Hamilton served as a troop processing center during the Mexican War and the Civil War. Robert E. Lee and "Stonewall" Jackson served there in the 1840's. It served as a staging area during the two World Wars and the Korean war and is still active today.

A rebuilding of the fort in the period 1954–63 destroyed most of the original structures. A portion of the original pier and the northeastern face of the inner fort, including its sally port and casemates, still remain. All other structures probably postdate the Civil War.

Fort Jay, New York

Location: New York County, on Governors Island, in New York Bay, New York City.

Fort Jay, begun by the city of New York late in the 18th century, was the earliest permanent fortification on Governors Island and remains an active military post today. It has never been attacked. Because of the threat of war with France in the early 1790's, the city of New York sought to strengthen existing harbor defenses and build others. In 1794 Congress appropriated money to the city for construction of a fort on Governors Island. Construction began that year, and additional appropriations in following years made possible completion of the fort by 1798. It was named Fort Jay, in honor of John Jay, Secretary for Foreign Affairs. In 1800 the city ceded the island to the United States, which in 1806 razed most of the fort and rebuilt it. Completed in 1808, it consisted of an enclosed pentagonal structure, having 4 bastions capable of mounting 100 guns. On its completion, officials renamed it Fort Columbus, but in 1904 the Secretary of War restored the original name.

The Army repaired the fort in 1833 and in 1836; it remains today much as it was then. It is open to the public each spring on Armed Forces Day. At other times, visits may be arranged with the Information Officer at Fort Jay.

Fort Ontario, New York

Location: Oswego County, on a secondary road, along U.S. 104, just east of Oswego.

This fort, a key post in the colonial struggle between England and France, was also involved in the War of 1812. The British built the original fort in 1755, but the following year the French destroyed it. In 1759 the British rebuilt it and used it as a base for a successful attack on Fort Niagara. The following year troops from the fort invaded Canada and captured Montreal. Abandoned in 1777, the fort was partially burned the following year by Continental troops. In 1782 the British regarrisoned it and held it until 1796. In 1803 and again in 1812–14 U.S. troops were stationed there. During the War of 1812 the fort served as a U.S. supply depot. In 1814 the British destroyed it. Between 1839 and 1844 the U.S. Army rebuilt it.

The fort, a pentagonal structure having bastions at each corner, is today a State-owned historic site and is open to the public. Most of the interior buildings date from the final rebuilding or later, but the ramparts are original. A museum on the second floor of the enlisted men's barracks interprets the history of the fort.

John Jay House, New York

Location: Westchester County, on N.Y. 22, between Bedford and Katonah.

John Jay built this home when he retired, in 1800, and lived in it until his death, in 1829. The house was thereafter occupied by five succeeding generations of the Jay family. The 1,000-acre tract of land on which Jay built the house had been purchased from an Indian chief by Jay's grandfather Jacobus Van Cortlandt. Jay distinguished himself as a lawyer early in his career and later held many high offices in the Federal Government. He was a Member of the First and Second Continental Congresses; author of "Address to the People of Great Britain," which protested England's mismanagement of her colonies; president of the Continental Congress; chairman of the committee that drafted the New York State constitution; one of the commissioners who negotiated the Treaty of Paris, ending the War for Independence; author of some of *The Federalist Papers;* the first Chief Justice of the U.S. Supreme Court, under President Washington; and negotiator of Jay's Treaty (1794), clarifying U.S. relations with Great Britain. In 1795 he was elected Governor of New York.

Jay's house, on a lovely site, is in nearly original condition. The wing built in 1922 contains many Jay possessions, including an outstanding collection of 18th-century oil paintings. Many of the furnishings are original, and documents and letters of historical importance are preserved. In 1958 Westchester County purchased the house and immediately turned it over to the State. It is open to the public.

Sackets Harbor, New York

Location: Jefferson County.

Founded by Augustus Sackett in 1801 on the shore of Lake Ontario, Sackets Harbor was first known as Sacketts Harbor. It became a center of trade with Canada and by 1812 consisted of about 50 houses. During the War of 1812 U.S. forces erected a base, Fort Tompkins, on the western side of the harbor and stored there naval and military supplies. A large shipyard in the village constructed naval vessels for use on the lake. In Sackets Harbor the northern campaign opened in the War of 1812. In July a British squadron of five vessels attacked the village. The British were determined to seize the U.S.S. *Oneida,* but the small U.S. force seriously damaged three of their vessels and soon compelled them to retreat. Another battle occurred in May 1813, when about 1,000 British regulars and Indians under Gov. Gen. Sir George Prevost attacked the garrison at Sackets Harbor. Jacob Jennings Brown, brigadier general of the New York Militia, commanded the defense, which drove off the British. Though never again attacked during the war, the town remained a key supply and shipbuilding center. The Sackets Harbor Battlefield is at the north end of Main Street, in a public park, overlooking Lake Ontario. It contains a monument to the memory of the soldiers who fought in the Battle of Sackets Harbor.

Fort Amanda Site, Ohio

Location: Auglaize County, just off Ohio 198, about 8 miles south-west of Lima.

Fort Amanda, built in 1812–13 by Col. Thomas Poague on orders from Gen. William Henry Harrison, was one of a series of fortified supply depots in Ohio planned by Harrison to help check the invading British Army, which had taken Detroit in the summer of 1812. It consisted of four two-story blockhouses, connecting palisades, and a central ware-house. Its primary purpose was to store supplies until Fort Meigs, farther north, required them. Following the British siege of Forts Meigs and

Stephenson, the Battle of Lake Erie, and the U.S. victory at the Battle of the Thames—all during 1813—Fort Amanda became a way station for troops returning from the north, a hospital, and a burial ground. Abandoned in 1814, it fell into ruins. In 1915 the site became a State memorial, and the State erected a 50-foot-obelisk dedicated to the men who served and died at the fort. The U.S. Government has marked the graves of the unknown dead with permanent headstones. The memorial is open to the public.

Fort Meigs Site, Ohio

> *Location: Wood County, on Ohio 65, about 1 mile southwest of Perrysburg.*

Early in 1813 Gen. William Henry Harrison built Fort Meigs as a defense against the invading British Army from Canada. Late in April the British occupied Fort Miami, 1 mile below Fort Meigs, and proceeded to build siege batteries facing Fort Meigs. For a few days the Americans held out alone against the overwhelming British force. Then some 1,200 Kentucky militiamen, under Harrison, dispersed the British. One group of about 800 pursued the British toward Fort Miami, but were caught in an ambush and all but about 150 killed. A second siege occurred in July, but Harrison forced the British to retreat. As a result of these actions, Fort Meigs became known as the "Gibraltar of the West." The site of Fort Meigs, containing 42 acres, is a State memorial. The only remains of the fort are earthworks, but an imposing granite shaft 61 feet high marks the site.

Fort Miami Site, Ohio

> *Location: Lucas County, Maumee.*

In 1794 the British built Fort Miami (Miamis) to block Gen. Anthony Wayne's advance on Detroit and to encourage the Ohio Indians in their resistance to U.S. penetration north and west of the Ohio River. The fort was a log stockade, which had four bastions, each capable of mounting four cannon, a river battery, barracks, officers' quarters, supply buildings, and various shops. A defensive ditch, 20 to 25 feet deep, ran along the land side of the fort.

Late in 1794 General Wayne and his troops marched northward toward Fort Miami from Fort Greenville. Just south of the fort, ambushed by the Indians and a small party of Canadian militia, he ordered a charge and dispersed his adversaries, in the Battle of Fallen Timbers. The Indians fled to Fort Miami, but the commander of the fort shut them out. Beaten and disillusioned, the Indians dispersed and 1 year later their chiefs gathered at Fort Greenville to negotiate with Wayne. The Treaty of Greenville opened most of the present State of Ohio and part of present Indiana to white settlement. In 1796, under the terms of Jay's Treaty (1794), the British abandoned Fort Miami. Wayne occupied and garrisoned it, but about 1799 U.S. troops abandoned it. During the War of 1812 Tecumseh, the Shawnee chief, and British officials maintained headquarters at the fort, from where they moved against Gen. William Henry Harrison at Fort Meigs.

In 1942 several Ohio civic and patriotic organizations acquired a part of the site of the old fort. Nothing remained of the original structure except parts of the earthworks. In 1953 the Ohio State Archaeological and Historical Society conducted preliminary excavations, and in 1957 the Historical Society of Northwestern Ohio placed a marker at the site, which remains undeveloped.

Fort Recovery, Ohio

Location: Mercer County, Wayne Street, town of Fort Recovery.

In 1793–94 Gen. Anthony Wayne erected Fort Recovery on the site of an Indian defeat of forces led by Maj. Gen. Arthur St. Clair, Governor of the Northwest Territory, in 1790. From the time of St. Clair's disaster to the time of Wayne's campaign, U.S. forces were trained and strengthened. In the fall of 1793 Wayne advanced into Indian territory. He buried the remains of St. Clair's men, recovered the cannon hidden by St. Clair's fleeing army, and built an outpost at the site. He named it Fort Recovery because his mission was one of recovery. In June 1794 at the gates of the fort about 2,000 Indians and a few British attacked a small convoy from Fort Greenville. The Americans beat off the attack.

Fort Recovery State Park contains a one-third scale replica of Wayne's fort and stockade. Overhanging tower rooms are at each end of the stockade. The fort is constructed entirely of wood and has firing platforms inside. Southwest of the fort is Fort Recovery Museum, a log

Scale replica of the stockade at Fort Recovery, erected in 1793–94 by Gen. Anthony Wayne. The replica is part of Fort Recovery State Park, which memorializes Wayne's role in quelling the Indians in the old Northwest and opening the area to white settlement.

structure that houses miscellaneous articles excavated at the site. Also in the park is a 93-foot-high monument, on a granite terrace 35 feet square, that commemorates the soldiers who lost their lives during the period 1791–94. A 9-foot-high figure of a frontiersman stands on the west base of the monument.

Greenville Treaty Site, Ohio

Location: Darke County, 114 West Main Street, Greenville.

The Greenville Treaty Site is also the site of Fort Greenville, built in 1793 by Gen. Anthony Wayne. In the winter of 1793–94 he carefully drilled his soldiers there and prepared for a campaign against the Indians in the Ohio country, which culminated in the defeat of the Indians and their Canadian allies at the Battle of Fallen Timbers (1794). The Treaty of Greenville (1795), signed by various tribes of the old Northwest, provided for the cessation of hostilities, the exchange of prisoners, and annual allotments of goods to the Indians. The Indians ceded to the United States lands comprising about three-quarters of the present State of Ohio and the southeastern corner of Indiana.

In 1805 Tecumseh and "The Prophet" founded an Indian settlement on the white man's side of the Greenville Treaty line. The settlement, adjoining the site of Fort Greenville, served as a base, where Tecumseh formulated his plan for an Indian confederacy. As the Indians moved west from Greenville, French, English, and German settlers moved in and a town grew up. A Fort Greenville Treaty Memorial is located on the site of the signing of the treaty. Tecumseh Memorial Boulder is situated near Mud Creek Bridge. Fort Greenville burial ground monument, at the southeast corner of West Third and Chestnut Streets, honors soldiers who died during General Wayne's campaign.

Marietta, Ohio

> *Location: Washington County.*

In April 1788, 47 New Englanders laid out Marietta, the first settlement in the Northwest Territory resulting from passage of the Ordinance of 1787. They were members of the Ohio Co. of Associates, which owned a 1,800,000-acre tract of land in the Muskingum and Hocking River Valleys and along the Ohio River. In July Gen. Arthur St. Clair, Governor of the Territory, arrived and set up a Territorial government. Campus Martius, a large fort, was at that time being built by Rufus Putnam, superintendent for the company, on high ground overlooking the settlement. When completed, it was a square stockade, whose walls were 180 feet in length. The blockhouse was 2 stories high. A sentry tower was located at each corner. The stockade housed many of the settlers until the Treaty of Greenville (1795) concluded the Indian wars in the region.

The settlement prospered, and soon local crafts and businesses sprang up. The location of the town on the Ohio River made it a center of shipping and shipbuilding. In 1800 workers completed the 104-ton brig *St. Clair,* which in 1801 cleared port for Havana, carrying a cargo of pork and flour. In the next 7 years local craftsmen built about 20 ocean-going brigs and schooners and a few Navy gunboats. As the frontier moved westward, Marietta, though superseded industrially and economically, remained a thriving river town.

In 1931 the State of Ohio completed the Campus Martius Museum on the site of the old fort. Its exhibits portray life in the frontier community of Marietta and tell the story of the early Northwest Territory.

The home of Rufus Putnam, the superintendent of the Ohio Co. of Associates, is enclosed in a wing of the museum. Putnam built it around 1788 and used it as his office for many years. Other exhibits in the museum interpret the history of the Ohio River. Exhibited on the Muskingum River, a few blocks away from the museum, is the *W. P. Snyder, Jr.,* a stern wheel towboat. The oldest office building in the Northwest Territory, the Ohio Land Co.'s Land Office, owned by the Colonial Dames of Ohio, stands on the grounds of the museum. A hand-hewn board house, 20 by 30 feet, it was the office in which the Ohio Co. produced the first maps of the Territory and sold and recorded lands. At 326 Front Street stands a 15-room brick house, built in the first decade of the 19th century by Return Jonathan Meigs, Jr., fourth Governor of Ohio, justice of the Ohio Supreme Court, U.S. Senator, and Postmaster General.

Fort Towson Site, Oklahoma

Location: Choctaw County, on U.S. 70, about 1 mile northeast of the town of Fort Towson.

In 1824 the U.S. Army built Fort Towson in the southeastern part of Indian country as a sister post to Fort Gibson, lying to the north. The post was built to aid Indians emigrating from the Southeast. In 1829 the Army abandoned it, but 1½ years later rebuilt it to protect the Choctaws emigrating from Mississippi. Throughout the 1830's it was one of a line of forts that guarded the frontier. It was active during the Mexican War, but, as the frontier moved westward, it was no longer needed. In 1854 the Army abandoned it. Except for brief occupations by Confederate and Union forces during the Civil War, it was no longer used. Only the ruins of several stone buildings remain today.

Daniel Boone Homestead, Pennsylvania

Location: Berks County, on a secondary road, 1 mile north of Baumstown.

Daniel Boone resided at this homestead in the wilderness from his birth, in 1734, until he was 16 years old, when his family moved to North Carolina. Boone's parents had settled at the homestead 4 years before his birth. Young Boone learned to hunt, trap, shoot, and develop other skills that he later used in his frontier explorations. Originally the homestead was a log cabin. Boone's father probably built part of the two-story stone house that now stands. The foundations of the Boone cabin formed part of the foundation wall of the present building. The Commonwealth of Pennsylvania has restored the homestead, which is open to the public. Nearby are a blacksmith shop and a bank barn. Planned for reconstruction are a log cabin, such as the one Boone lived in, a typical frontier village, and a gristmill.

Flagship *Niagara* Replica, Pennsylvania

> *Location: Erie County, at the foot of State Street, in Niagara Park, Erie.*

The *Niagara* was Oliver Hazard Perry's second flagship in the Battle of Lake Erie, during the War of 1812. On September 10, 1813, Perry met a British fleet near Put-in-Bay, Ohio. Enemy guns battered his flagship *Lawrence* so badly that Perry had to transfer, under heavy fire, to the *Niagara*. Soon after the transfer the British commander, his flagship destroyed and his other ships disabled, surrendered. Perry reported to Gen. William Henry Harrison, the military commander, "We have met

Replica of the *Niagara*, at Erie, Pennsylvania. During the Battle of Lake Erie (1813), Commodore Oliver Hazard Perry, USN, used two flagships, the *Lawrence* and the *Niagara*.

the enemy and they are ours." Perry's victory, Harrison's success at the Battle of the Thames, and Thomas Macdonough's triumph in 1814 at the Battle of Plattsburgh Bay, on Lake Champlain, blocked British invasion efforts from Canada. The present replica of the *Niagara* is the second reconstruction of the vessel and is open to the public. It contains a 78-foot section of the original black keel.

S-Bridge, National Road, Pennsylvania

Location: Washington County, just off U.S. 40, about 6 miles west of Washington.

This bridge is one of the few remaining landmarks in Pennsylvania that commemorates the National (Cumberland) Road, over which once passed thousands of westward emigrants. Begun in 1811, the road originated at Cumberland, Md., and by 1817 it had reached Uniontown, Pa. In 1818 it reached the Ohio River at Wheeling, W. Va., which remained its western terminus for several years. In 1836 the Federal Government turned over Pennsylvania's section of the road, consisting of about 75 miles, to the Commonwealth, which charged tolls. In the 20th century, the realinement of U.S. 40 bypassed the bridge. At that time its west end was damaged, and the structure is now only in fair condition. Sitting just off U.S. 40, it may be visited by the public.

S-Bridge, Pennsylvania, was one of several along the National Road. The route today is followed generally by U.S. 40. Courtesy, Pennsylvania Historical and Museum Commission.

Rocky Mount, Tennessee

> *Location: Washington County, on U.S. 11E, about 5 miles north-west of Johnson City.*

Rocky Mount, built about 1770 by William Cobb, was one of the first homes in Tennessee and served for a time as the residence of William Blount, Governor of the Southwest Territory. Blount arrived in present Tennessee late in 1790 and set up temporary headquarters in Cobb's log house. For 18 months Rocky Mount served as temporary capitol of the Territory. In the summer of 1791 Blount founded Knoxville, where he constructed a permanent residence. Rocky Mount subsequently served as a stopping place on the stagecoach line from Baltimore, Md., to Memphis, Tenn. Andrew Jackson, a relative of Cobb's, once spent 6 weeks at the house, while waiting for his license to practice law in Jonesboro. From 1838 to 1847 the house served as a U.S. post office.

The State of Tennessee purchased Rocky Mount and in 1959 authorized the Rocky Mount Historical Association to restore and maintain it. It is a two-story structure of white oak logs. The logs are hewn, notched, and chinked with clay. One large hipped chimney of brick stands in an ell at the back of the house. The large fireplaces, mantels, and woodwork are of pine. The stairway and front door are paneled. The house is furnished with period pieces and several of Cobb's possessions. Reconstructed kitchen and scullery buildings stand on the grounds, as does a brick museum containing exhibits of pioneer life in Tennessee. Rocky Mount is open to the public.

Aquia Creek Quarries, Virginia

> *Location: Stafford County, on a secondary road, Wigginton's Island.*

Sandstone from these quarries was used in constructing the Capitol and the White House. Early in the winter of 1791–92 Maj. Pierre Charles L'Enfant, designer of the Capital City, went to Aquia, Va., and on behalf of the Government purchased Wigginton's Island and leased for a 10-year period land along Aquia Creek. On this land, workers quarried the sandstone used for the outer walls of the Capitol and the White House and in other Government buildings. Today, Wigginton's Island is difficult to reach by land, via a causeway. The approach road is impassable in some places. The vegetation is thick, and only a few quarry sites show evidence of stonecutting.

Ash Lawn, Virginia

Location: Albemarle County, just off County 795, about 4 miles south of Charlottesville.

Ash Lawn, situated on a hilltop about 2 miles from Jefferson's Monticello, was the home of James Monroe from November 1799 until near the end of his first term as President, in 1820. Because of his busy career, he stayed at the home only intermittently. Jefferson supervised construction, which began in 1796 during Monroe's absence as Minister to France. Built on a rather steep slope, the house was a modest, seven-room structure, having one story in front and two behind. Several outbuildings stood on the 3,500-acre estate. The landscaping, which Monroe supervised, included a boxwood garden. The present house stands at the head of a long wooded lawn. Its main section is a two-story addition to Monroe's original house, which is connected to the back of the main section. The house is privately owned, but is open to the public.

This small rear section of the present mansion at Ash Lawn, Virginia, was the home of President James Monroe for more than 20 years. The two-story front part, partly visible in this photograph, is a later addition.

Aerial view of Fort Norfolk, Virginia. This fort, one of the Nation's earliest coastal defenses, was erected because of French and English attacks on U.S. shipping in the 1790's. Courtesy, U.S. Army.

Fort Norfolk, Virginia

> *Location: Nansemond County, east side of Elizabeth River, at the western end of Front Street, Norfolk.*

In 1794 Congress authorized the building of Fort Norfolk as a defense for Norfolk and the upper reaches of the Elizabeth River. The fort was one of a series of coastal defenses erected because of French and English attacks on U.S. shipping. In 1795 construction began. In 1802 Secretary of War Henry Dearborn visited Norfolk and ordered the fort dismantled and a new one constructed at Ferry Point. In 1807 the *Chesapeake* embarked from Norfolk, but was intercepted about 10 miles off Cape Henry by the British frigate *Leopard,* which opened fire. The *Chesapeake's* commander struck his flag, and the *Leopard* officers boarded the ship and removed three U.S. sailors and a British deserter. This incident outraged Norfolk citizens, who persuaded the Federal Government to reactivate Fort Norfolk. During the War of 1812 troops from the fort reconstructed a redoubt on Craney Island, where they repelled a British attack on Norfolk. Several Civil War actions also occurred at the fort.

The irregular-shaped fort is about 400 feet long and 250 feet wide.

On the west side, facing the main river approach, the parapet is in the shape of a half moon; on the northwest, it forms an acute angle; on the northeast, a full bastion; and, on the southeast, a bastion of irregular design. The face of the fort is brick, but the terreplein and the banquettes are of sodded dirt. Traces of a ditch may be seen on the land side in front of the northeast bastion. Inside the fort are numerous buildings, probably once used as magazines, storehouses, barracks, and officers' quarters. All are in a good state of repair. The fort, which is owned and maintained by the U.S. Army, is open to the public.

James Monroe Law Office, Virginia

Location: Spotsylvania County, Charles Street, Fredericksburg.

This quaint 1½-story building represents a typical late 18th-century law office. Inside are housed a collection of furniture, portraits, and personal possessions of James Monroe. Built in 1758, the building was the first and only private law office of Monroe. After serving in the War for Independence, Monroe studied law in Richmond, and by 1786, when he moved to Fredericksburg, had become a member of the Virginia Assembly, the State Executive Council, and the Continental Congress. He practiced law in this office from 1786 until 1789, when he was elected U.S. Senator. He later served as Minister to France, Spain, and England; Governor of Virginia for two terms; Secretary of War; Secretary of State; and President for two terms.

Many of Monroe's possessions have been removed from his Oak Hill estate to the law office, where they are displayed. Among the exhibits is the Louis XVI desk, having secret compartments, on which Monroe signed the message to Congress that contained the Monroe Doctrine. Behind the law office is an old-fashioned garden containing a century-old mulberry tree at the center. At the end of the boxwood-lined walks stands a bronze bust of Monroe. In 1927 Monroe's descendants opened the building to the public and in 1947 presented it to the James Monroe Memorial Foundation. In 1961 a two-story memorial library wing was added to the rear of the office. In 1964 the foundation donated the structure to the University of Virginia. It is open to the public.

[When this volume was in an advanced stage of publication, the Advisory Board declared the James Monroe Law Office to be eligible for the Registry of National Historic Landmarks.]

Shadwell, Virginia

Location: Albemarle County, on U.S. 250, about 2 miles east of Charlottesville.

Shadwell was the plantation home in which Thomas Jefferson was born, in 1743. About 1737 Jefferson's father, Peter, had built it on land he had purchased 1 year or so earlier from William Randolph. Jefferson lived in it for the first 2 years of his life, and again during the years 1752–70, on an intermittent basis. Fire destroyed the home in 1770, and the site was subsequently lost. In 1955, however, archeologists, after a 14-year search, located it. The style of the original house is unknown, but architects, under the auspices of the Jefferson Birthplace Memorial Park Commission, designed and built a 1½-story clapboard home faithful to the era and mode of life of Jefferson's parents. This home, which stands today as a memorial to Jefferson, is open to the public.

Woodlawn Plantation, Virginia

Location: Fairfax County, on U.S. 1, about 3 miles west of Mount Vernon, approximately 7 miles southwest of Alexandria.

This estate was selected and surveyed by George Washington and presented as a wedding gift to his adopted daughter, Eleanor Parke (Nelly) Custis, who married his nephew Lawrence Lewis. It consisted of 2,000 acres of Washington's Mount Vernon lands. As a house site Washington recommended the hill overlooking Dogue Creek, the Potomac River, and the mansion at Mount Vernon. Dr. William Thornton, first architect of the U.S. Capitol, designed a mansion for the young couple, who lived at Mount Vernon until 1802, when they moved into the uncompleted mansion. In 1805 it was completed. The Lewises lived there until Lawrence's death, in 1839, when Nelly abandoned the estate, which then fell into ruin. Beginning in 1846 it passed through many ownerships. In 1948 the Woodlawn Public Foundation purchased the mansion and grounds and 9 years later turned them over to the National Trust for Historic Preservation, which directed restoration of the mansion, furnished it, and opened it to the public.

The mansion is of five-part construction—a central portion with two

Mansion at Woodlawn Plantation, Virginia. Designed by architect William Thornton, it was the home of George Washington's adopted daughter, Nelly, after her marriage to Lawrence Lewis.

flanking wings and connecting hyphens. Beyond it are a smokehouse and a dairy, both linked to the wings by brick walls, penetrated by solid wooden doors. The mansion is built of brick, burned on the grounds, and trimmed with local Aquia sandstone. The river facade is noteworthy for its handsome portico and columns, marble floor, and double stairway leading to the garden. Within the mansion are imported mantelpieces of carved marble and molded compo ornaments in classic design. The woodwork is handsomely detailed. The winding stair and carved mahogany rail in the central hall are noteworthy. Restoration includes original paint colors for the walls. Mementos of Nelly Lewis' years at Mount Vernon are displayed, as well as memorabilia of the Washington and Lewis families.

Blennerhassett Island, West Virginia

Location: Wood County, in the Ohio River, 2 miles south of Parkersburg.

In 1805 Harman Blennerhassett and Aaron Burr, meeting at Blennerhassett's mansion on this island, made plans for setting up an empire in the old Southwest. In 1797 Blennerhassett, a wealthy Irishman who had come to the United States with his young bride in search of a refuge where he could live undisturbed and carry on his experiments in the natural sciences, had acquired 170 acres at one end of the island. Three years later he completed a long, semicircular, stone mansion, where he entertained local socialites. Burr, on hearing of Blennerhassett's wealth and influence, visited him and persuaded him to support his plot to create a Southwestern empire. He convinced Blennerhassett that, under the empire, his home would become a Utopia surrounded by intelligentsia.

In December 1806 Blennerhassett and a company of adventurers, planning to meet Burr at Natchez, started down the Ohio River in a small fleet of river boats. Rumors of treason had reached President Jefferson, who sent the Virginia Militia to the island to arrest the conspirators. Before the militia arrived, Mrs. Blennerhassett and the children had fled. Not finding anyone on the island, the troops partially destroyed the mansion and confiscated all of Blennerhassett's property. Burr and Blennerhassett were subsequently captured in the Southwest. The court in Richmond, chaired by Chief Justice of the Supreme Court John Marshall, acquitted Burr; and Blennerhassett, although never brought to trial, was held in custody to answer any indictment against him. By the time authorities released him, creditors had seized his estate, and in 1811 fire destroyed what remained of the mansion. A few dwellings hidden in the overgrowth of willow trees are on the island today, but only some foundation stones and a well remain of the mansion. The island, owned by the State of West Virginia, is accessible only by boat.

SUGGESTED READING

General Works

CUNLIFFE, MARCUS. *The Nation Takes Shape, 1789–1837* (The Chicago History of American Civilization Series). Chicago: University of Chicago Press, 1959; available in paperback. A concise and readable analysis of the development and nature of the American character by a noted English historian.

DE TOCQUEVILLE, ALEXIS. *Democracy in America.* The Henry Rowe text as revised by Francis Bowen; edited by Phillips Bradley, 2 vols. New York: Knopf, 1945; available in paperback. This classic work, originally published in 1835, records the highly perceptive impressions of the Frenchman de Tocqueville during his visit to the United States, in 1831–32.

HOFSTADTER, RICHARD. *The American Political Tradition and the Men Who Made It.* New York: Knopf, 1948; available in paperback. Consists of 12 essays that offer a provocative interpretation of the political philosophies and contributions of statesmen from the Founding Fathers to Franklin D. Roosevelt.

KROUT, JOHN A. and DIXON R. FOX. *The Completion of Independence, 1790–1830* (Volume V of the *History of American Life Series*). New York: Macmillan, 1944. Contains much excellent factual information. Emphasizes social history.

MORISON, SAMUEL E. *An Hour of American History.* Boston: Beacon Press, 1960; paperback; first published by J. B. Lippincott Co., 1929. More than an hour is required to read this brief volume, but it provides an excellent introduction to U.S. history.

NYE, RUSSELL B. *The Cultural Life of the New Nation, 1776–1830* (The New American Nation Series). New York: Harper, 1960; available in paperback. A valuable account of the diverse cultural activities of Americans during the formative years.

WILTSE, CHARLES M. *The New Nation, 1800–1845.* New York: Hill and Wang, 1961; available in paperback. One of the best introductions to the Jeffersonian-Jacksonian period. Includes an extensive bibliographical essay.

The Formative Years

ADAMS, HENRY. *The History of the United States during the Administrations of Jefferson and Madison.* Abridged, 2 vols.; introduction by George Dangerfield and Otley M. Scruggs. Englewood Cliffs, N.J.: Prentice-Hall, 1963; available in paperback. One of the best of several abridgements of Adams' classic 9-volume study.

———. *The United States in 1800.* Ithaca, N.Y.: Cornell University Press; paperback. A reprint of the first six chapters of Adams' *History,* cited above. These chapters are noted for their superb description of the United States at the dawn of the 19th century.

BURNETT, EDMUND C. *The Continental Congress.* New York: Macmillan, 1941; available in paperback. The last seven chapters trace activities of the Congress from the peace treaty ending the War for Independence to the inauguration of the Government under the Constitution.

FARRAND, MAX. *The Framing of the Constitution of the United States.* New Haven: Yale University Press, 1913; available in paperback. An older work that is still useful, interesting, and easy to read.

FREEMAN, DOUGLAS S. *George Washington—A Biography.* Seven vols., New York: Scribner's, 1948–54. Volume VI of this classic study, and Volume VII, completed after Freeman's death by John Alexander Carroll and Mary Wells Ashworth, treat Washington's years as a statesman after the War for Independence. One of many fine biographies of the Founding Fathers and other early national leaders.

HAMILTON, ALEXANDER, JOHN JAY, and JAMES MADISON. *The Federalist; A Commentary of the Constitution of the United States: Being a Collection of Essays Written in Support of the Constitution Agreed Upon September 17, 1787, by the Federal Convention.* Available in many complete and abridged editions, including paperback. This series of 18th-century newspaper essays is still one of the most penetrating analyses of politics and representative government ever written.

JENSEN, MERRILL. *The New Nation.* New York: Knopf, 1950; available in paperback. Suggests that what 19th-century historian John Fiske called the "Critical Period,"—the years immediately after the War for Independence, when the movement for change in the national government produced the Constitution— was not really so critical.

MILLER, JOHN C. *The Federalist Era, 1789–1801* (The New American Nation Series). New York: Harper, 1960; available in paperback. A readable and scholarly synthesis of recent scholarship, including that of the author, on the years from the launching of the Government under the Constitution to the election of Jefferson.

PETERSON, MERRILL D. *The Jefferson Image in the American Mind.* New York: Oxford University Press, 1960; available in paperback. Traces the changing image of Jefferson in the minds of succeeding generations of Americans.

RUTLAND, ROBERT A. *The Birth of the Bill of Rights, 1776–1791.* Chapel Hill, N.C.: University of North Carolina Press, 1955; available in paperback. Studies the origins and structure of the 18th-century concept of individual liberties and the process by which they were incorporated into the Constitution.

The War of 1812

BEIRNE, FRANCIS F. *The War of 1812.* New York: Dutton, 1949. One of the best balanced general accounts of the war.

COLES, HARRY L. *The War of 1812* (The Chicago History of American Civilization Series). Chicago: University of Chicago Press, 1965. A concise and readable account of the war. Emphasizes the military campaigns, but also contrasts the Canadian and American points of view on the war.

PERKINS, BRADFORD, ed. *The Causes of the War of 1812—National Honor or National Interest?* (The American Problem Series). New York: Holt, Rinehart, and Winston, 1962; paperback. Contains representative samples of the various interpretations of the causes of the war.

An Emergent Nationalism

DANGERFIELD, GEORGE. *The Awakening of American Nationalism, 1815–1828* (The New American Nation Series). New York: Harper and Row, 1965; available in paperback. Synthesizes recent studies of the principal themes and personalities of the period. Dangerfield is an expert on the diplomacy of the era.

JAMES, MARQUIS. *Andrew Jackson, Border Captain.* New York: Bobbs-Merrill, 1933; available in paperback. A Pulitzer-Prize-winning biography that describes Jackson's military exploits. Concludes with

Jackson's return to The Hermitage after he concluded his service in Florida.

PERKINS, DEXTER. *A History of the Monroe Doctrine.* Boston: Little, Brown, rev. ed. 1955; available in paperback. Summarizes in a readable manner the history of the Monroe Doctrine and its diplomatic applications from its beginnings to the 20th century.

SYDNOR, CHARLES S. *The Development of Southern Sectionalism, 1819–1848* (Volume V of the *History of the South Series*). Baton Rouge, La.: Louisiana State University Press, 1948. Surveys the development of a distinct Southern civilization in the ante bellum years.

TAYLOR, GEORGE R. *The Transportation Revolution, 1815–1860* (Volume IV of the *Economic History of the United States* series). New York: Holt, Rinehart, and Winston, 1951. A readable book about a difficult subject.

The Westward Movement

BILLINGTON, RAY A. *Westward Expansion.* New York: Macmillan, 1949. A readable and comprehensive work on the westward movement.

SMITH, HENRY N. *Virgin Land—The American West as Symbol and Myth.* Cambridge, Mass.: Harvard University Press, 1950; available in paperback. A pioneering study that deals with the influence of the West on the national mind and imagination.

TURNER, FREDERICK J. *Rise of the New West.* New York: Macmillan, 1906; available in paperback. A classic study by the founder of the "frontier thesis" in U.S. history.

VAN EVERY, DALE. *Ark of Empire—the American Frontier, 1784–1803.* New York: Morrow, 1963; available in paperback. A popular account of the early westward movement. Discusses the part played by the first three Presidents in westward expansion. Other volumes in this series on the frontier are also of interest.

WADE, RICHARD C. *The Urban Frontier.* Cambridge: Harvard University Press, 1959; available in paperback. Provides a fresh approach to interpreting the frontier process. Stresses the importance of western towns as points of defense and as agents for the spread of civilization.

CRITERIA FOR SELECTION
OF HISTORIC SITES
OF EXCEPTIONAL VALUE

1. Structures or sites at which events occurred that have made a significant contribution to, and are identified prominently with, or which outstandingly represent, the broad cultural, political, economic, military, or social history of the Nation, and from which an understanding and appreciation of the larger patterns of our American heritage may be gained.

2. Structures or sites associated importantly with the lives of persons nationally significant in the history of the United States.

3. Structures or sites associated significantly with an important event that outstandingly represents some great idea or ideal of the American people.

4. Structures that embody the distinguishing characteristics of an architectural type specimen, exceptionally valuable for a study of a period style or method of construction; or a notable structure representing the work of a master builder, designer, or architect.

5. Objects that figured prominently in nationally significant events; or that were prominently associated with nationally significant persons; or that outstandingly represent some great idea or ideal of the American people; or that embody distinguishing characteristics of a type specimen, exceptionally valuable for study of a period style or method of construction; or that are notable as representations of the work of master workers or designers.

6. Archeological sites that have produced information of major scientific importance by revealing new cultures, or by shedding light upon periods of occupation over large areas of the United States. Such sites are those which have produced, or which may reasonably be expected to produce, data affecting theories, concepts, and ideas to a major degree.

7. When preserved or restored as integral parts of the environment, historic buildings not sufficiently significant individually by reason of historical

224-051 O - 67 - 23

association or architectural merit to warrant recognition may collectively compose a "historic district" that is of historical significance to the Nation in commemorating or illustrating a way of life in its developing culture.

8. To possess national significance, a historic or prehistoric structure, district, site, or object must possess integrity:

For a historic or prehistoric structure, integrity is a composite quality derived from original workmanship, original location, and intangible elements of feeling and association. (A structure no longer on the original site may possess national significance if the person or event associated with it was of transcendent importance in the Nation's history and the association consequential.)

For a historic district, integrity is a composite quality derived from original workmanship, original location, and intangible elements of feeling and association.

For a historic or prehistoric site, integrity requires original location and intangible elements of feeling and association. (The site of a structure no longer standing may possess national significance if the person or event associated with the structure was of transcendent historical importance in the Nation's history and the association consequential.)

For a historic object, integrity requires basic original workmanship.

9. Structures or sites which are primarily of significance in the field of religion or to religious bodies but are not of national importance in other fields of the history of the United States, such as political, military, or architectural history, will not be eligible for consideration.

10. Birthplaces, graves, burials, and cemeteries, as a general rule, are not eligible for consideration and recognition except in cases of historical figures of transcendent importance. Historic sites associated with the actual careers and contributions of outstanding historical personages usually are more important than their birthplaces and burial places.

11. Structures, sites, and objects achieving historical importance within the past 50 years will not as a general rule be considered unless associated with persons or events of transcendent significance.

12. Structures, sites, and objects proposed for addition to the National Park System must also meet standards of suitability and feasibility.

ACKNOWLEDGMENTS

Advisory Board on National Parks, Historic Sites, Buildings, and Monuments (1959–60)

Edward B. Danson, Jr., Museum of Northern Arizona.
Harold P. Fabian, Utah State Park and Recreation Commission.
E. Raymond Hall, University of Kansas.
Walter L. Huber, San Francisco, Calif.
John A. Krout, Columbia University.
Frank E. Masland, Jr., Carlisle, Pa.
John B. Oakes, New York City.
Sigurd F. Olson, Ely, Minn.
Earl H. Reed, American Institute of Architects.
Fred Smith, Newark, N.J.
Robert G. Sproul, Berkeley, Calif.
Harold S. Wagner, Akron, Ohio.
Carl I. Wheat, Menlo Park, Calif.

Consulting Committee for the National Survey of Historic Sites and Buildings (1959–60)

J. O. Brew, Peabody Museum of Archaeology and Ethnology.
Eric Gugler, American Scenic and Historic Preservation Society.
Richard Howland, Smithsonian Institution.
Frederick Johnson, Robert S. Peabody Foundation for Archaeology, Phillips Academy.
Waldo G. Leland, American Council of Learned Societies.
Earl H. Reed, American Institute of Architects.
S. K. Stevens, Pennsylvania Historical and Museum Commission.
Louis B. Wright, Folger Shakespeare Library.

National Park Service

Roy E. Appleman, Historian, Division of Interpretation and Visitor Services.
Edwin C. Bearss, Historian, Division of History Studies.

[321

Frederick R. Bell, Picture Librarian, Office of Information.

James H. Charleton, Student Research Assistant.

Vincent L. Gleason, Chief of Publications, Division of Interpretation and Visitor Services.

Herbert E. Kahler, Chief (retired), Division of History and Archeology.

Ronald F. Lee, Chief (retired), Division of Interpretation.

Steven H. Lewis, Historian, Division of History Studies.

Mrs. Carol J. Smith, Public Information Officer, National Capital Region.

John W. Walker, Archeologist, National Survey of Historic Sites and Buildings.

Mrs. Lucy Wheeler, Division of History Studies.

Rogers W. Young, Chief, Branch of Park History Studies, Division of History Studies.

Other Individuals

Dr. William T. Alderson, Executive Secretary, Tennessee Historical Commission, Nashville.

George W. Anderson, Tennessee Eastman Corporation, Kingsport.

Dr. Lewis Beeson, Executive Secretary, Michigan Historical Commission, Lansing.

Dr. Peter A. Brannon, Director, Department of Archives and History, Montgomery, Ala.

Waldo S. Carrell, Pensacola Chamber of Commerce, Fla.

William Center, Fort Smith Chamber of Commerce, Ark.

Dr. Walter L. Creese, President, Society of Architectural Historians, Urbana, Ill.

Thomas N. DeLashmutt, Oak Hill Farms, Aldie, Va.

Miss Milburn Divine, Association for the Preservation of Tennessee Antiquities, Johnson City.

Robert O. Dougan, Librarian, Huntington Library and Art Gallery, San Marino, Calif.

C. L. Dvorecka, Public Information Officer, Springfield Armory, Springfield, Mass.

Thomas S. Eader, Assistant Librarian, Maryland Historical Society, Baltimore.

Mrs. Josephine M. Elliott, Librarian, Workingmen's Institution, New Harmony, Ind.

Lawrence J. Flynn, Director, Vacation/Travel Promotion, Massachusetts Department of Commerce, Boston.

Mrs. John M. Gilchrist, Society of Architectural Historians, Mount Vernon, New York.

Mrs. June L. Goldman, 9307 Wadsworth Drive, Bethesda, Md.

Ralph P. Grant, Kingsport, Tenn.

Frederick J. Griffiths, Director, Gunston Hall, Lorton, Va.

Charles F. Hinds, Executive Secretary, Kentucky Historical Society, Frankfort.

Jay W. Johns, Charlottesville, Va.

Milton Kaplan, Prints and Photographs Division, Library of Congress, Washington, D.C.

Miss Gussie Killian, Portersville, Ala.

Dr. Richard C. Knopf, Research Historian, Anthony Wayne Parkway Board, Columbus, Ohio.

Dr. George S. May, Historic Sites Specialist, Michigan Historical Commission, Lansing.

Mrs. Florence Miller, Office Manager, U.S. Capitol Historical Society, Washington, D.C.

Mrs. Margaret Palmer, Clemson, S.C.

J. C. Parker, Kingston, Tenn.

Eugene T. Peterson, Mackinac Island State Park Commission, Lansing, Mich.

Earle R. Poorbaugh, Information Officer, Maryland Department of Economic Development, Annapolis.

J. Reese Price, Jefferson County Historical Society, Watertown, N.Y.

Miss Charlotte M. Read, Genesee County Historian, East Pembroke, N.Y.

Mrs. Edith S. Reiter, Campus Martius Museum, Marietta, Ohio.

Mrs. Marion duPont Scott, Montpelier, Orange County, Va.

Mrs. Lorrain Seay, Executive Secretary, Henry Clay Memorial Foundation, Lexington, Ky.

Raymond S. Sivesind, Chief, Historic Sites and Markers Division, Wisconsin State Historical Society, Madison.

Dr. S. K. Stevens, Executive Director, Pennsylvania Historical and Museum Commission, Harrisburg.

Mrs. Florian H. Thayn, Librarian, Office of the Architect of the U.S. Capitol.

Dr. G. R. Turrentine, Registrar, Arkansas Polytechnic College, Russellville.

Dr. R. W. C. Vail, Director, New-York Historical Society, New York City.

Charles C. Wall, Resident Director, Mount Vernon, Va.

Mrs. Harry T. Watts, Sr., Chairman of Restoration for "Grouseland," Vincennes, Ind.

Clark Wilcox, Chemung County Historical Society, Inc., Elmira, N.Y.

Dr. Erwin Zepp, Director, Ohio State Historical Society, Columbus.

Index

Abolitionists, and Gallatin, 249; antagonist of, 251; in U.S. Congress, 74–75. *See also* Slavery.

Absinthe House (New Orleans), 274

Academies, military, proposed, 235–236. *See also* United States Military Academy.

"Acropolus" ("Grove on the Hill") estate, D.C., 280

"Act for the Punishment of Certain Crimes" (An), *see* Alien and Sedition Acts

Acts of Congress, *see* Continental Congress; Law and laws; United States Congress

Adams, Abigail, *see* Adams, Mrs. John

Adams, Brooks, career of, 131, 134; father of, 134; residence of, *see* Adams Mansion and Adams National Historic Site

Adams, Charles Francis, career of, 133–134; father and grandfather of, 133; residence of, *see* Adams Mansion and Adams National Historic Site; sons of, 133, 134

Adams, Charles Francis, Jr., career of, 134; father of, 134

Adams, "Deacon" John, and Adams (John) Birthplace, 211; son of, 211

Adams, Henry, career of, 131, 134; father of, 134; residence of, *see* Adams Mansion and Adams National Historic Site

Adams, John, achievements of, 98; and Alien and Sedition Acts, 36, 37; and foreign recognition of U.S., 132; and Great Seal of the United States, 132; and Hamilton, 34, 39; and Harrison, 189; and Indiana Territory, 189; and Jefferson and Jeffersonians, 5, 26; and Judiciary Act of *1800*, 41; and Mason, 260; and party warfare, 26; and Washington (George), 132; and West, 6; and XYZ affair, 34–35; antagonists and political rivals of, 34, 39; as Federalist, 26; as first White House occupant, 38, 112; as lawyer, 211, 213; as leader in Continental Congress, 131; as Vice President, 131, 132; biographer of, 133–134; birthplace of, *see* Adams (John) Birthplace; brother of, 212; Cabinet and appointments of, 34, 41, 260; dies, 132, 134; diplomatic career of, 15, 21, 132, 134, 205, 211, 212, 213; does not attend Constitutional Convention, 21; domestic policies and programs of, 4, 26, 36–38; education of, 131; entertained, 179; father of, *see* Adams, "Deacon" John; foreign policies and programs of, 4, 26, 34–36, 38, 132, 281; friends and supporters of, 34, 260; helps draft Declaration of Independence, 116, 132; inaugurated as President, 153; marries, 210–211, 213; opposes Stamp Act, 131; participates in in-

(Rear end paper)

Scene along the Mohawk River, New York. Lithographed by Bichebois, figures by V. Adams, from the drawing "Road and Bridge over the Mohawk," by Jacques G. Milbert. Courtesy, Library of Congress.